Postcard History Series

Genesee River

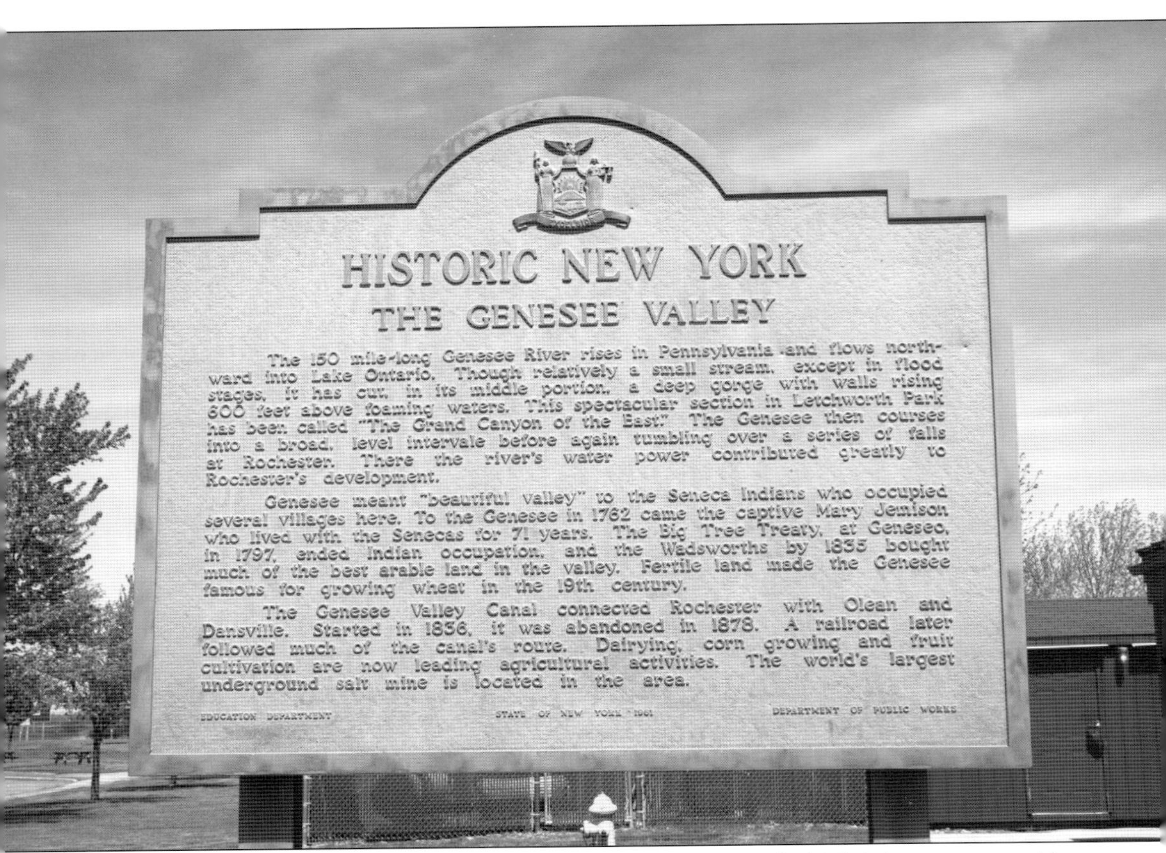

The Genesee River Valley is unique in many ways, the first of which is its unsurpassed beauty. The Seneca Indian word for it meant "Beautiful Valley." The area is rich in Indian and colonial history as well as agricultural productivity. The valley was and still is a major north/south transportation route. This historic marker is at the Geneseo Rest Area off Interstate 390 North. (Author's collection.)

On the Front Cover: Pictured are the Upper Falls of the Genesee River in Rochester, New York, in the early 1900s. (Author's collection.)

On the Back Cover: Pictured is a view of Ontario Beach Park at the mouth of the Genesee River. (Rochester Public Library.)

POSTCARD HISTORY SERIES

Genesee River

John and Sue Babbitt
Foreword by Craig R. Braack

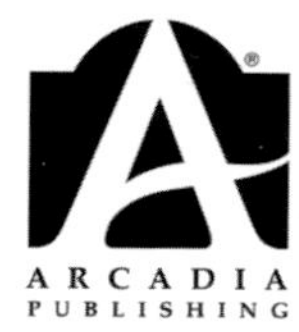

ISBN 978-0-7385-9782-9

Published by Arcadia Publishing
Charleston, South Carolina

Printed in the United States of America

Library of Congress Control Number: 2012941766

For all general information contact Arcadia Publishing at:
Telephone 843-853-2070
Fax 843-853-0044
E-mail sales@arcadiapublishing.com
For customer service and orders:
Toll-Free 1-888-313-2665

Visit us on the Internet at www.arcadiapublishing.com

This book is dedicated to those individuals who inspired our love for local history.

Contents

FOREWORD

Just over 200 years ago, when our first settlers moved into the Genesee Valley, they experienced vast, virgin wilderness as far as the eye could see. They soon felled the forests, cleared the fields, and opened roads to their future. They gave us a legacy of hard work and an indomitable spirit of harnessing the power and value of our Genesee River. One cannot help but wonder what these people would feel and say if they were here today.

Starting from a spring on a farm in the hamlet of Gold, Pennsylvania, our river peacefully meanders north through the farmlands of Pennsylvania into the historic oil fields of Allegany County, New York. Just into Wyoming County, the river's calm meandering abruptly ends with the roar of three magnificent waterfalls in Letchworth State Park. At Mount Morris, our river reenters its ancient bed and continues its inexorable, calm flow north to the city of Rochester, where it roars over its last three major waterfalls. It is these latter falls that helped create the great city of Rochester as our first settlers harnessed the river's power to grind grain from the rich soils of the valley.

No doubt many thousands of photographs have been created over the years depicting the myriad array of employment and recreational opportunities our region offers. The Babbitts have captured the essence of our valley with the few photographs and captions space has allowed. Enjoy the book as it invites you to visualize the pioneers as they heralded the arrival of the Erie Canal in 1825, quickly followed by the New York Central Railroad, changing Rochester from the "Flour City" to the "Flower City." Advancements in photography and printing in the early 1900s allowed valley residents to send, near and far, magnificent postcards of industrialization and growth.

Please consider exploring the length of our Genesee River Valley in person and visiting the many museums our region has to offer. One could then fully understand and appreciate why the Seneca Indians called this "The Beautiful Valley."

Respectfully submitted,
Craig R. Braack
Allegany County Historian

Acknowledgments

A book of this scope would not be possible without the support of many individuals who loaned us their personal postcard collections and who offered their extensive knowledge. The images in this book were produced from a number of different media that documented life along the river over the years. They have included early photographs, postcards, glass plates, stereo cards, and maps.

Many thanks to my wife, Sue, who journeyed with me on many research expeditions and was my chief proofreader, and to those who loaned us their personal postcard collections: Craig R. Braack (CRB), Thomas S. Cook (TC), Jane Schryver, and Paul Hoffman (JS). Many others kindly got out the keys, opened the doors to small village museums, sat down with us, pulled out scrapbooks, and looked through records to find just that image or bit of information we needed: Judy Wightman, Avoca Historical Society (AHS); Amie Alden, Livingston County Museum (LCM); the Gold General Store (GGS); Jeannette Buck (JB) in Gold, Pennsylvania; Jim Pomeroy (JP) in Rushford; Kay Brownell Reed, Potter County Historical Society, Pennsylvania (PCHS); Eileen Tecza, David A Howe Public Library, Wellsville, New York (HPL); Tom Wenzel, Mount Morris Dam (ACE) in Letchworth State Park, whose persistence with the Army Corps of Engineers resulted in some spectacular 1972 flood photographs; Jean Richmond (JR) in Wellsville; James Potter (JP) in Wellsville; CoraBelle Lounsberry (CL); Scio Historical Society (SHS); Norm Annis (NA); Ron Taylor, Allegany County History Society (ACHS); Belfast Historical Society (BHS); New York State Museum (NYSM); John S. Babbitt (JSB); and many from the collection of the Rochester Public Library Local History Division (RPL). All images not otherwise designated are from our personal collection.

Several publications, which we found invaluable, are the Arch Merrill books: *Land of the Senecas*, *River Ramble*, *Rochester Sketchbook*, and *White Woman and Her Valley*.

We deeply appreciate the assistance and encouragement from everyone, especially our tech-support friends, Steve Cotton and Adrian Morling. You all have had an important part in this challenging endeavor.

—John and Sue Babbitt

Introduction

The history of the Genesee River Valley is rich and colorful. Long before the coming of humans, the country was covered with an extensive ice sheet. As it melted, the retreating ice produced much of the beautiful scenery we find along the river, including six magnificent waterfalls.

It was the nations of the Iroquois Confederacy that first occupied the river basin. The coming of the white man from Europe to New York State wrought considerable changes, and soon after the Revolutionary War, the Indians became dependent upon or were pushed out by the white man.

Each of the towns along the Genesee has a colorful history, and together they are credited with helping form our country's history. The larger of these early settlements are centered around Rochester, Geneseo, and Mount Morris. Their factories were tethered to the river by the need for waterpower. Early trails, canals, tributaries, and railroads all played a part in the growth of these river towns.

The path of the Genesee River wound through four educational institutions: Houghton College, SUNY Geneseo, Rochester Institute of Technology, and the University of Rochester.

Arch Merrill (1894–1974), an American journalist, poet, and adventurer, was fascinated by the Genesee River and the stories surrounding it. During the summer of 1943, Arch began to walk the entire length from the spring in a farmer's barnyard in Gold, Pennsylvania, to its mouth at Charlotte on Lake Ontario. As Arch commented, "Oh, I made the trip all right, the 130 odd miles, plus some detours." Kindhearted people along the way were generous with offers of rides, many entertaining him with their river stories. His book *River Ramble* is the result.

Today, the Genesee is a vastly different river from that of the 1700s and 1800s. As we traveled Arch Merrill's path along the river, we also caught a bit of his sense of adventure and discovery. Here are just a few of the events that make the Genesee River Valley an exciting place to live in or to visit. In this book, we hope to capture the magnificence and power as well as many aspects of the history of the Genesee River. We have tried to mirror the flow of the river as it meandered from south to north.

One

The Early Genesee
Potter County, Pennsylvania

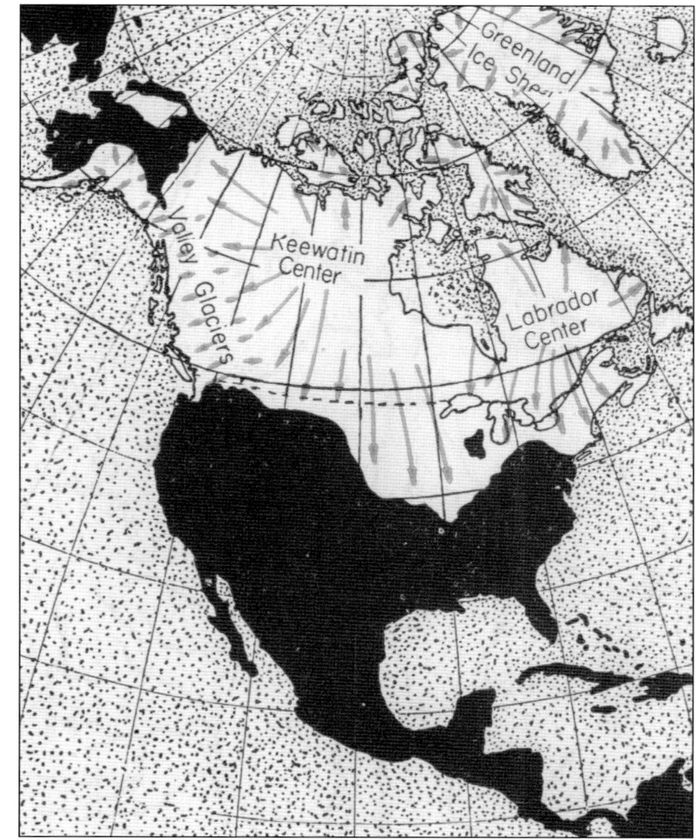

Roughly 10,000 years ago, the Wisconsin Ice Age produced powerful glaciers, which scraped along the earth, pushing and dragging huge volumes of rock and soil. The ice sheet that covered the Genesee River Valley originated in Labrador. As the glaciers melted, the beginning of today's Genesee took form. Large deposits of glacial soil and debris were left behind, forcing the Genesee to establish its old route. One branch was forced west near Avon, while the second branch was established near Portageville, creating a deep canyon called Letchworth State Park today. New York State areas suffered greatly under the weight of this scraping, but the result is the beautiful landscape enjoyed today.

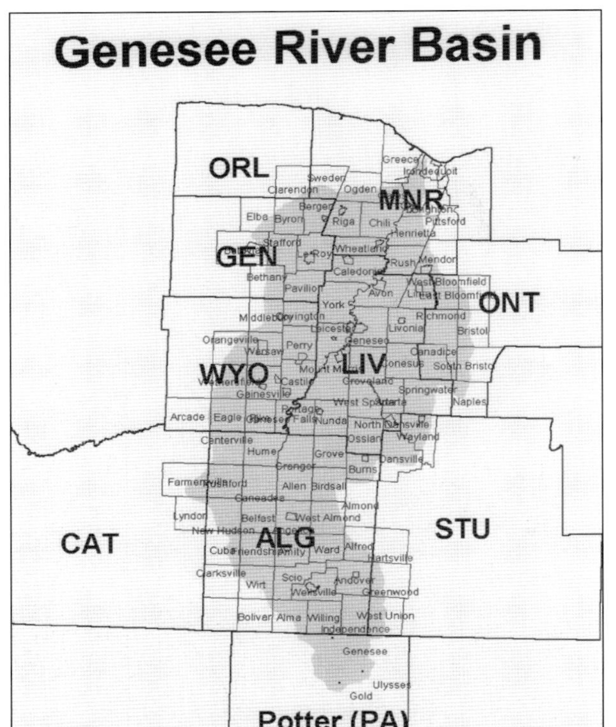

The Genesee River is 157 miles long from its source in Gold, Pennsylvania, to Lake Ontario in New York State. The watershed drains an area of 2,400 square miles. Unlike most rivers, this one runs south to north. The watershed is a river system of great beauty, high points being Letchworth State Park, known as "The Grand Canyon of the East," and the Mount Morris Dam area.

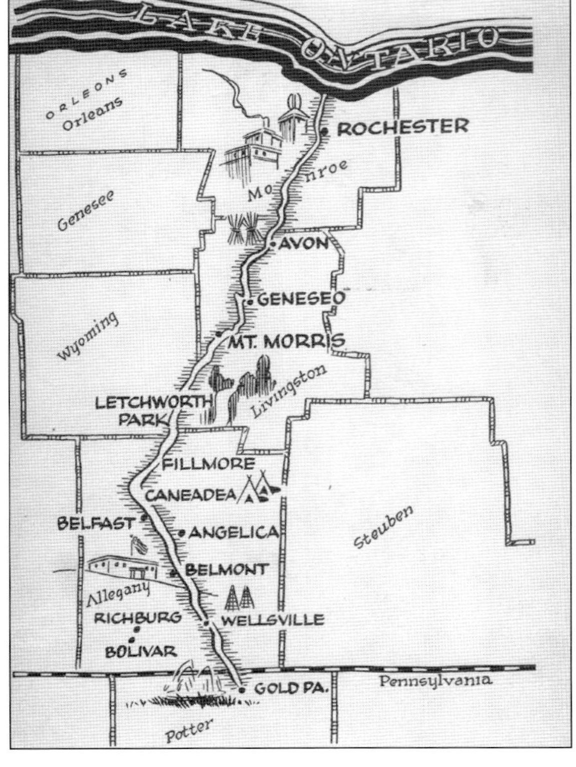

Arch Merrill began his "rambling" along the Genesee, traveling first through Potter County, Pennsylvania, then crossing into Allegany County in New York State, then Wyoming and Livingston Counties, and finally ending with the city of Rochester in Monroe County. Notice that Letchworth State Park lies about halfway along the river, stretching a length of 17 miles and covering 14,350 acres.

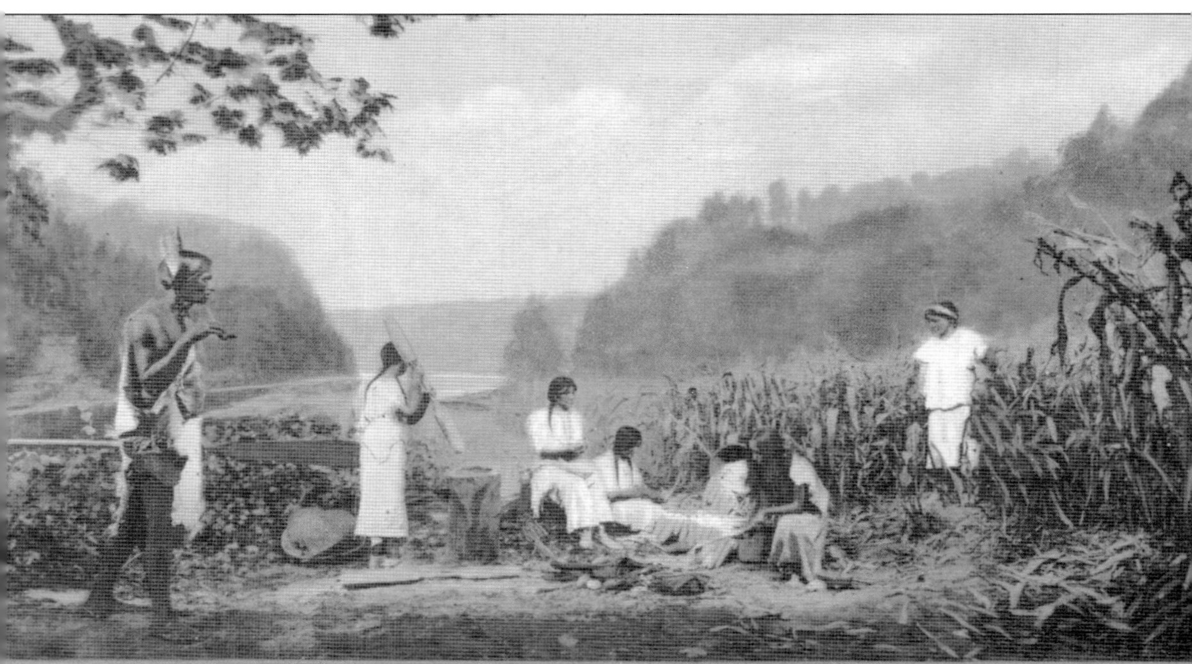

Iroquois Indian Exhibit—The Corn Harvest—Scene, High Banks of the Genesee River
State Museum, Education Building, Albany, N. Y.

Early residents in the valley were the Native American tribes who eventually joined, forming the Iroquois Confederacy in the 1570s. They called the Genesee "The Little River of the Senecas." The river valley was their livelihood, both as a source of fish and transportation, as well as irrigation for farming. The fertile soil provided bountiful harvests as well as hunting grounds for the native tribes, and as European settlers began to come into the area in the 1600s and 1700s, they too discovered the fertile land. The white settlers craved the land, and gradually the tribes began to be pushed out. (JSB.)

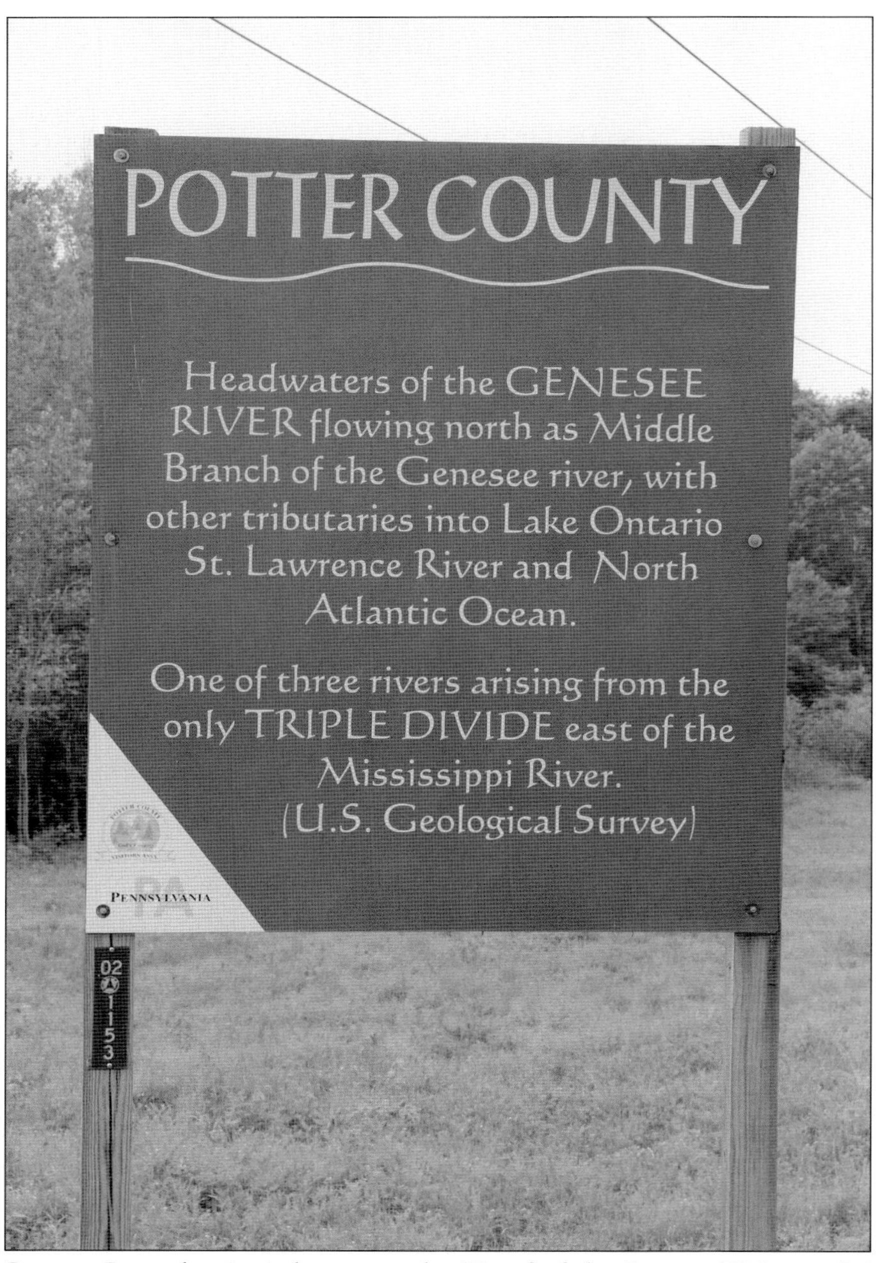

Potter County, Pennsylvania, is known as the "Roof of the Eastern US," containing the headwaters of three rivers: the Genesee River, which flows north through Rochester, New York, and empties into Lake Ontario; the Allegheny River, which begins here with two branches and eventually flows westward to join the Monongahela River in Pittsburg, Pennsylvania; and the Cowanesque River, which rises in the northeast of the county and eventually joins the Susquehanna River and empties into Chesapeake Bay. This hilltop is called the Allegheny Plateau and is located just 12 miles south of the New York state line. It has an elevation of 2,500 feet. The hamlet of Gold is less than half a mile from this sign in the western part of Ulysses Township. (JSB.)

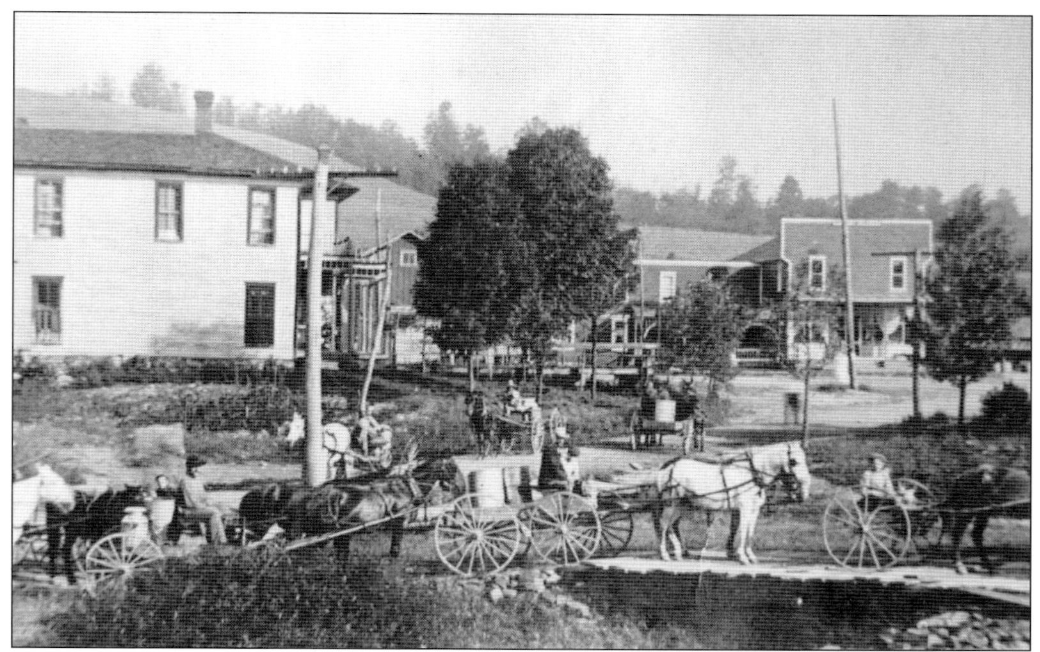

Some people in Potter County today probably think life must have been simpler 100 plus years ago. Maybe in some ways that is true, but the line up of milk wagons every morning headed for the cheese factory shows that farm life was a busy one. It looks like quite a traffic jam here at the only crossroads in the middle of Gold. (JB.)

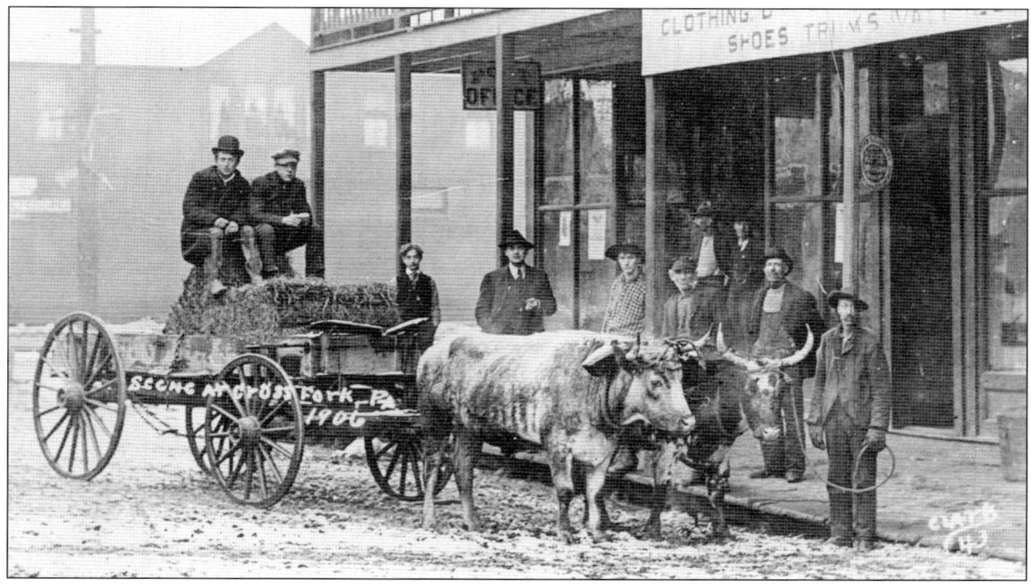

Located at the intersection of Pennsylvania Routes No. 49 and No. 449, the Gold General Store was built in 1902. Some years later it burned and then was rebuilt. It has been a hub of town activity and information for 110 years. Today, it is a combination residence, general store, restaurant, and gathering place for folks who want to share and learn local news. (JSB.)

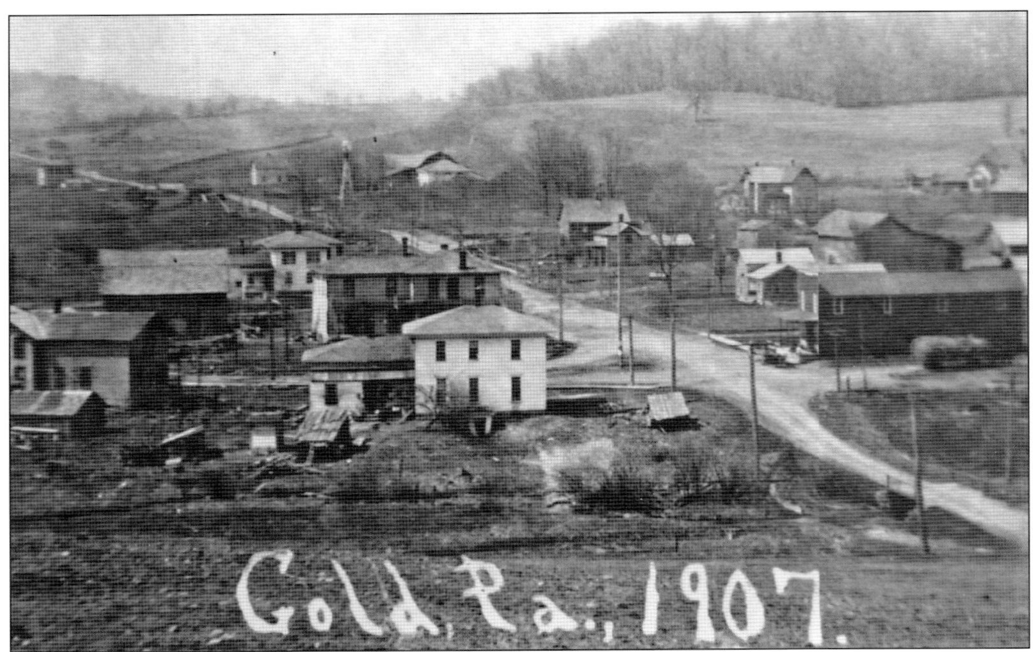

The residents of Gold, Pennsylvania, are proud of their "Living Sign," planted in the 1950s by a troop of Boy Scouts. It was originally named East Raymond, but in 1881 when the residents wanted their own post office, they needed a new name. There are two stories of how the town got its name. One is that it was from the wealth that came from the rich lumbering industry. Another version is that residents were asked to submit suggestions for the name. A little girl was asked to draw the winning slip of paper—gold! (Above, JB; below, GGS.)

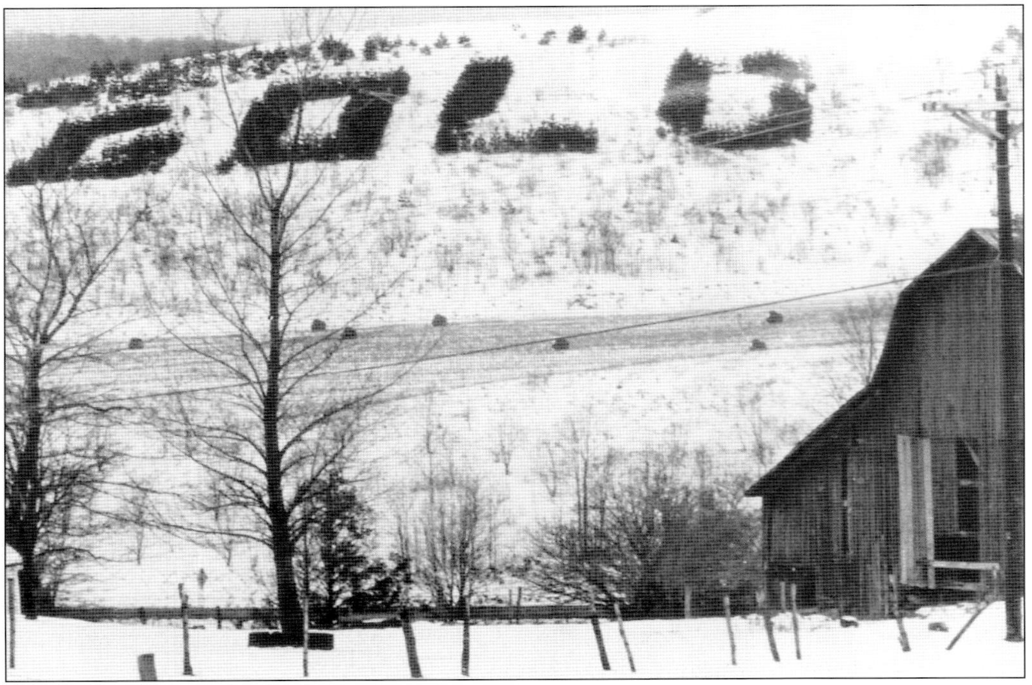

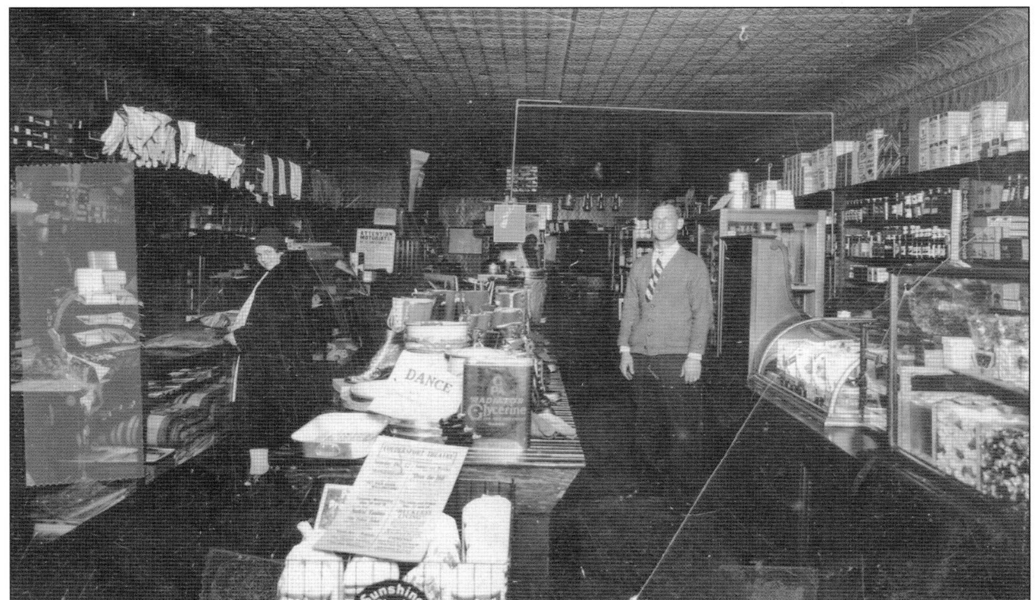

In its early years, Gold was a bustling community with five stores, a blacksmith shop, gas station, and numerous saw mills and gristmills, as well as a thriving cheese factory. It is unusual to see the interior of a store, but interesting to note the multitude of products available over a century ago. (JB.)

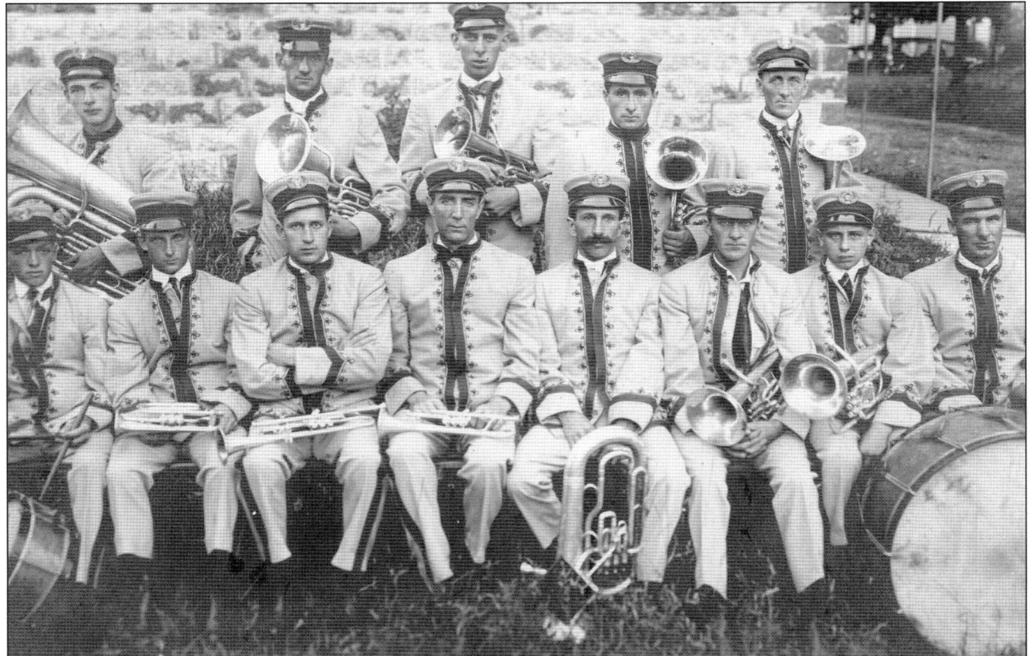

Community bands have been popular ever since the Civil War. Many villages promoted this activity as shown by this beautiful photo card of the town-sponsored band of Gold. Just as they do now, the mostly amateur musicians performed in local celebrations, marched in parades, and were a source of community pride. (JB.)

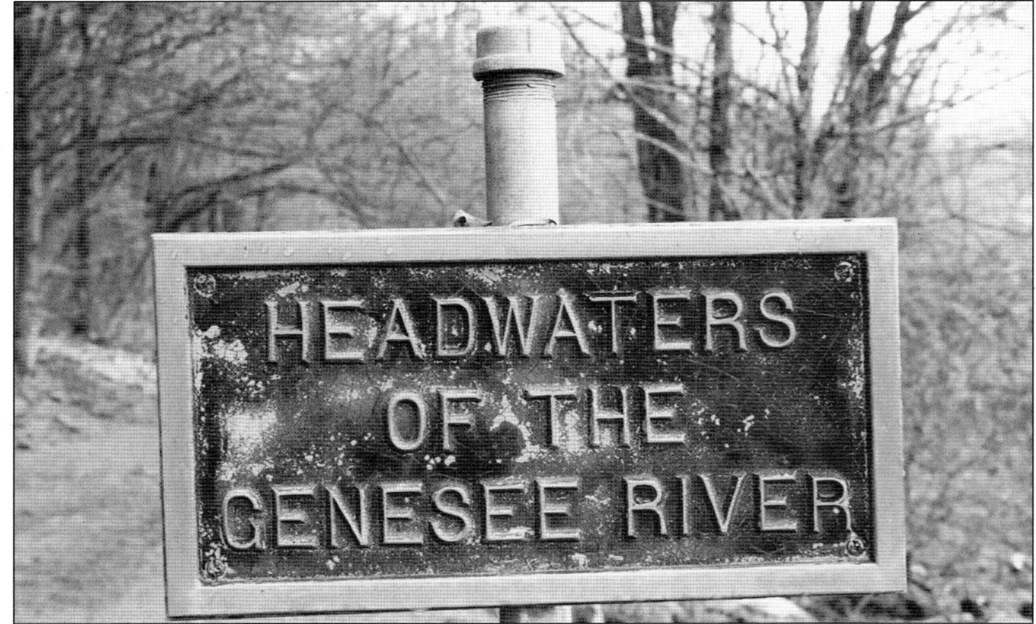

This marker indicates the source of the Genesee River is on land owned by the Slaybaugh family. They are accustomed to visitors wanting to view the humble beginnings of the great river; therefore, the path down to the cistern is kept mowed. The water trickles into several rivulets down the hillside, but they are small enough to step over. (JSB.)

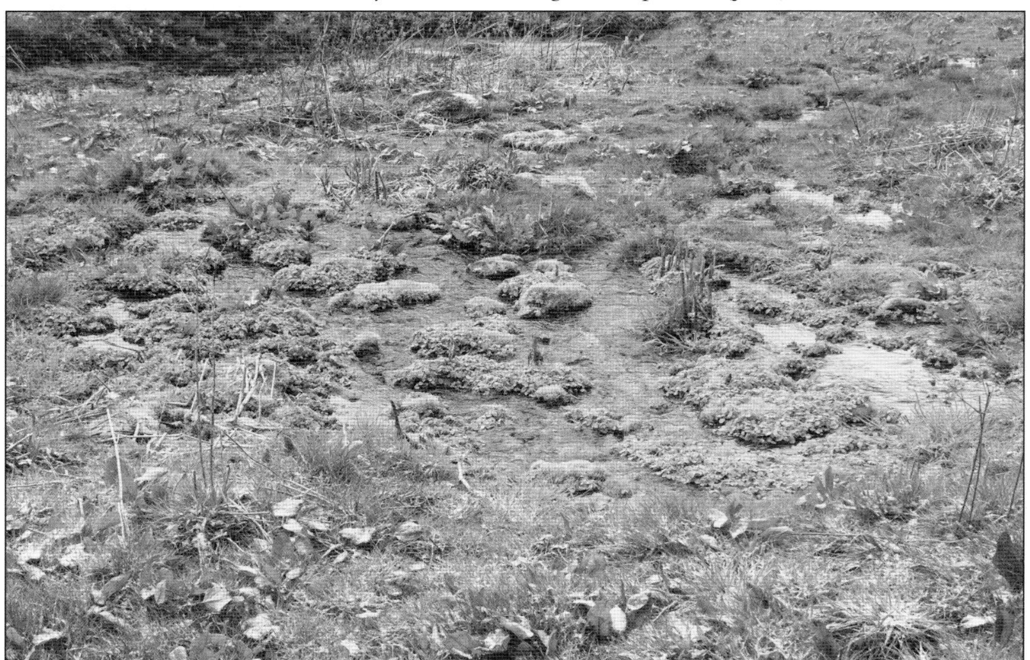

Arch Merrill, an assistant city editor for the *Rochester Democrat and Chronicle*, hiked along the river off and on in 1943 during World War II. He wrote, "The water that bubbles out of that spring that is the birthplace of the Genesee is cold and clear." (JSB.)

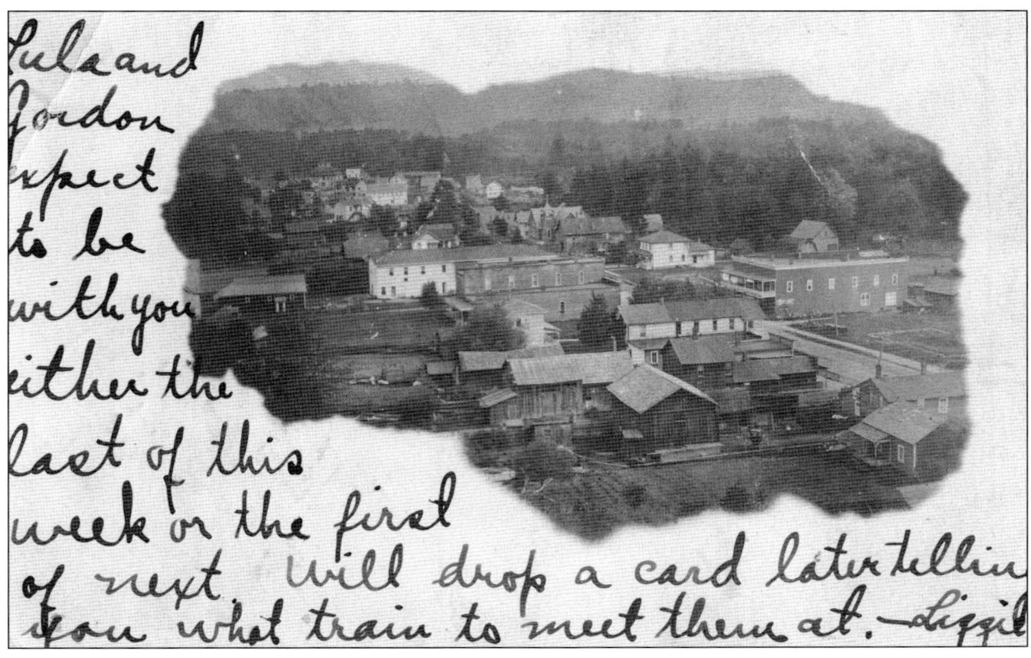

Genesee, Pennsylvania, located in Genesee Township, was named for the river that runs through its center. The town was founded in 1853 and was originally known as Genesee Forks. The confluence of the west, east, and middle branches of the river occurs within the village. During the late 1800s and early 1900s, the lumbering industry was flourishing. The town boasted several hotels, along with several sand, gravel, and brick industries. As a result, the population continued to grow, and today, many of the brick buildings still stand. However, the industries are not still there, and the population, according to the 2000 census, was 789. (CRB.)

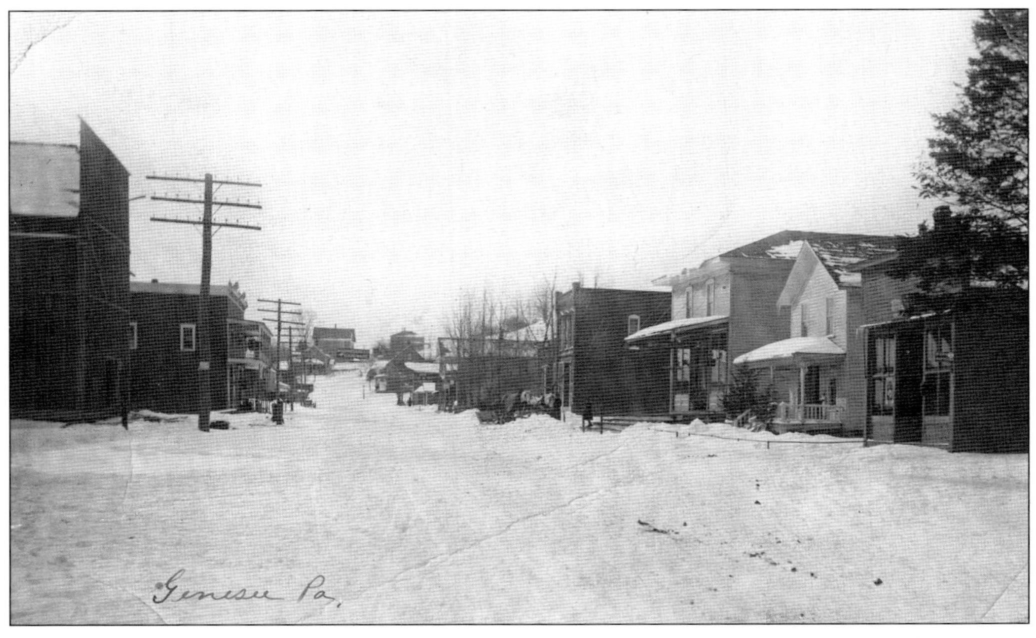

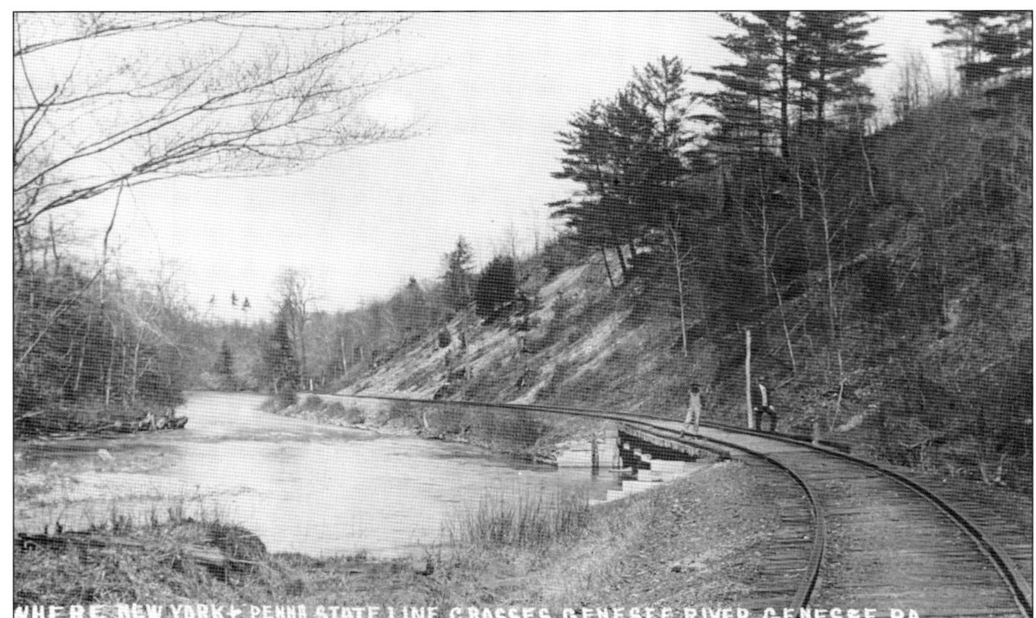

As the Genesee begins its meander north, it passes slowly through mostly rural farming communities. Sometimes a farmer had to construct his own bridge or pick the easiest place to ford the stream, if it cut into his farmyard or pasture. One main industry in the early years was lumbering. The river was a convenient way to get the timber to markets in the northern towns and cities. Workers built rafts called arks and floated the wood downstream. When they arrived at the market, the arks were dismantled and also sold. The men would then buy horses and ride back home with their profits. In later years, modern highways and railroads have often followed the river's course. (CRB.)

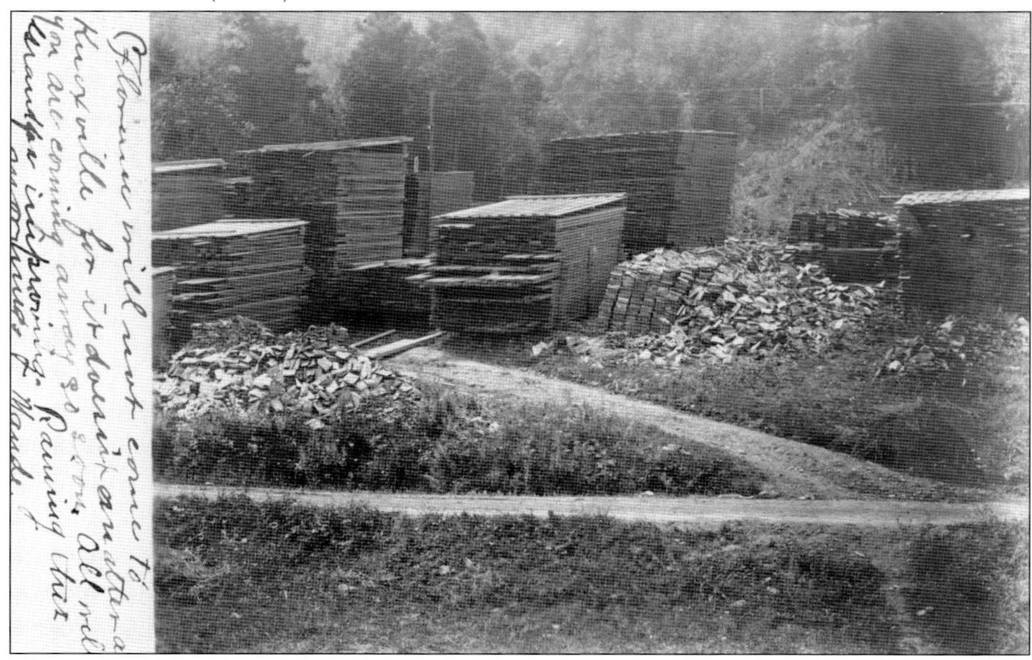

Two

Allegany County
The Oil Boom

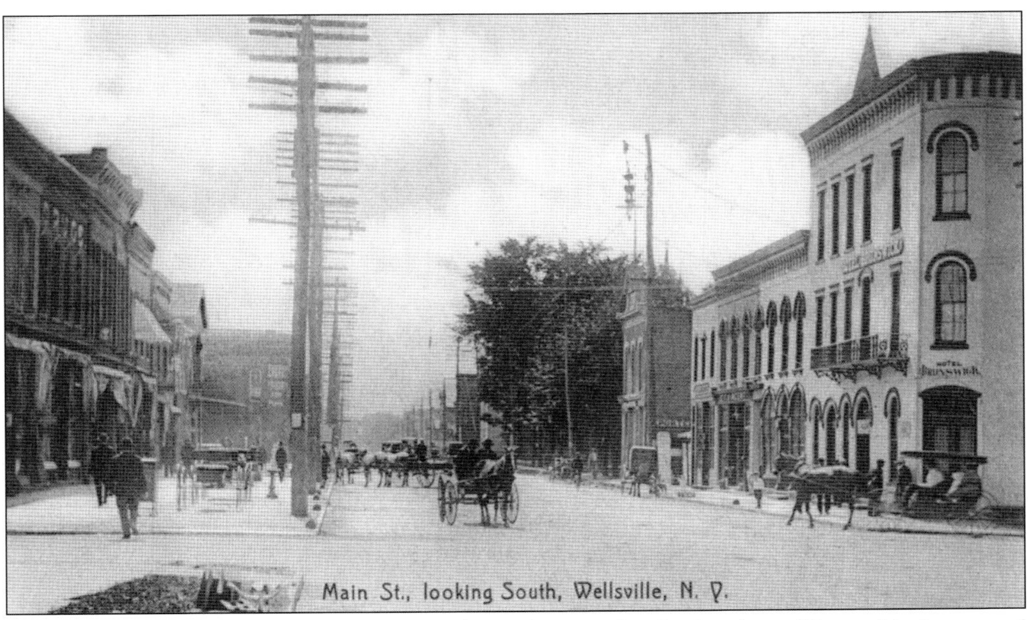
Main St., looking South, Wellsville, N. Y.

Wellsville, New York, has long been an industrial center for the Southern Tier and is the second largest community straddling the Genesee River. The village is located in Allegany County, which was formed in 1806 from Genesee County. The first settler in the area was Nathaniel Dike, a captain in the Revolutionary War under George Washington. Arriving in 1795, Dike built a gristmill, sawmill, and tannery on a stream that is today called Dykes Creek. People might think that the name Wellsville came from the booming oil industry there, but it was really named for a major landowner named Gardiner Wells. For a brief time in the early 1870s, the town was called Genesee; however, after much political wrangling, the name Wellsville was agreed upon, supposedly because Gardiner Wells was the only prominent resident who did not show up at the meeting. (CRB.)

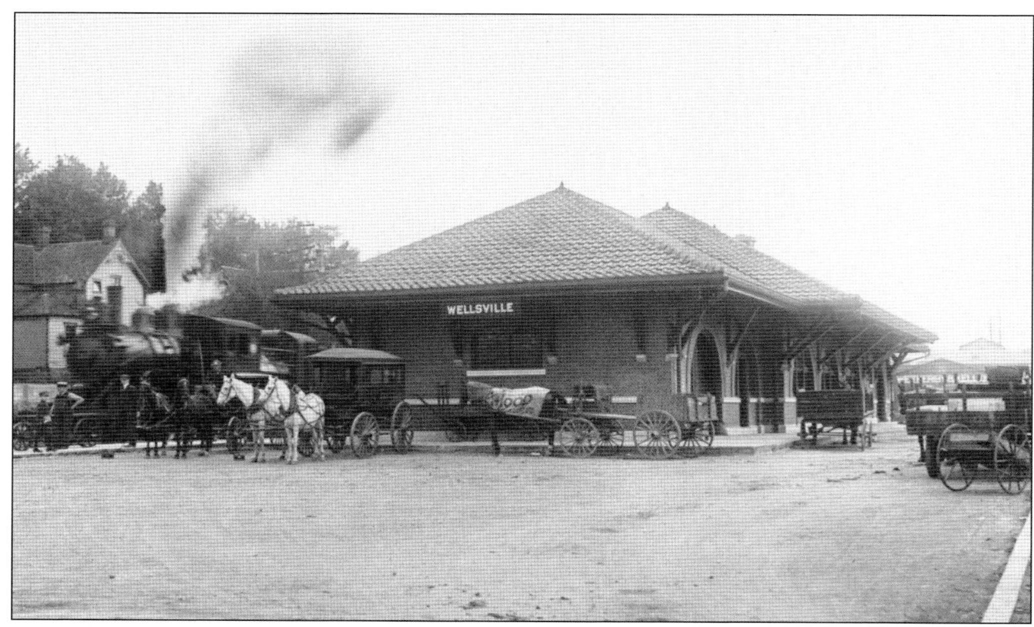

The Wellsville Depot was constructed in 1911 for the Erie Railroad. Its one-story structure displayed elements of Queen Anne and Romanesque Revival styles, both popular in the late 19th and early 20th centuries. Wellsville soon became an important link on the Allegany division of the Erie Railroad routes out of New York City. (CRB.)

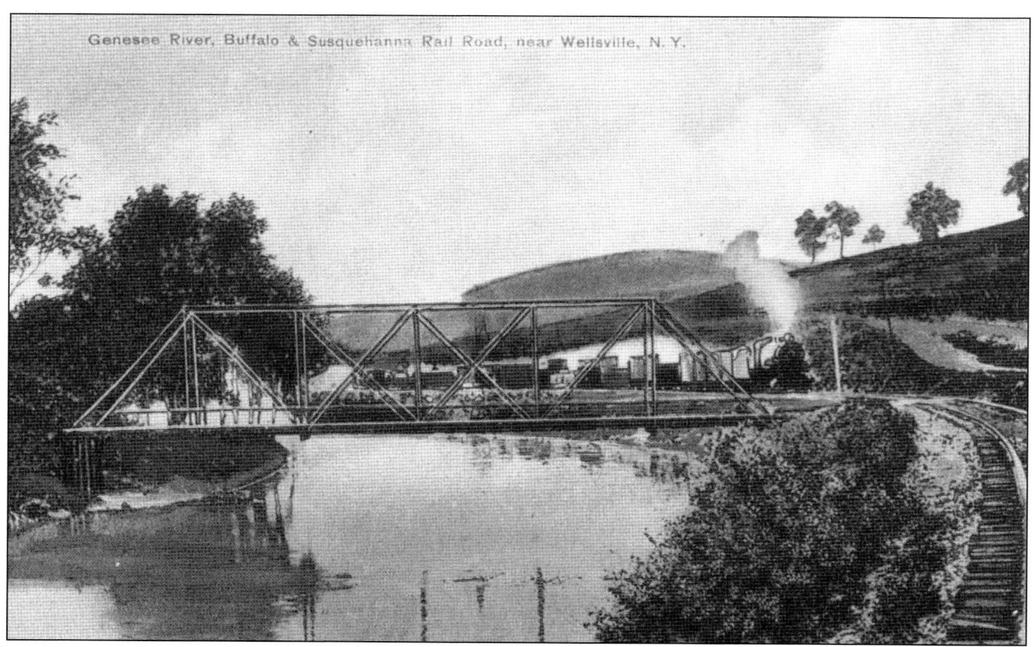

The trains first came to Wellsville in the early 1850s. The trains that followed the Genesee River gave lumbermen a new and more efficient means to get their products to market. Previously, logs had to be floated on the river or on canals. (CRB.)

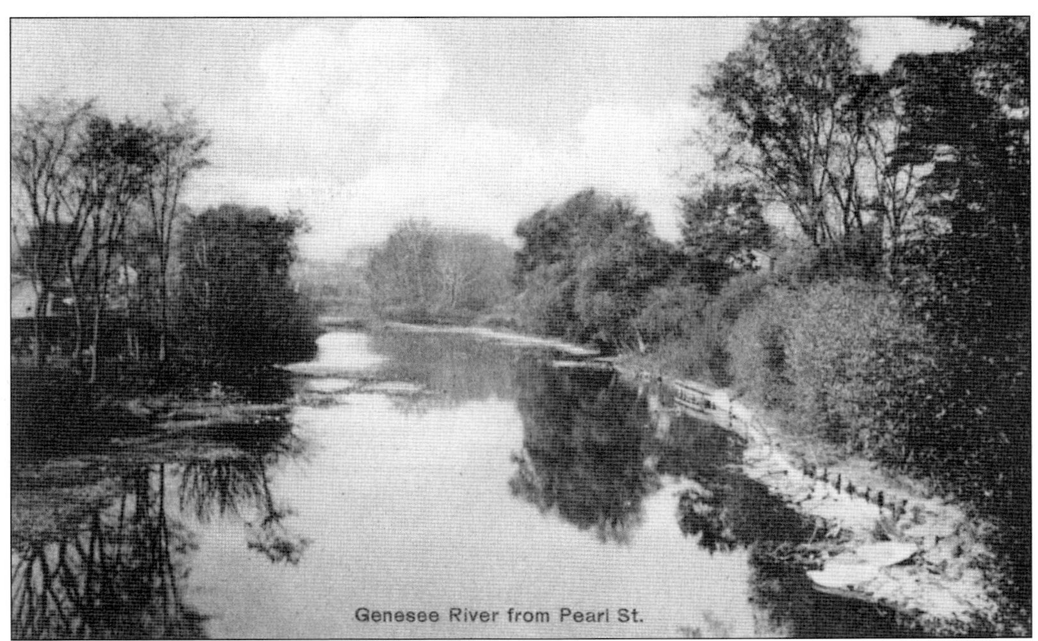

Wellsville is near the junction of many small feeder streams into the Genesee River. Its unique geography in the watershed places it near the source, resulting in clean, pure water. In the farther outlying areas around Wellsville, the water might flow in any one of three directions: north (down the Genesee River into Lake Ontario and eventually into the Atlantic Ocean; southeast (down the Susquehanna River and eventually into the Atlantic Ocean at Baltimore); or southwest (down the Allegheny River to the Mississippi River and the Gulf of Mexico). (CRB.)

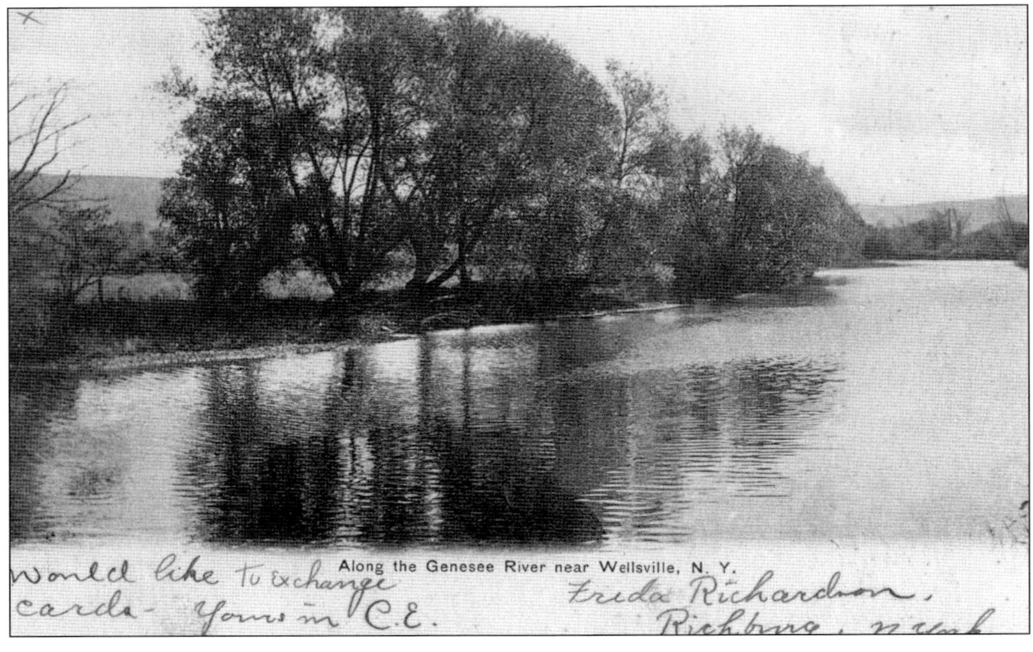

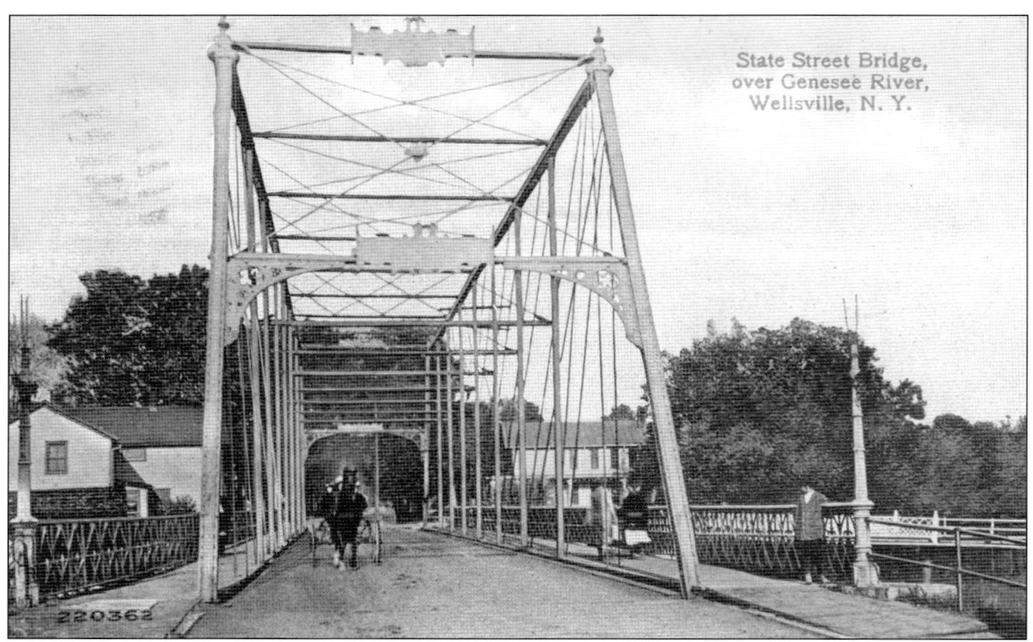

The State Street Bridge is one of the many spans across the Genesee in Wellsville as the river bisects the village. The water usually flows very gently through town, so it is often a place where casual boating, wading, and fun will occur. Sometimes more organized entertainment is planned, such as the annual fishing derby and the Great Wellsville Balloon Rally, which just concluded its 37th annual event. (Above, JR; below, CRB.)

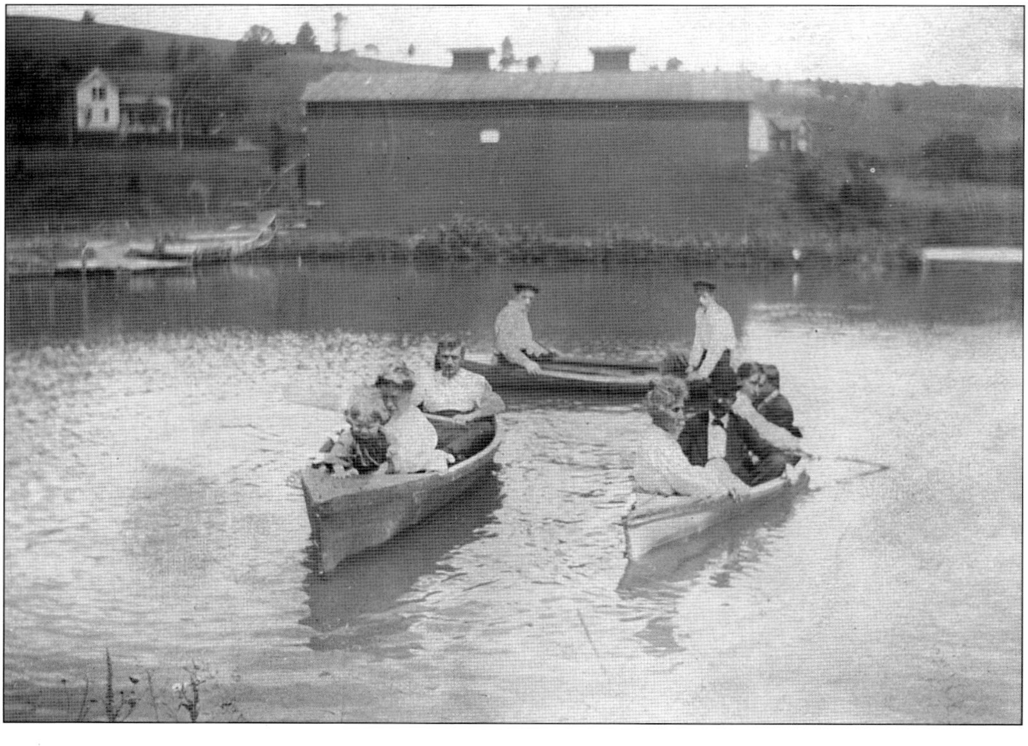

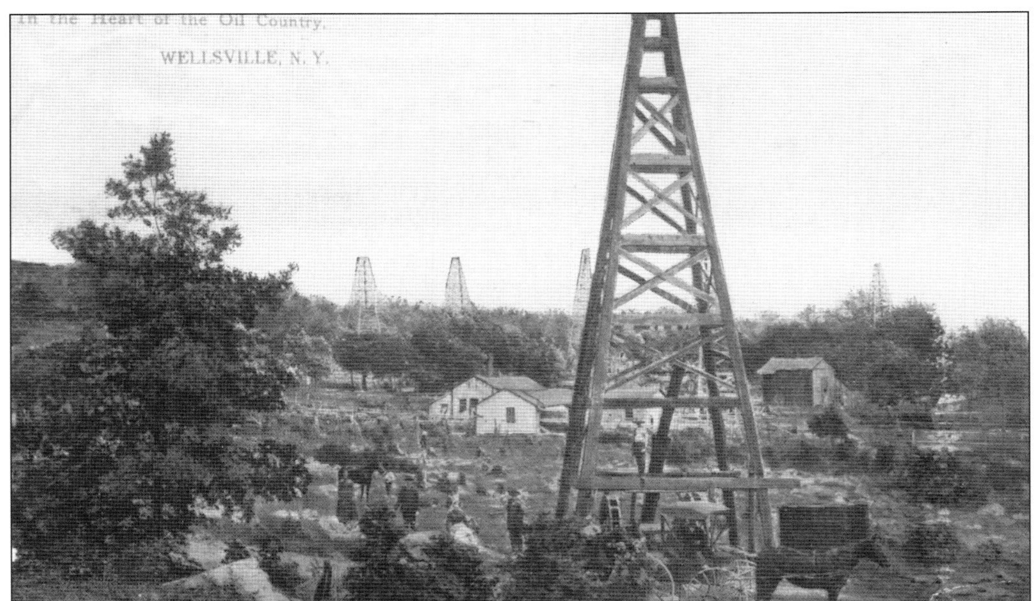

Wellsville played an important role in the oil industry in the northeast United States. One of the richest oil fields in the Empire State was located in the southwest corner of Allegany County. The discovery of oil near Wellsville in 1879 began an era of boomtown growth to the area. (CRB.)

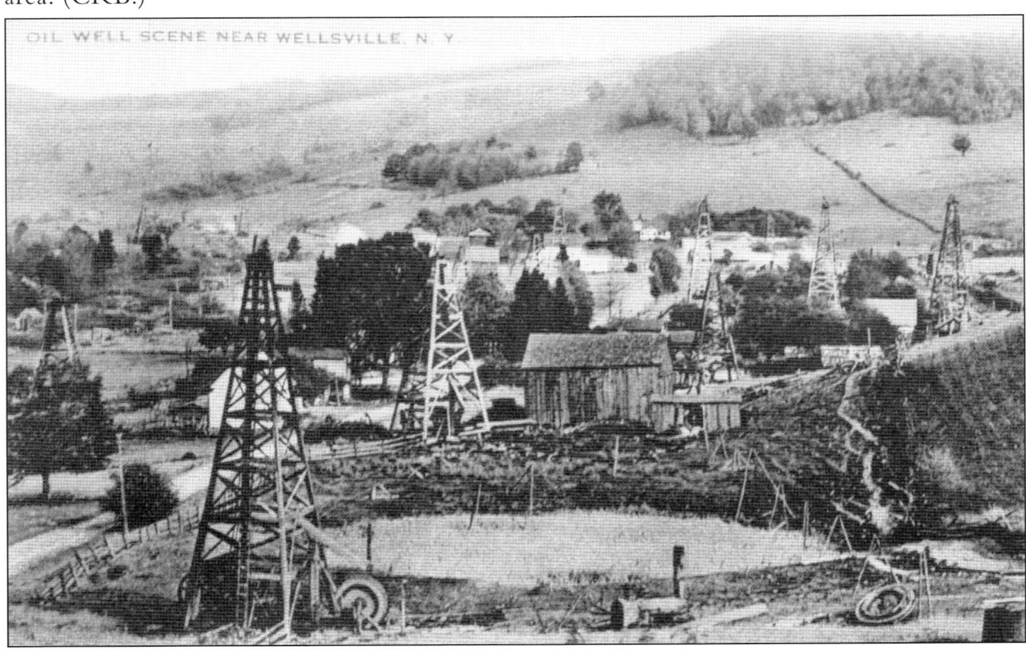

In the early 1900s, Wellsville was known as the "capital of the oil fields," as this November 15, 1915, postcard shows. The Sinclair Refinery, once one of the largest refineries in the Pennsylvania-New York crude oil fields, operated in Wellsville until 1958. Oil pump apparatus still dots the hillsides, but few are pumping actively. The oil industry left behind a number of beautiful and stately public buildings and private residences. (CRB.)

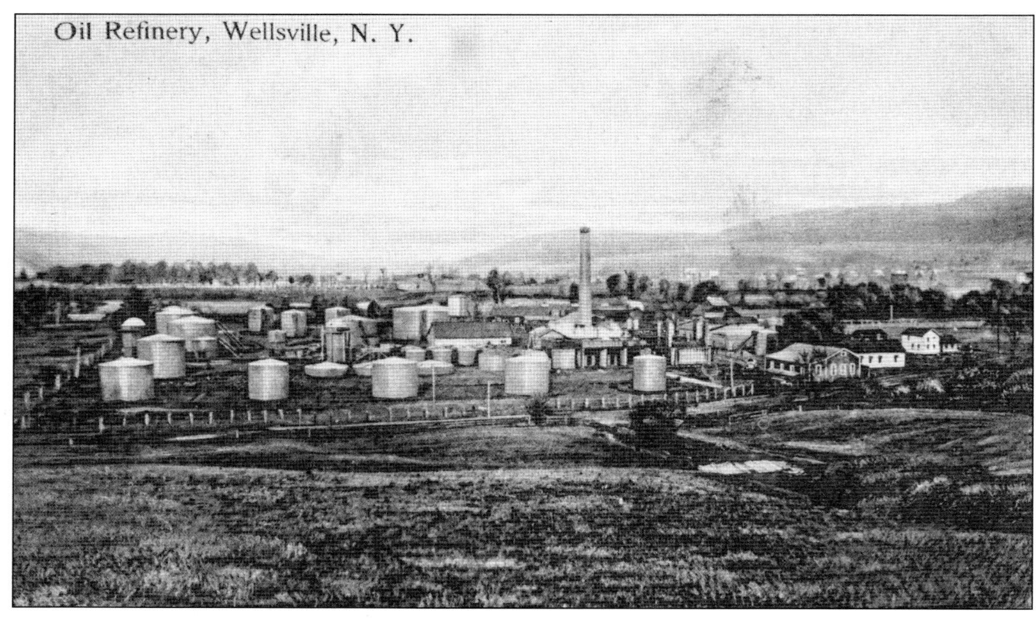

These two 1915 postcards show that the oil refineries were a big part of the area's landscape. Through the oil boom years of the late 1800s and early 1900s, Wellsville made itself the center for much of the industry's infrastructure: the sources of oil nearby, equipment, marketing, management offices, and more. It also became home to a good portion of the labor pool. Many of the wealthier families who made millions in gas and oil built beautiful homes in Wellsville and the surrounding communities. (Above, CRB; below, JP.)

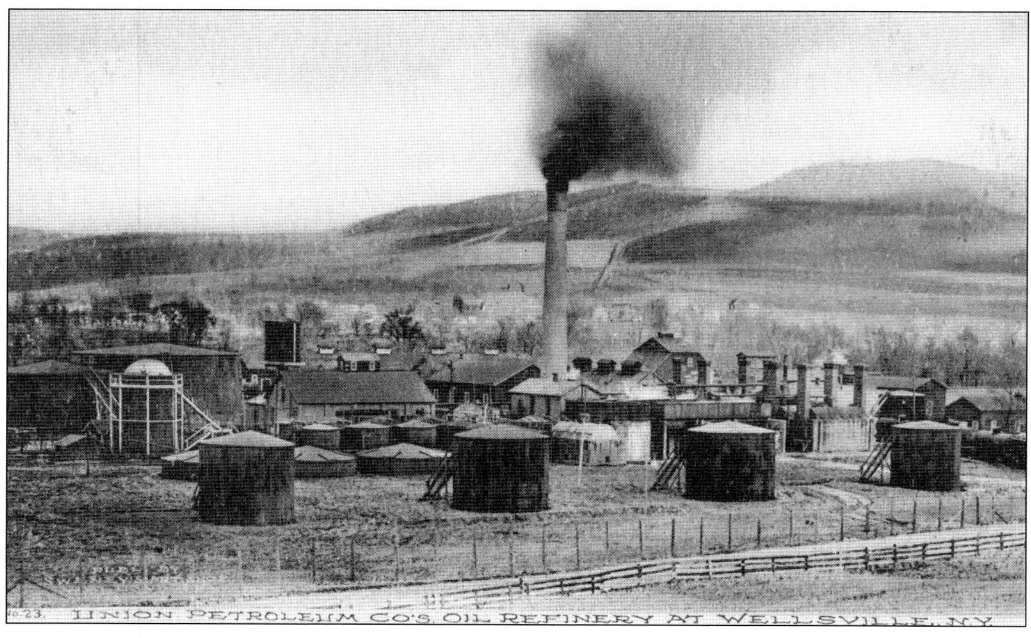

The oil business was a risky one as shown in this postcard. Torpedoing a well was a technique the oil workers used. An explosive agent was fired into the well to fracture the surrounding rock layer and stimulate the flow of oil. (JR.)

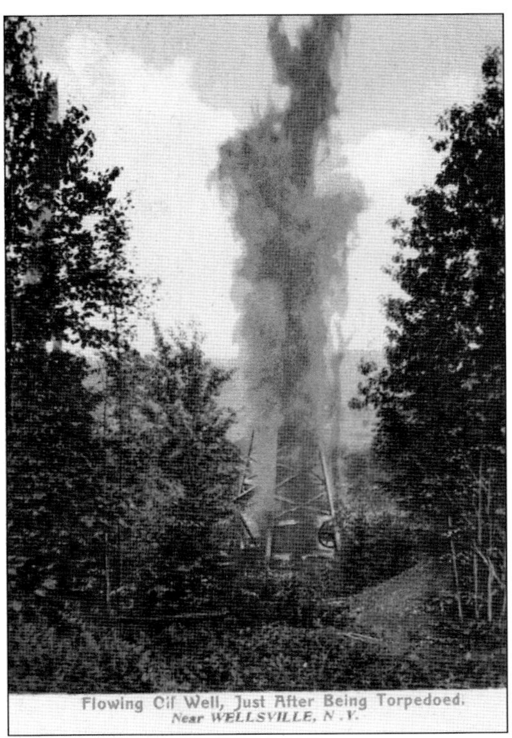

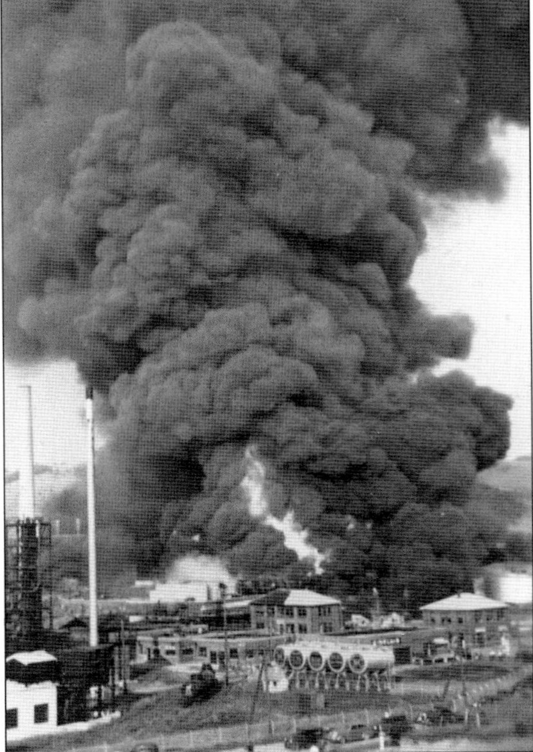

This three-day fire broke out at 4:00 p.m. on Sunday, July 17, 1938, in the de-waxing plant at the Sinclair Refinery in Wellsville. It finally burned out by Tuesday afternoon due to the use of foam and running out of fuel. It was the largest fire in the history of Allegany County in both size and expense. The company's loss was estimated to be over $1 million. (CRB.)

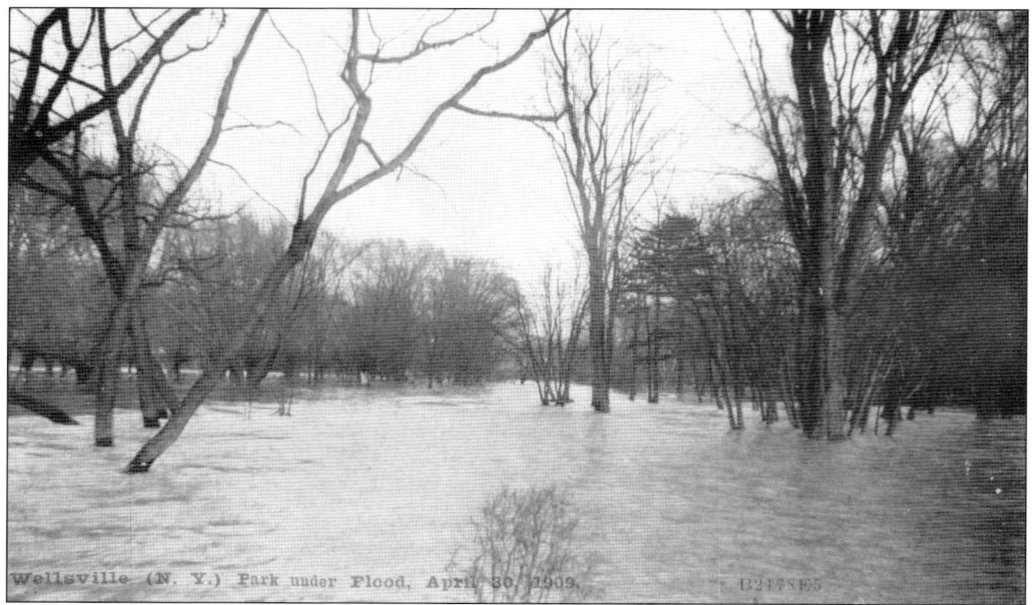

According to the May 7, 1909, issue of the *Belmont Dispatch*, the events of this flood took place quickly. On Wednesday, April 28, the Wellsville area was hit by a big snowstorm. This was followed by heavy rains the next day. These two events resulted in severe flooding conditions throughout the area. (CRB.)

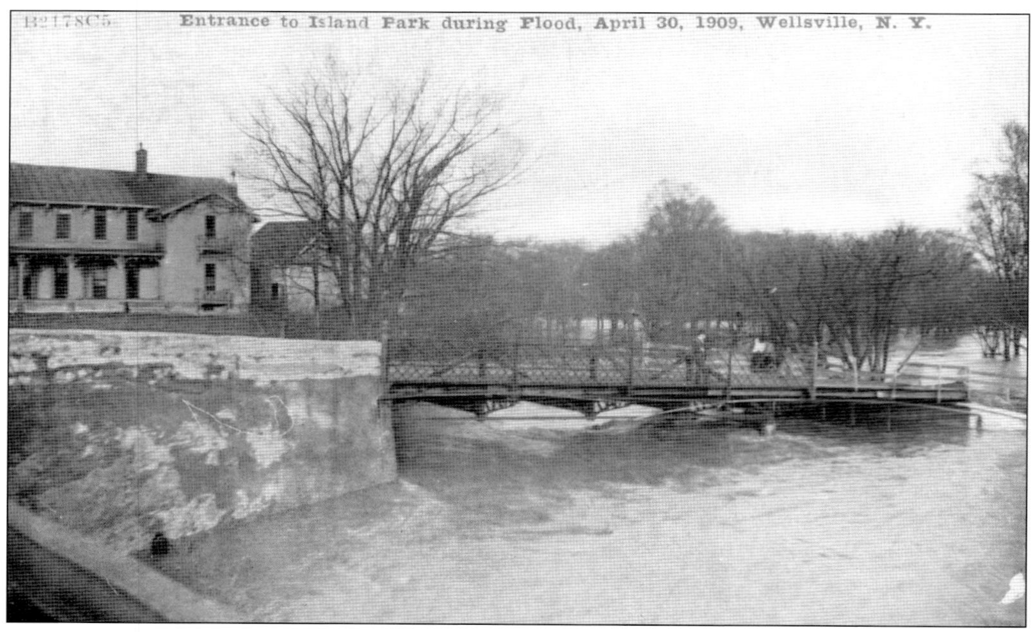

This postcard shows the entrance to Island Park during the devastating flash flood of April 30, 1909. The floodwaters took out the bridge on South Main Street in Wellsville. Residents had to be rescued and taken out by boat in the Ward Annex section of the village. Island Park and the Wellsville GAR Hall on Island Park were badly damaged. (CRB.)

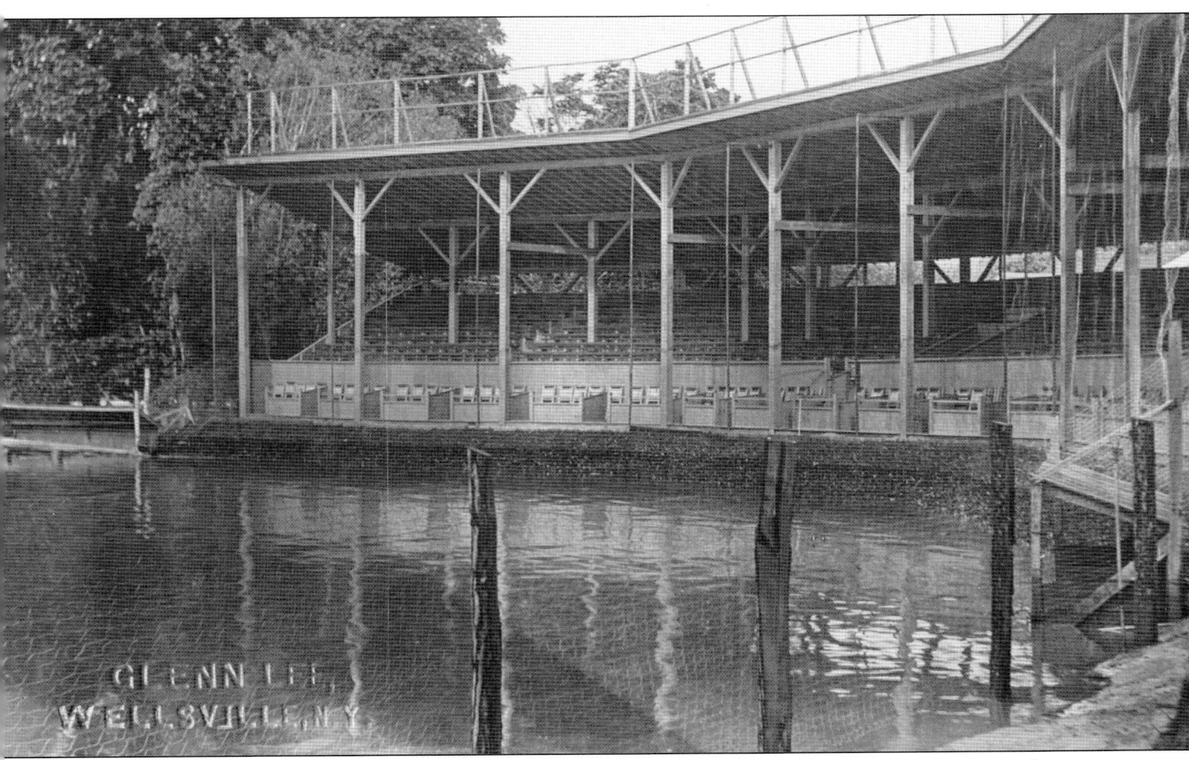

This is a fine example of a photo postcard showing Tullar Field during the flood of 1913. This type of documentation could be made quickly and distributed the same day. Enterprising America at its finest! Photographer Glenn Lee was based in Wellsville. The ballpark is a popular field in use today. (CRB.)

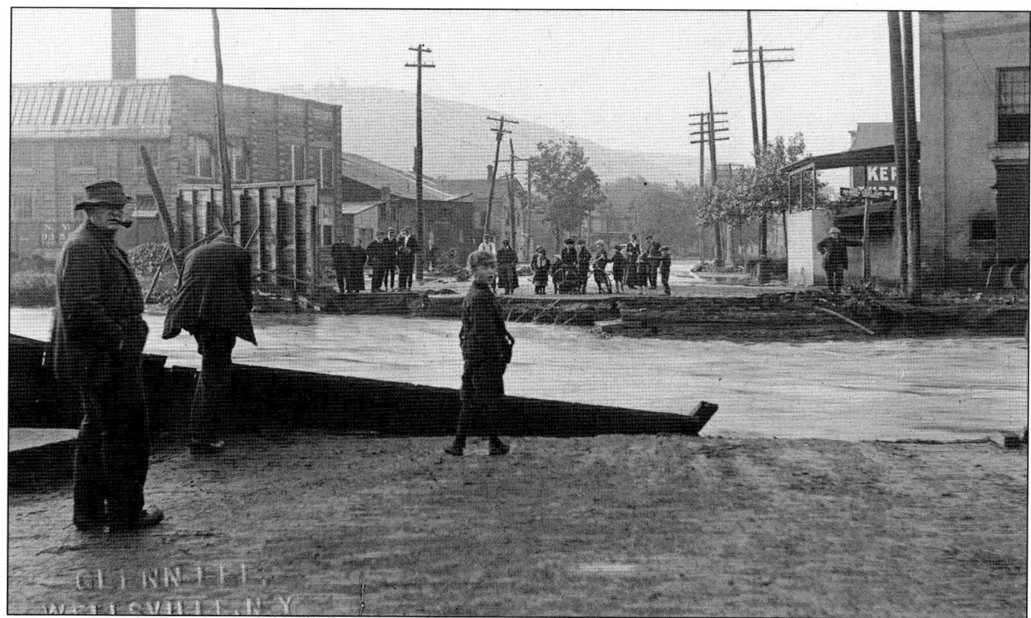

Local photographer Glenn Lee captured the events of the day in these beautiful photo postcards showing the extent of the flood in Wellsville. The flood of 1913 occurred on March 25. Extensive damage occurred in the west end of Angelica. The Pennsylvania railroad suffered three washouts between Belfast and Cuba. There were no deaths in Allegany County but one death in Hornell and one in Olean as a result of the flood. (JR.)

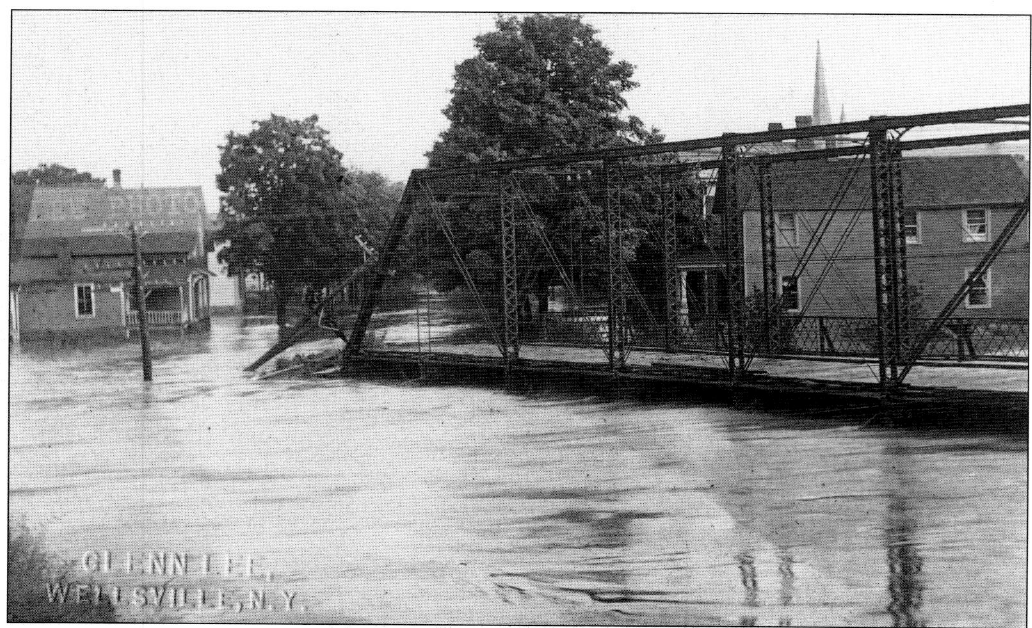

The overflow of the Genesee River during the flood of 1913 created havoc on many small bridges in the area. This beautiful photo postcard illustrates the depth of the floodwaters passing under a bridge in Wellsville. (JR.)

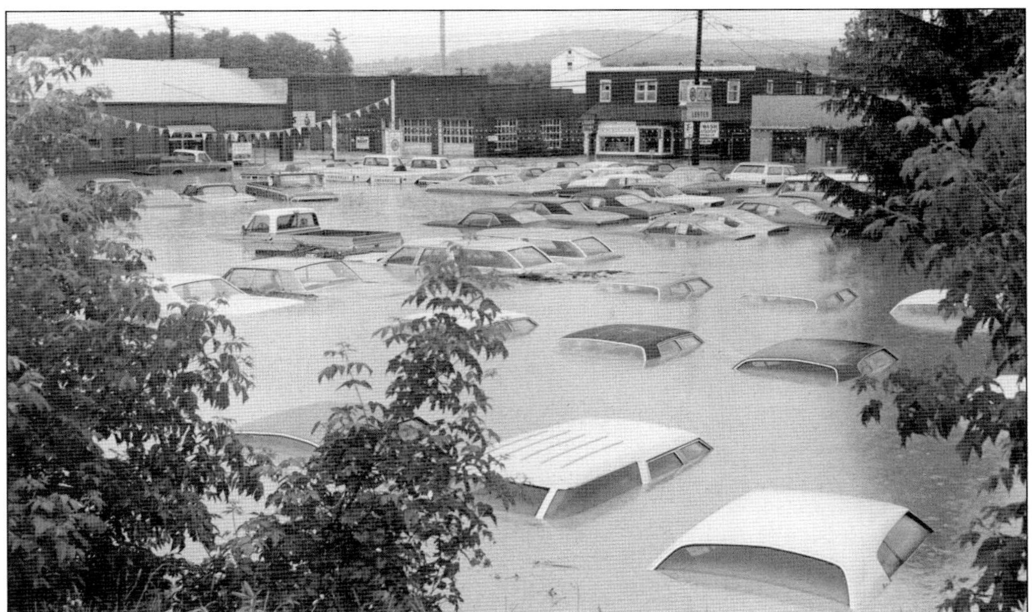

In western New York State, the flood of 1972 began with light showers beginning around 8:00 p.m. on June 20. Hurricane Agnes began on June 14 in the Caribbean, and then swept on up the eastern United States coastline. As she sailed into New York State, she seemed to slow and circle around the central part of the state, dropping copious amounts of water over the next five days. This photograph looks down South Main Street toward Lester Chevrolet. Rainfall totals in Wellsville reached 13.7 inches. (Allegany County History Society.)

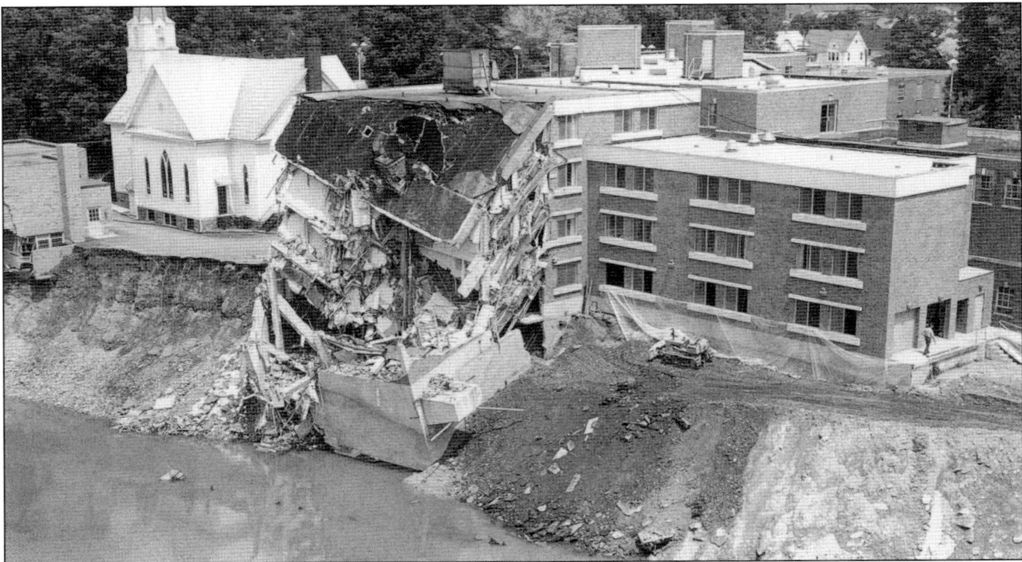

Wellsville was the hardest hit community in Allegany County in the flood of 1972. The Genesee River crested at 24 feet at 4:00 a.m. on Friday, June 23. At 6:40 a.m., the west wing of Jones Memorial Hospital collapsed into the swollen river. Five floors with 25 beds were lost, resulting in $1.9 million in damage. The Trinity Lutheran Parish Hall, to the left of the hospital, also collapsed. (Allegany County History Society.)

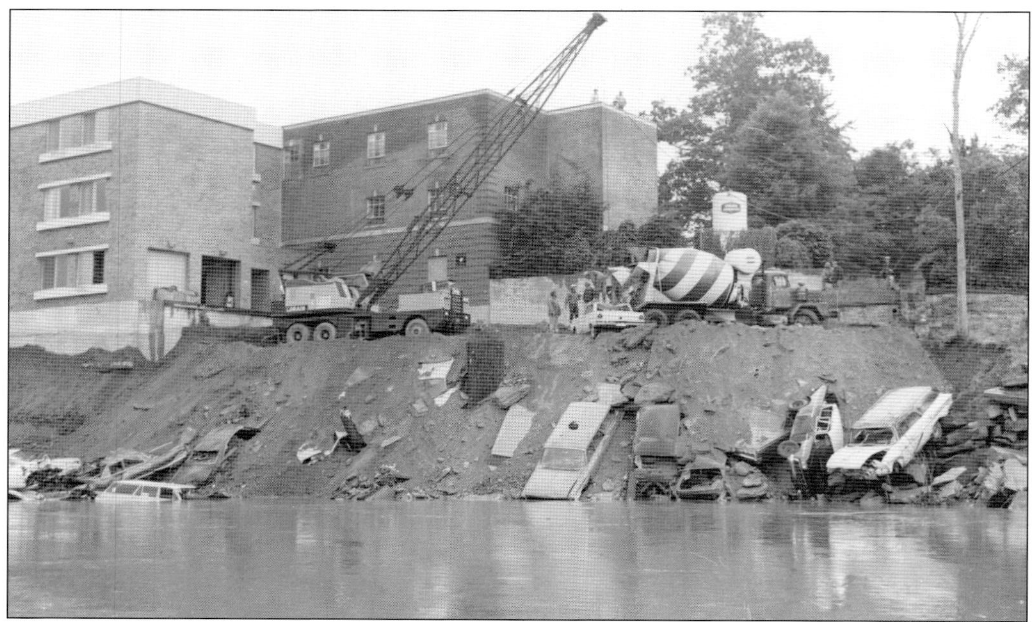

The most destructive widespread flooding to happen in the eastern United States occurred in June 1972 as a result of Hurricane Agnes. In this photograph are some of the numerous vehicles that were placed along the Genesee River bank to stem the erosion. (Allegany County History Society.)

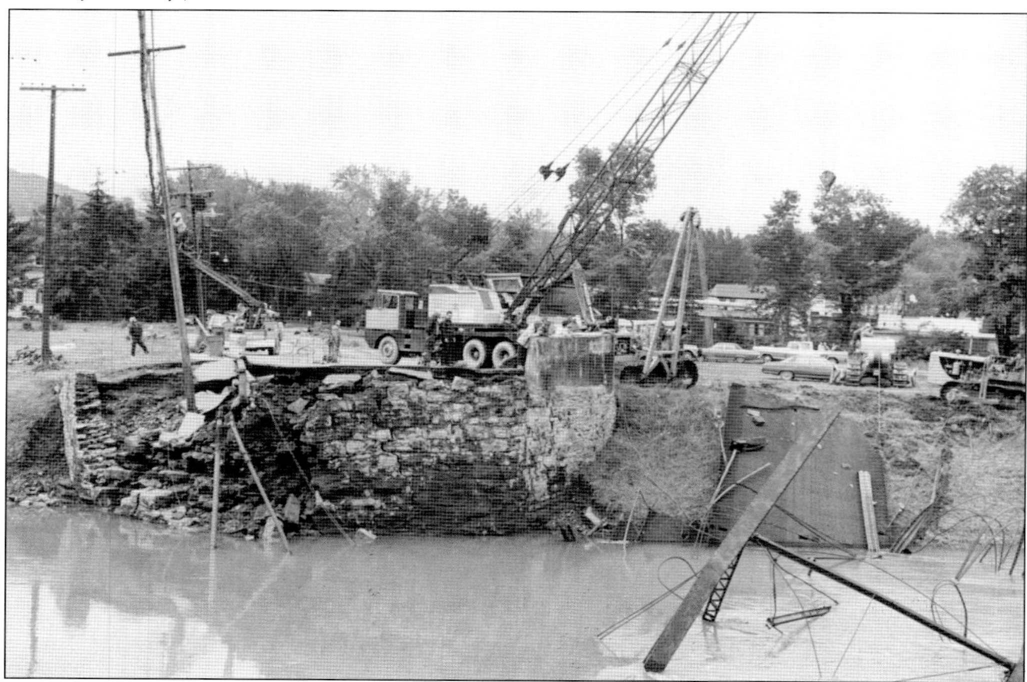

On a normal day, the Genesee River flows at 3,000 cubic feet per second. During this catastrophic flood, the flow was 72,000 cubic feet per second. Here is one of the many bridges destroyed by the raging waters. (Allegany County History Society.)

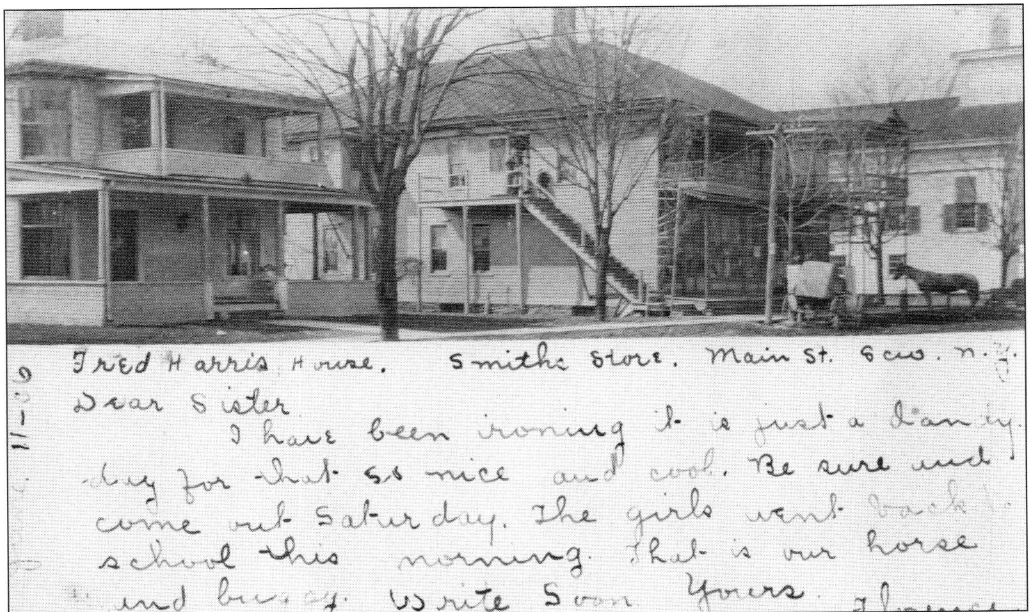

The first settlement in Scio was made at the mouth of Knights Creek in 1805 by Joseph Knight, a minuteman in the American Revolution, and his son Silas from Oneida County. The town of Scio was formed from the larger town of Angelica on January 31, 1823. (CL.)

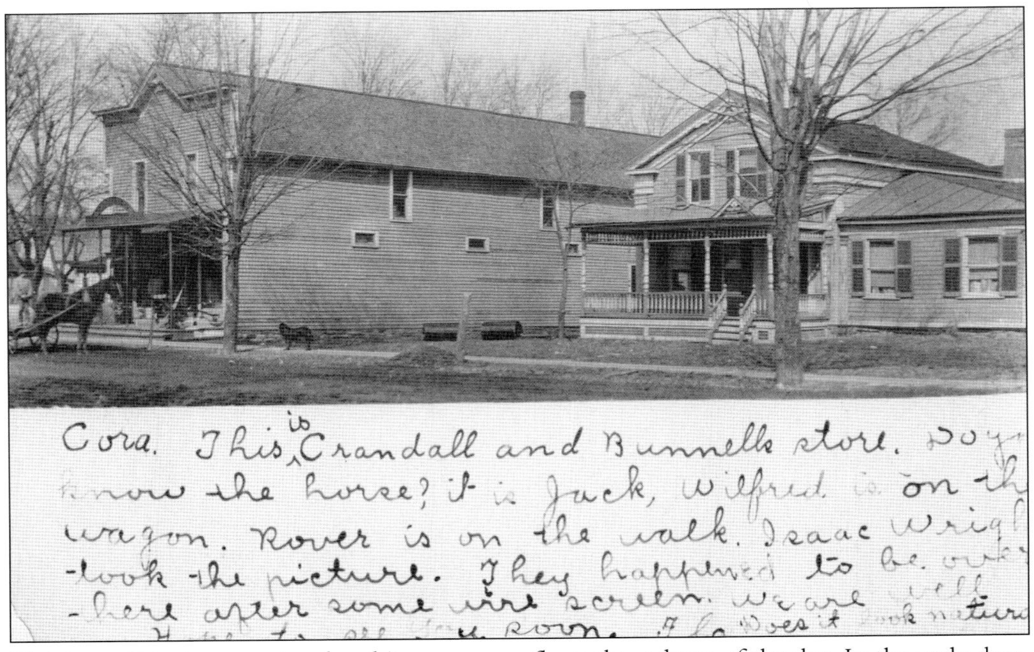

This beautiful photo postcard and its message reflects the culture of the day. In the early days, only the address was allowed on the back of the card; any message had to be written on the front. (CL.)

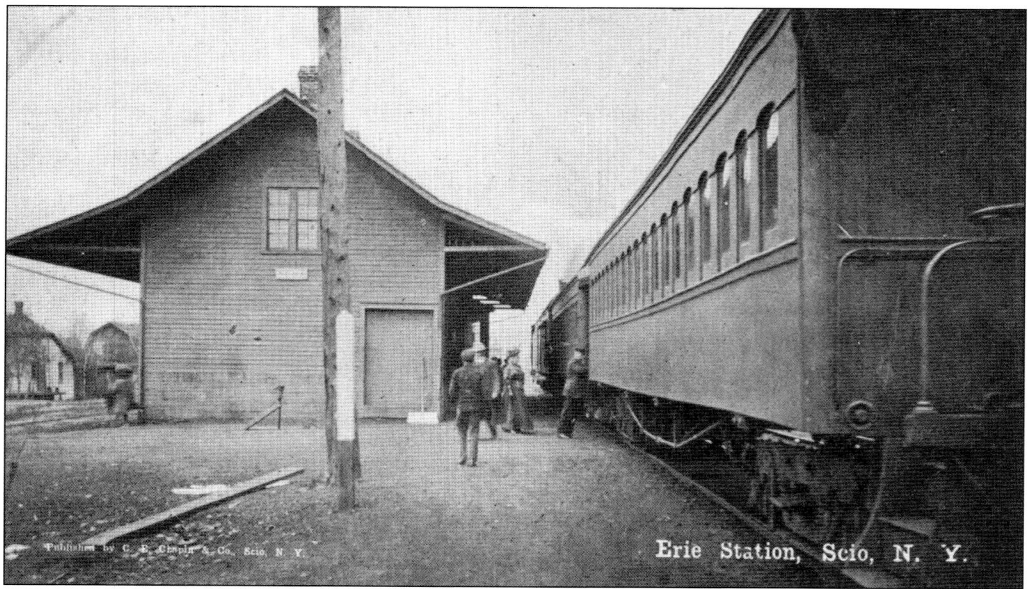

The first sawmill was erected in 1822 and the first gristmill in 1823 by Benjamin Palmer. The real growth to businesses in Scio was the coming of the Erie Railroad in May 1851. The arrival of the Erie was one of the greatest events in the history of the Southern Tier. (JR.)

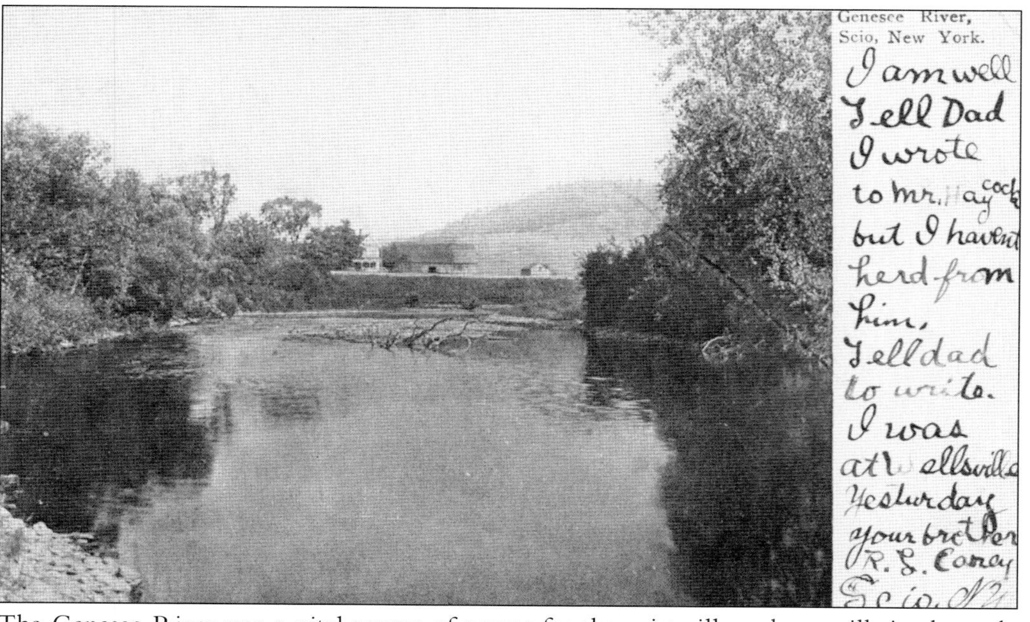

The Genesee River was a vital source of power for the gristmills and sawmills in the early 1800s. The postcard shows just one of many check dams that spanned the Genesee, diverting water to power nearby gristmills. Again, writings are on the front of the postcard due to postal regulations allowing only the address on the reverse side. (CRB.)

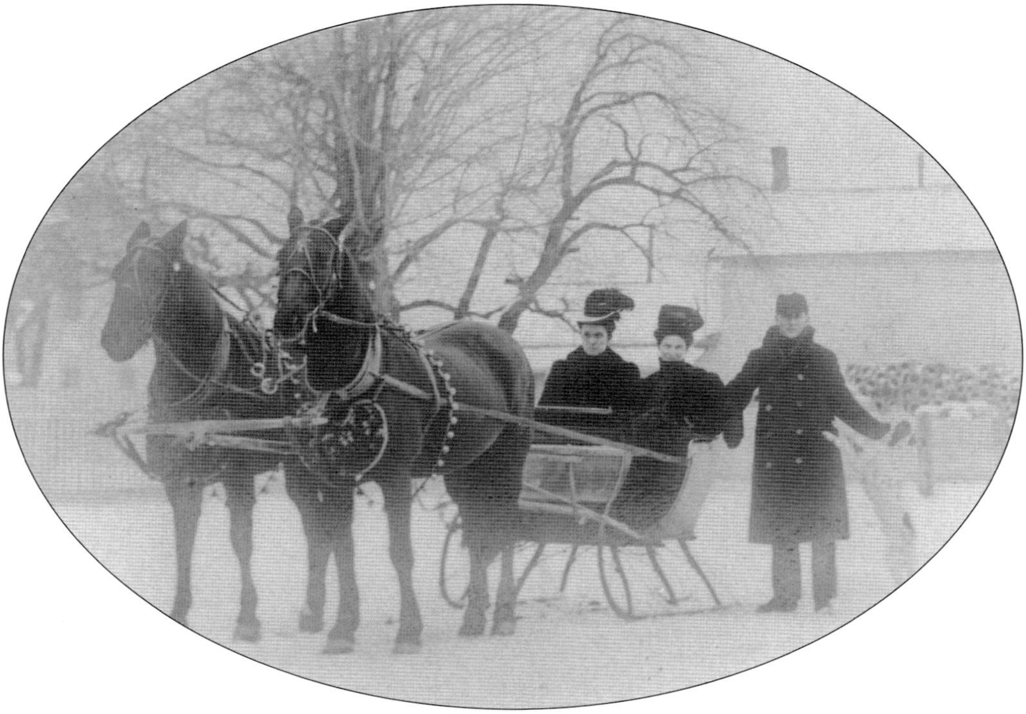

Life was simple in the early 1800s. Horse-drawn sleighs were used in the wintertime, and teams of horses were helping with the farmwork in spring and summer. Settlers cleared land along the Genesee for homes and farmland. Sadly, modern technology has made these scenes just memories today, except where Amish families have settled in small clusters throughout the valley. (CRB.)

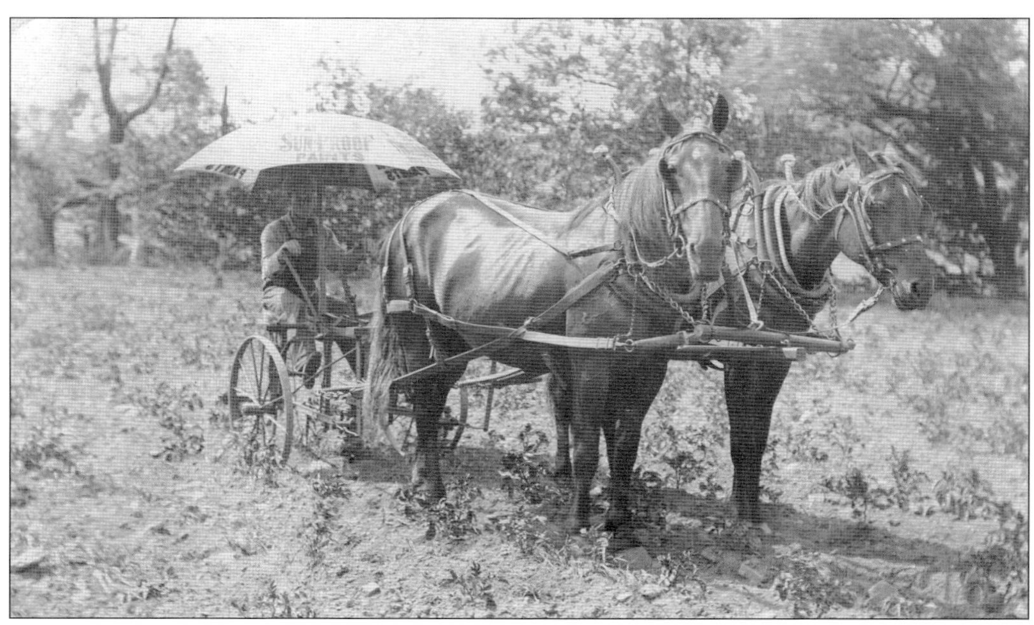

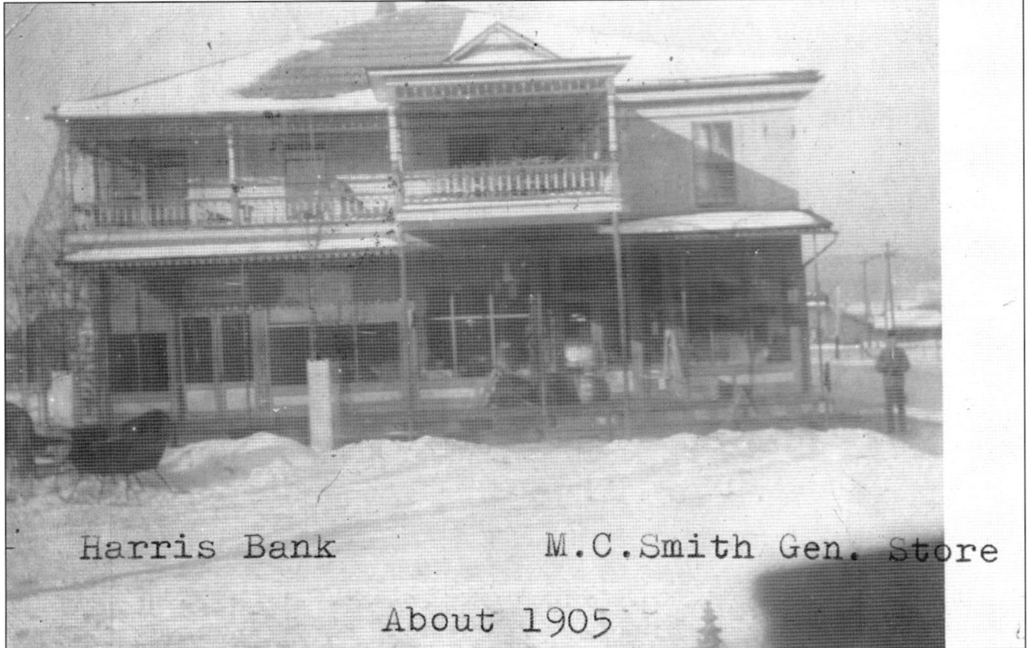

This beautiful photo postcard of Scio in 1905 shows a building used for multiple purposes. The Harris Bank is on the left side, and the M.C. Smith General Store is on the right. What great documentation when the sender had the foresight to add details to a postcard. (SPL.)

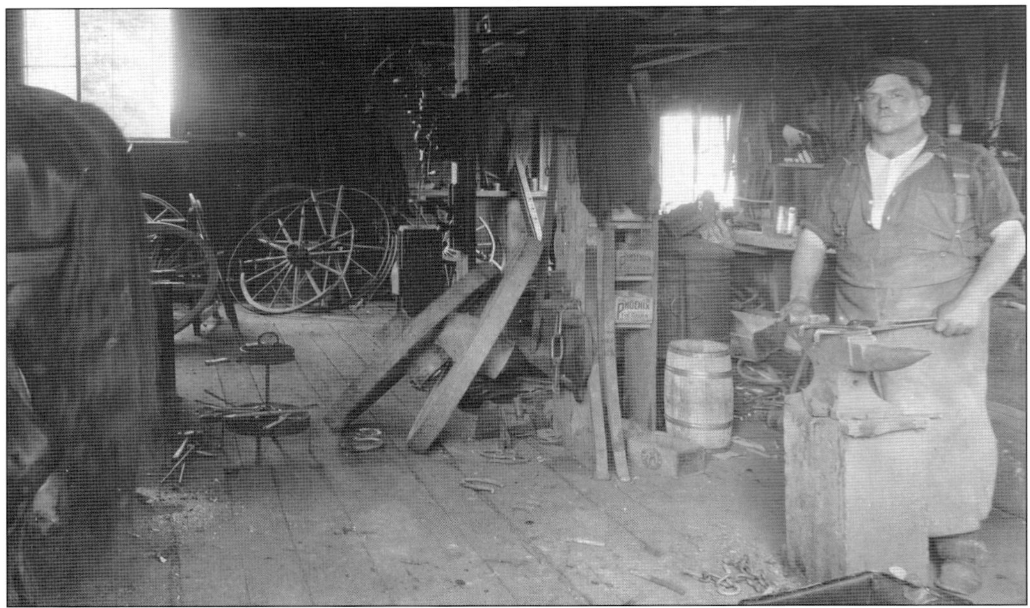

The role of the blacksmith in these early settlement days cannot be overestimated. A man could not place an order for machinery and tools easily or call the local repairman to come fix his equipment. However, the blacksmith working with iron would make and repair tools for other craftsmen. He fixed carts and wagons and made and mended household utensils. Eventually everyone in the countryside and villages needed the services of the blacksmith. (SPL.)

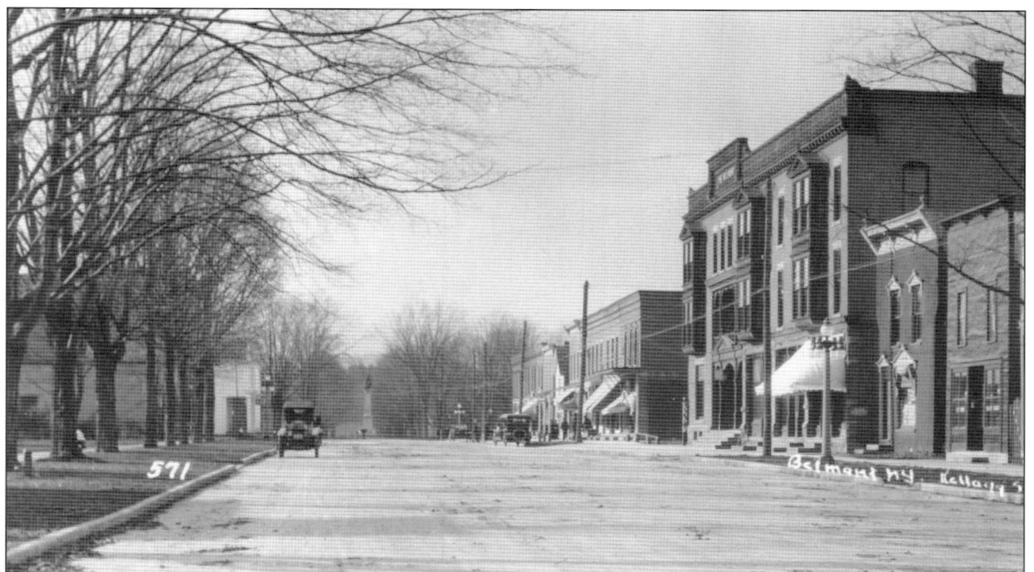

The Village of Belmont, New York, was incorporated in 1853 and was originally called Philipsville after Philip Church. It became the county seat for Allegany County in 1859, replacing Angelica. When the railroads began to come through the area, Belmont was on the rail line and Angelica was not. Then when the village absorbed the community of Miltonville on the east side of the Genesee River, it was renamed Belmont, meaning "Beautiful Hill." The population in 2010 was 969 people. (CRB.)

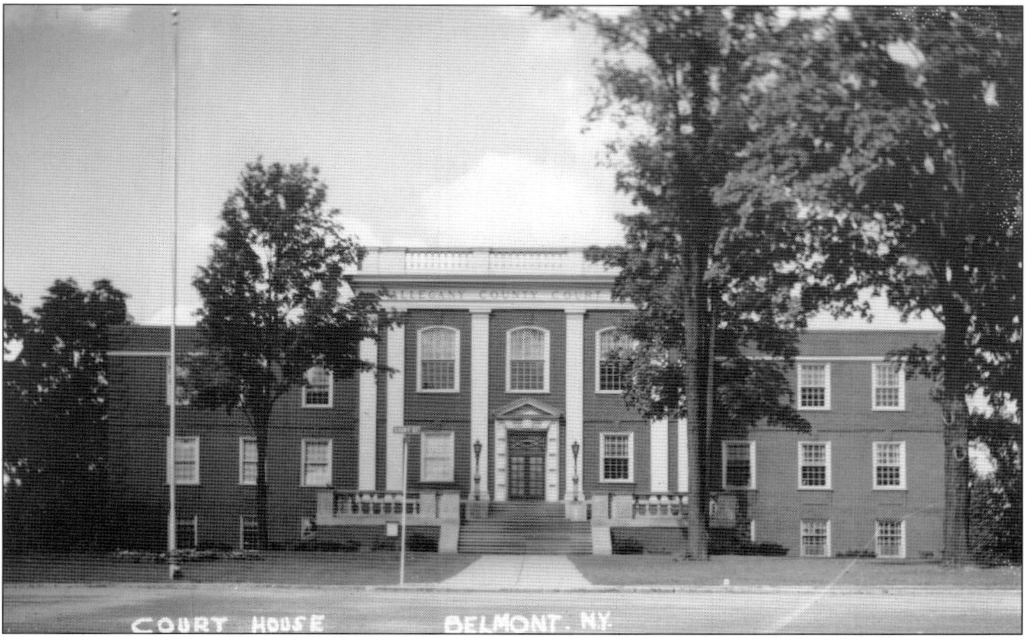

Belmont became the county seat of Allegany County in 1859, and a new courthouse was built. This building was torn down to make way for a new courthouse shown here, constructed in 1937. Inside the main courtroom is one of the most beautifully decorated courtrooms in the state. Today, the building houses part of the county court system and county offices. (CRB.)

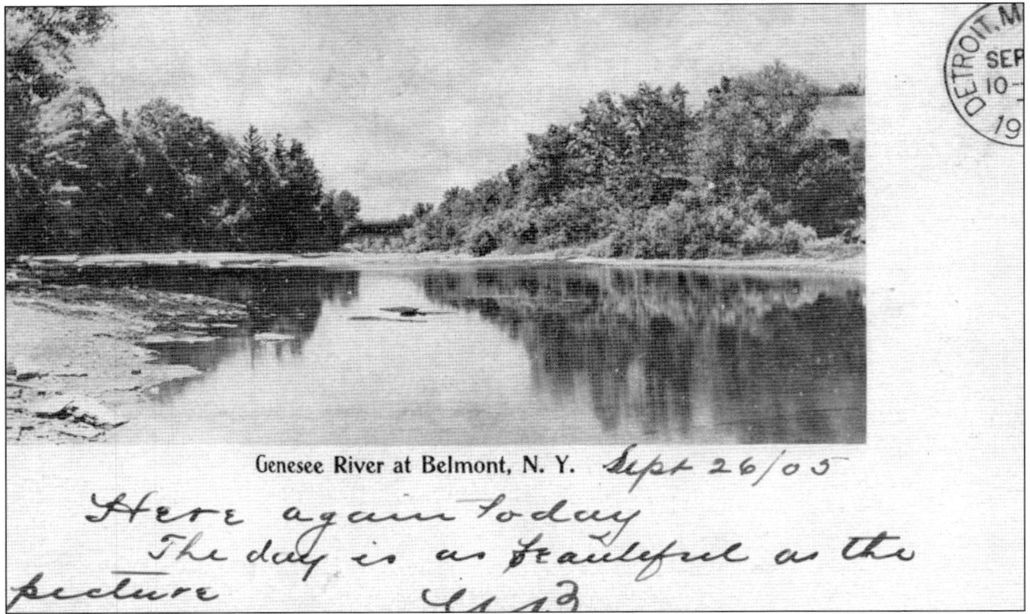

This 1905 postcard shows a serene view of the Genesee River as it flows through the middle of Belmont. Area residents and visitors alike have always appreciated the beautiful river in their backyards when it is peaceful like this. (CRB.)

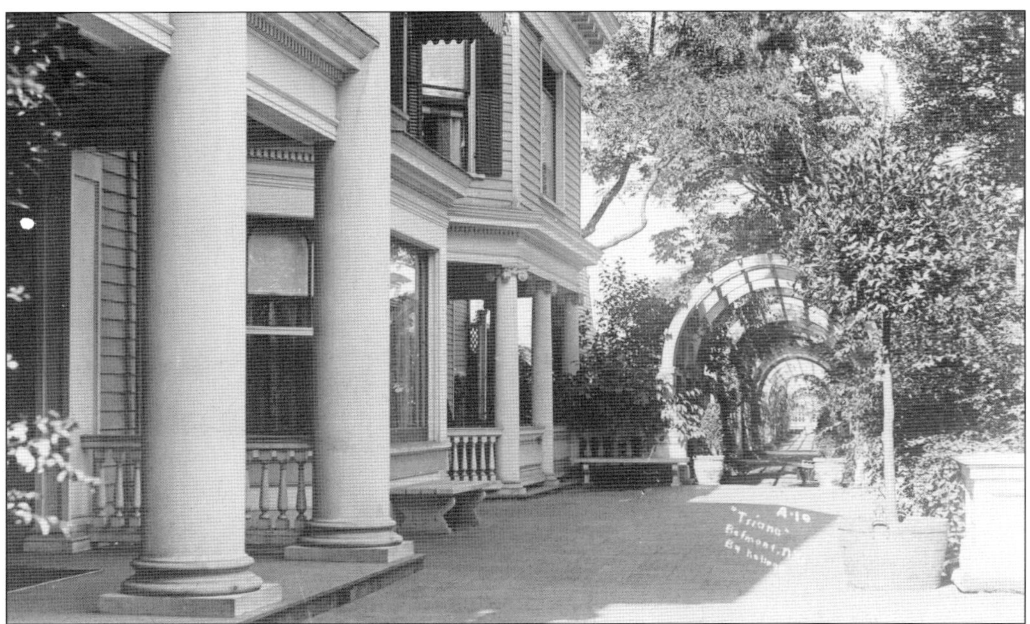

This beautiful Belmont Victorian mansion proudly stands on Willetts Avenue today. The home was owned by Elmore Willetts, founder of the Bank of Belmont. Today, the bank is a branch of Steuben Trust Company. (CRB.)

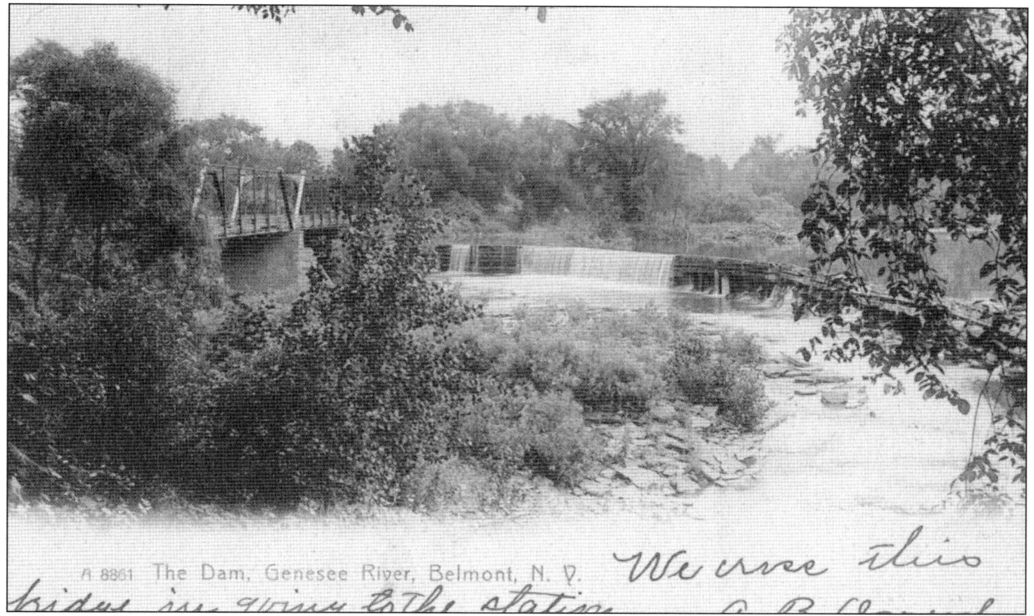

The early settlers were drawn to the Genesee River Valley by the availability of tremendous waterpower and the fertile soil along the river. In this postcard view, the Genesee River cascades over a small dam in the village of Belmont. In the 1800s, a dam on this location diverted water to operate a nearby mill. (CRB.)

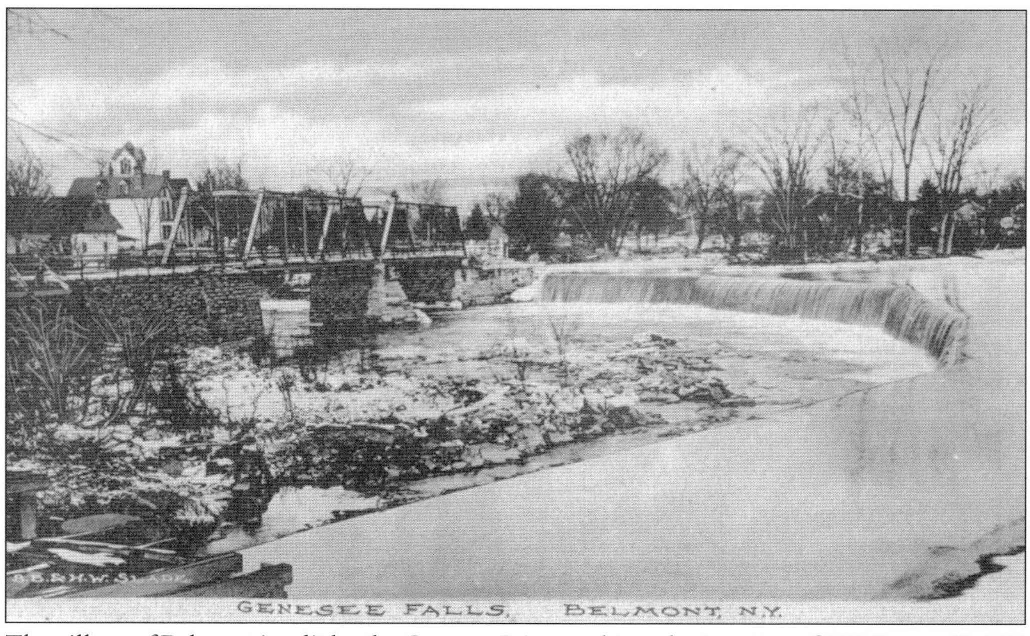

The village of Belmont is split by the Genesee River and is at the junction of NY Route 19, NY Route 244, and County Road 48. This horseshoe falls/dam in Belmont is only a couple of feet high, but its impressive curve is viewed by every traveler passing through the village. (CRB.)

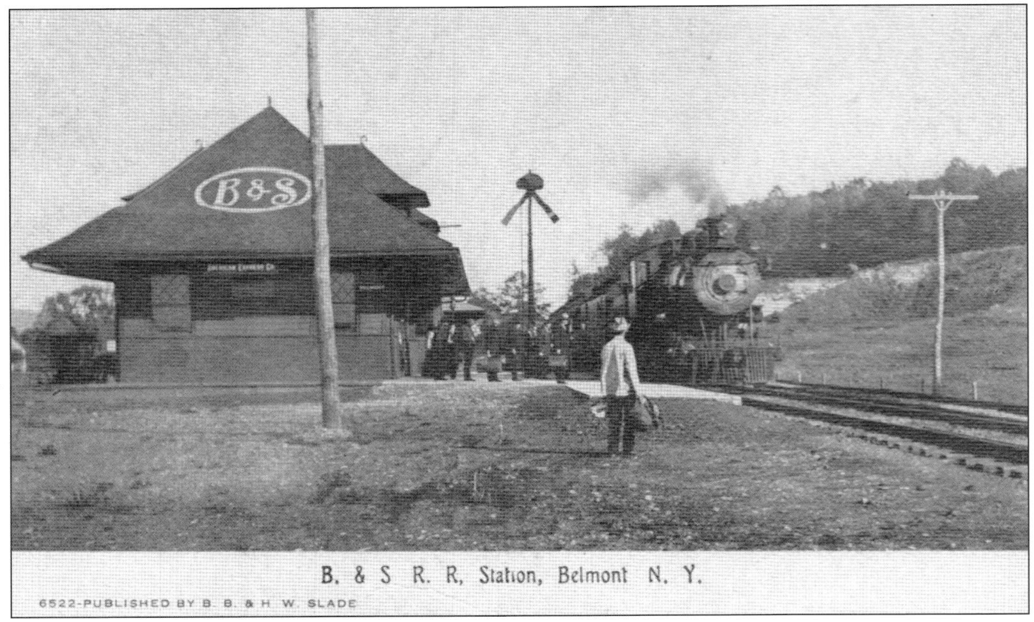

The Buffalo & Susquehanna Railroad was a railroad company that formerly operated in western and north central Pennsylvania and western New York State. It was created in 1893 by the merger and consolidation of several smaller logging railroads. The B&S reached Belmont in the early 1900s. It was a main route connecting Buffalo on the Great Lakes, through the Susquehanna Valley, to the Atlantic seaboard in Baltimore. The north and south tracks connected many depots along the Genesee that included Scio, Belfast, and Wellsville. (CRB.)

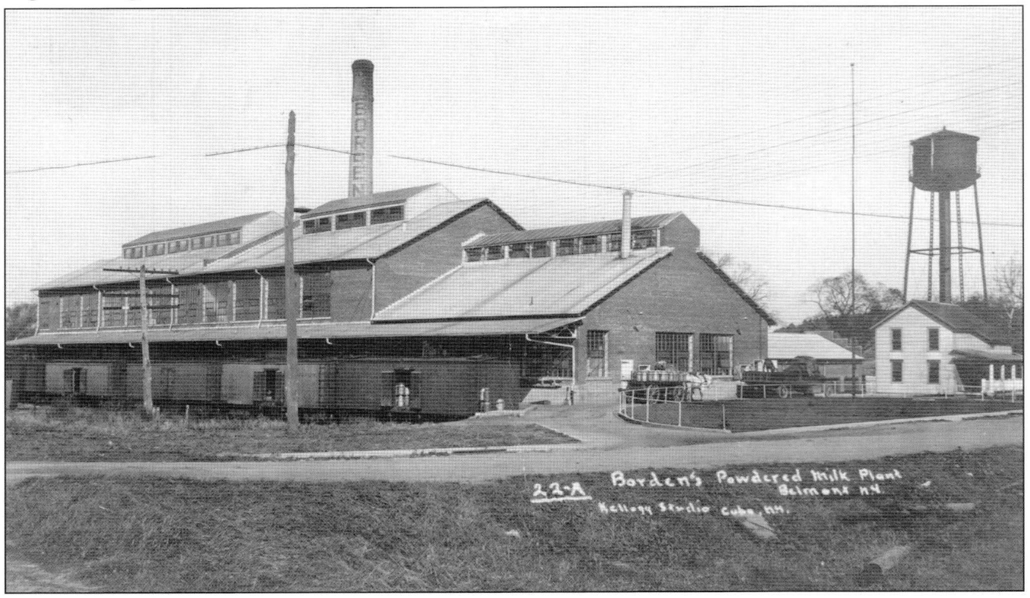

This postcard features the Borden's Powered Milk Plant in Belmont, New York, later known as the Borden Condensery. It was one of the areas biggest employers due to its location near the railroad. The building still stands today and over the years has been used by a number of industries. (CRB.)

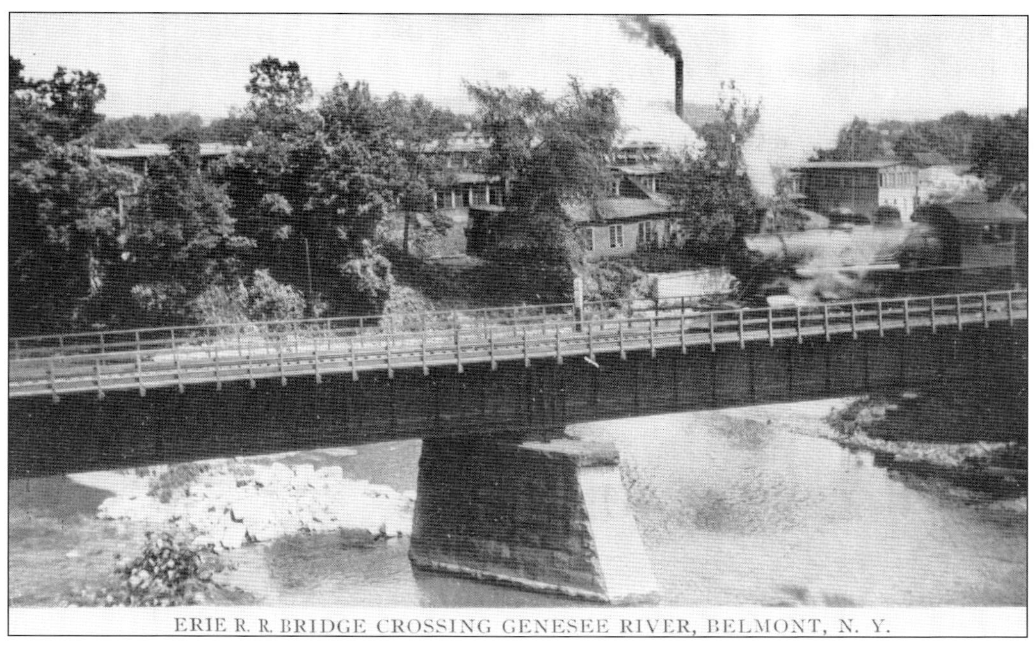

A principle reason for the rapid growth in population in the Belmont region was the arrival of the Erie Railroad through the Genesee Valley in 1851. This bridge still stands today and is in use for the Norfolk Southern Railroad. (CRB.)

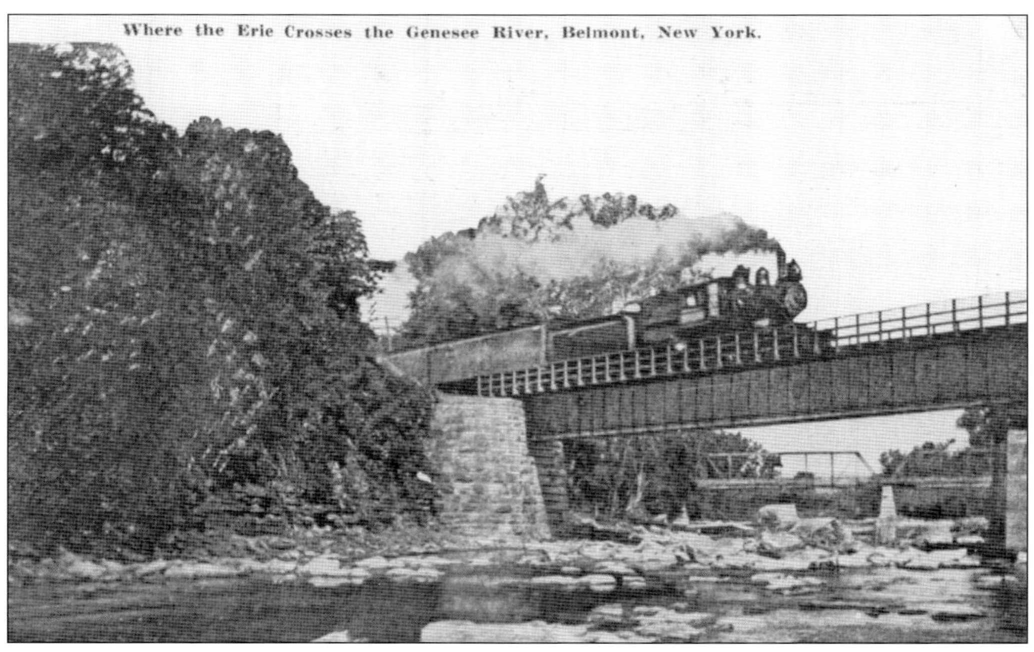

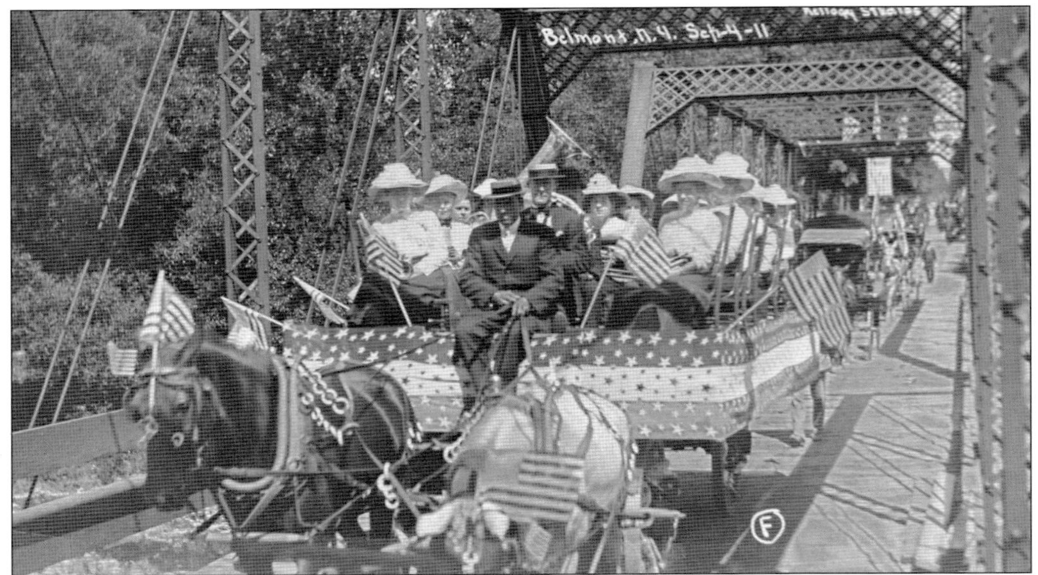

The two spectacular photo cards on this page show America at its finest. The scenes are a Labor Day parade on September 14, 1911. A beautifully decorated wagon pulled by a team of horses has on board a women's band that is made up of Josephine Rutherford and Bessie Ford, among other ladies, with George Williams as the conductor. (BHS.)

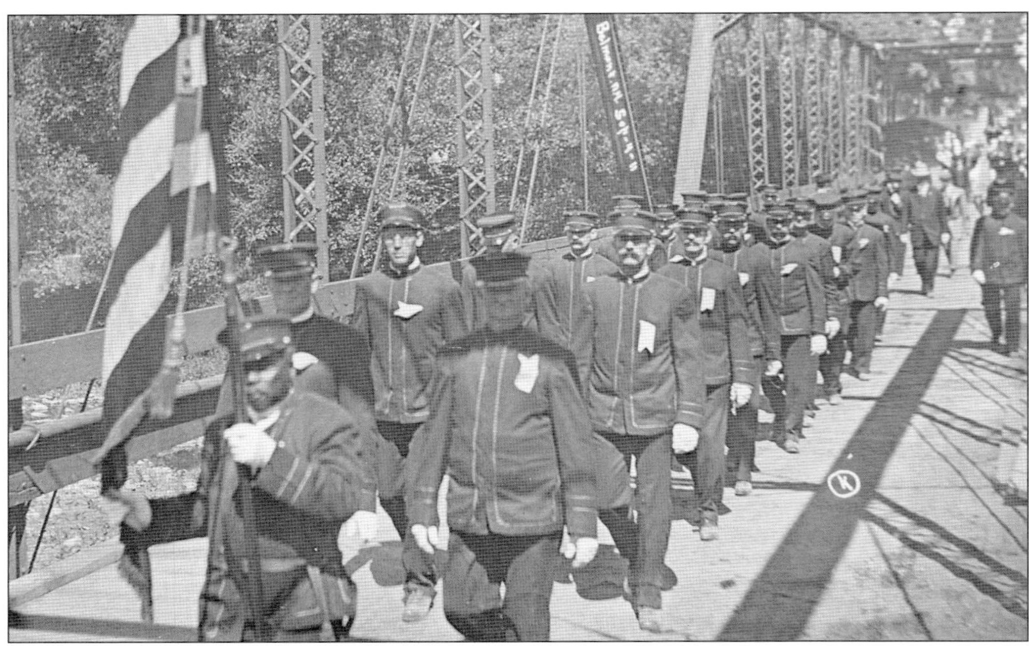

Parade spectators have long enjoyed watching their fire department members march in resplendent dress uniforms and witnessing friendly competition between departments. In this image, a group of Belfast firemen parades in dress uniform as they cross the Genesee Street Bridge, now Route 244, over the Genesee River. (BHS.)

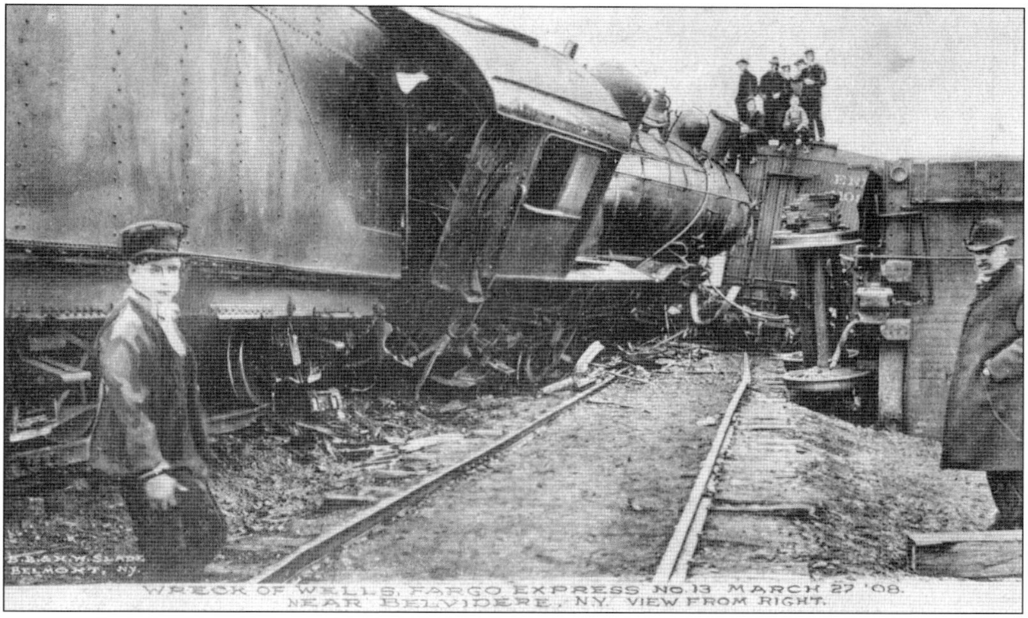

On March 27, 1908, the Wells Fargo Express Train No. 13 wrecked near Belvidere, New York. A head-on collision between the Wells Fargo Express Train No. 13 and the second section of train 82, near the JX Tower, two miles west of Belvidere on the morning of March 27, resulted in the death of engineer H.L. Helmer of Hornell, New York, and fireman James Cannon of Andover. Engineer Helmer was one of the best-known men in the city and had been a faithful and very efficient engineer. His popularity was evident when over 200 Erie employees attended his funeral on Sunday, March 29. (CL.)

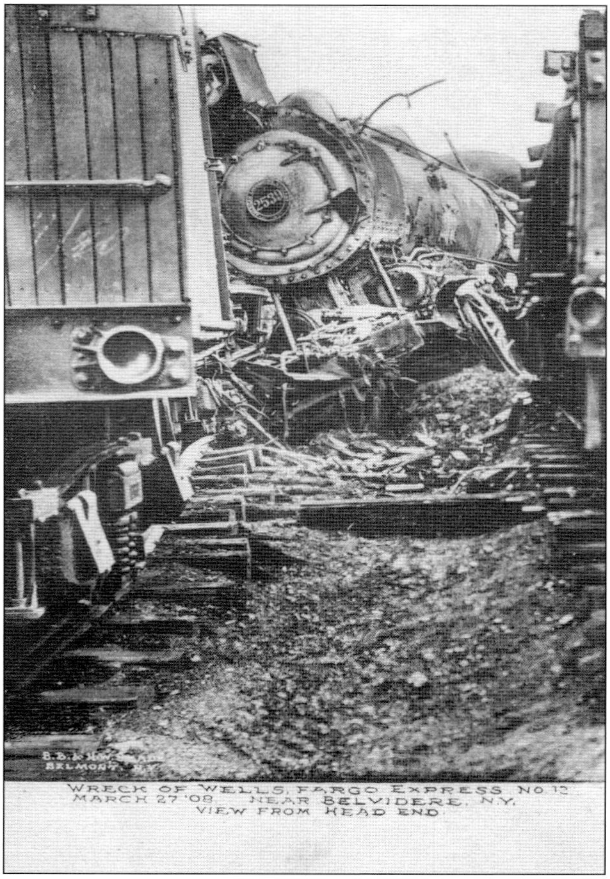

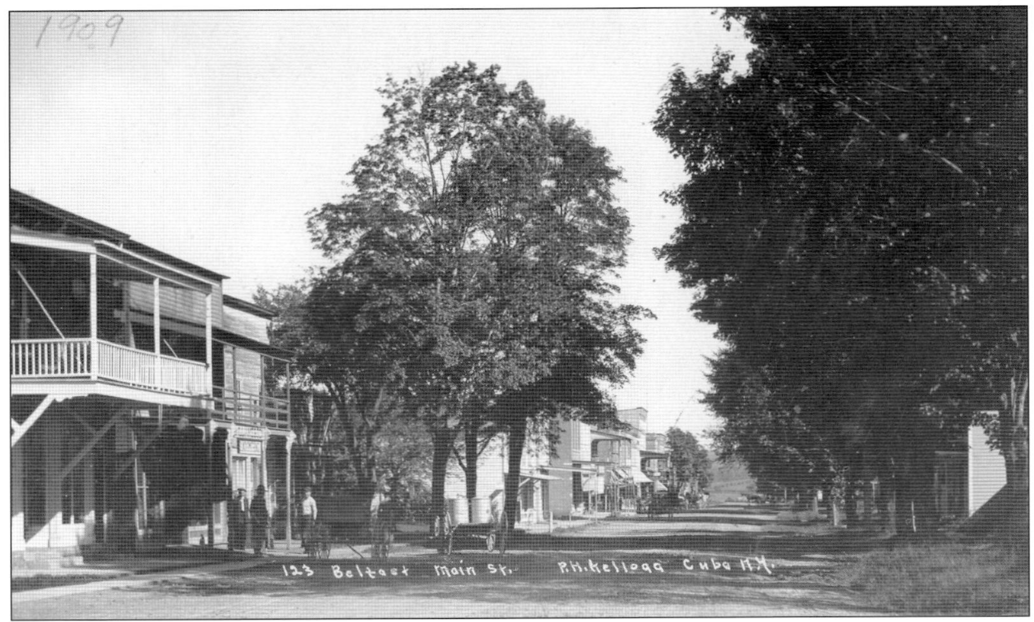

The first settlers arrived in the Belfast, New York, area in 1804. The Town of Belfast was established in 1824. It became primarily a mill town using the mighty power of the Genesee. (CRB.)

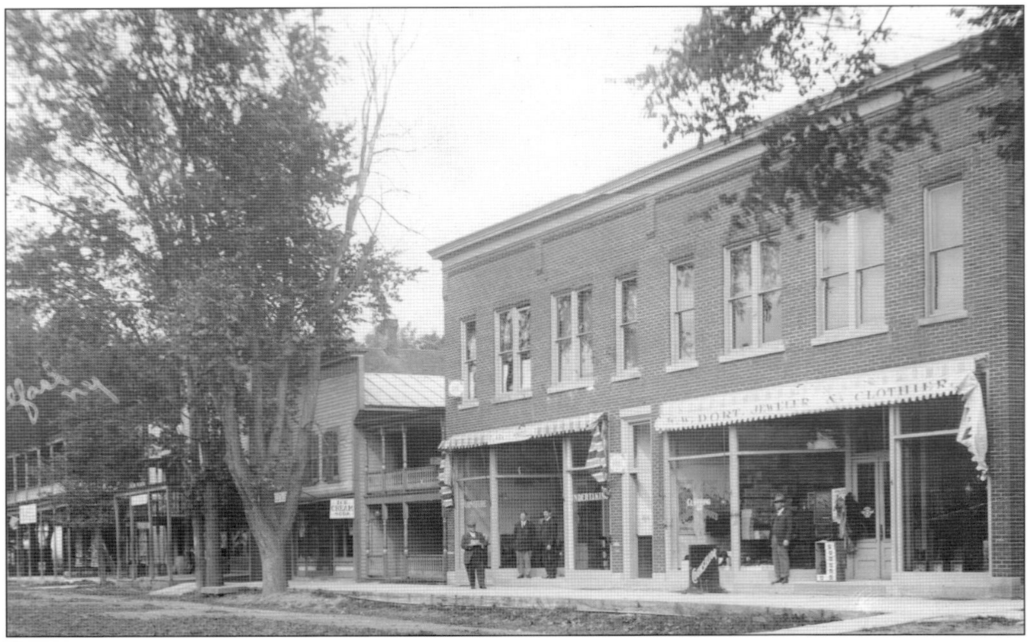

Belfast, a hamlet located on Route 19 on the west bank of the Genesee, was originally called Orrinsburgh. It has been the center of a farming community, a canal town, and a main line on the antislavery Underground Railroad prior to the Civil War. (CRB.)

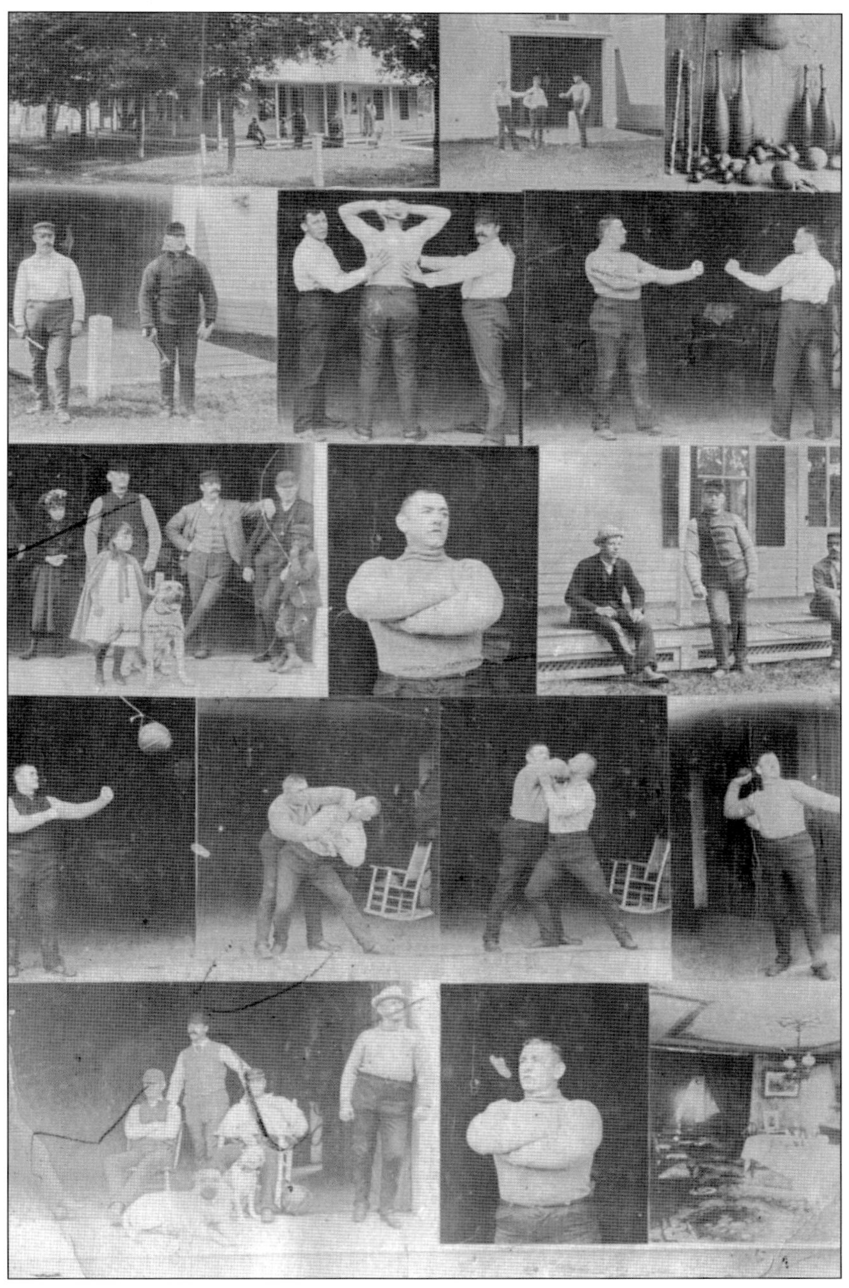

In 1889, John L. Sullivan, a world famous prizefighter, came to Belfast and established a camp to train for the last bare knuckle boxing Championship of the World. He was managed by Belfast native William Muldoon. His impressive career included 35 wins, one loss, and two draws, with 30 of those wins by knockout. In 1990, Sullivan was inducted into the International Boxing Hall of Fame. He was the last bare knuckle boxing champion in the world. Muldoon's barns have stood virtually untouched for more than 120 years. In 2009, the converted horse barns where Sullivan trained have been restored and are now the home of the Bare Knuckle Boxing Hall of Fame. (CRB.)

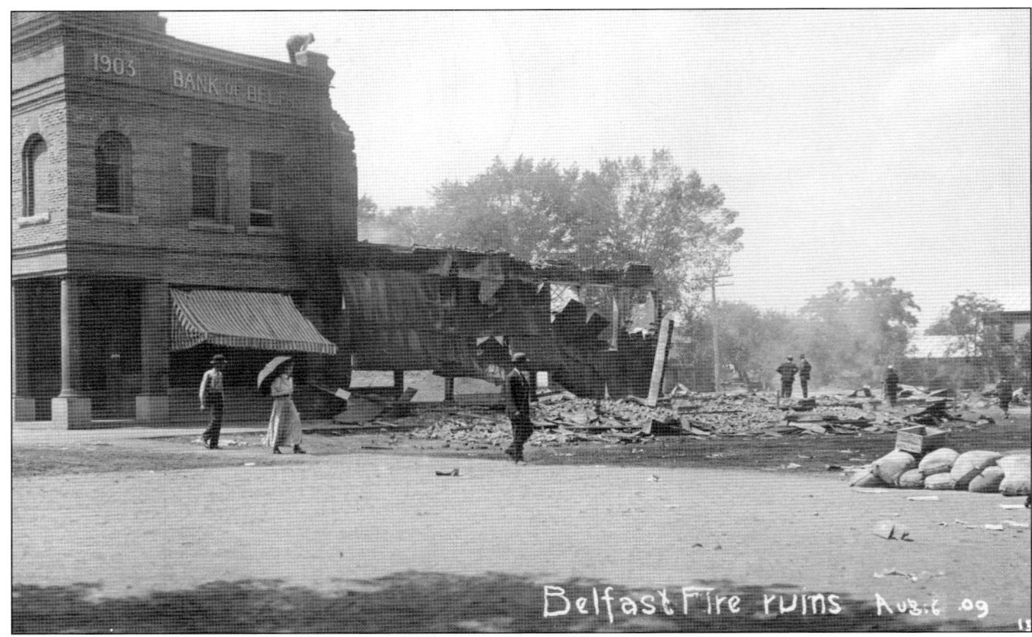

Almost every early community suffered extensively from fire at one time or another. This was mostly based on having wooden structures. Belfast residents here are observing with dismay the burned out wreckage of their main business block. The fire took place in August 1909 and burned the lower end of the Main Street business block to the bank. (CRB.)

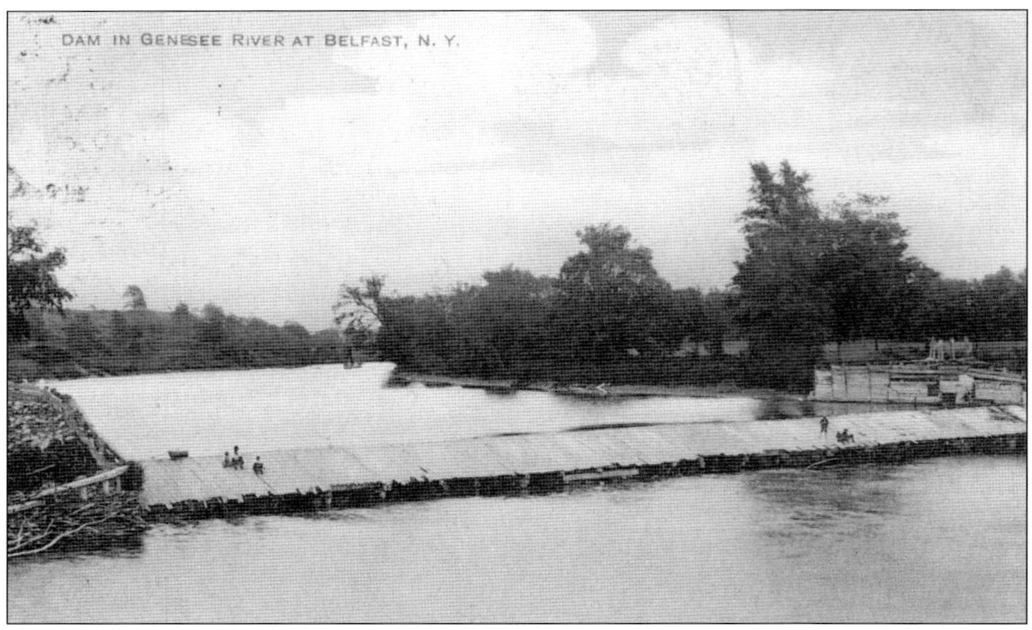

Here is a small check dam in the Genesee near Belfast. These small dams were common in many towns along the Genesee River. They were used to divert water from the river to nearby gristmills. (CRB.)

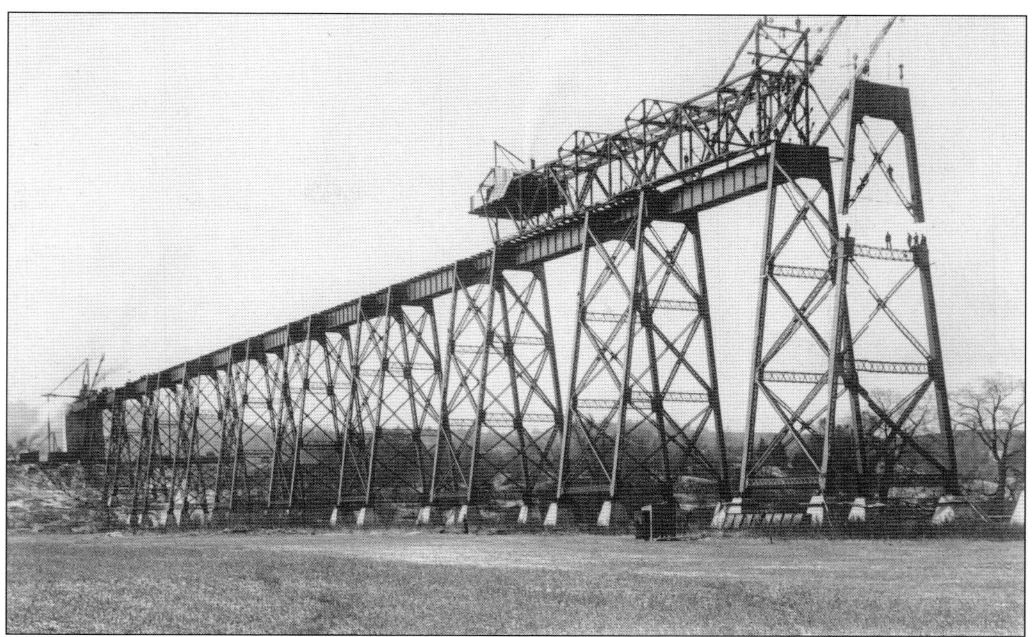

The Erie-Lackawanna Viaduct was a magnificent landmark for residents and visitors in Allegany County traveling along Route 19 between Belfast and the hamlet of Oramel. Notice that the relative size of the men in the foreground clearly shows how immense the Erie trestle in Belfast was. During the flood of June 1972, this amazingly constructed bridge stood firm. (CRB.)

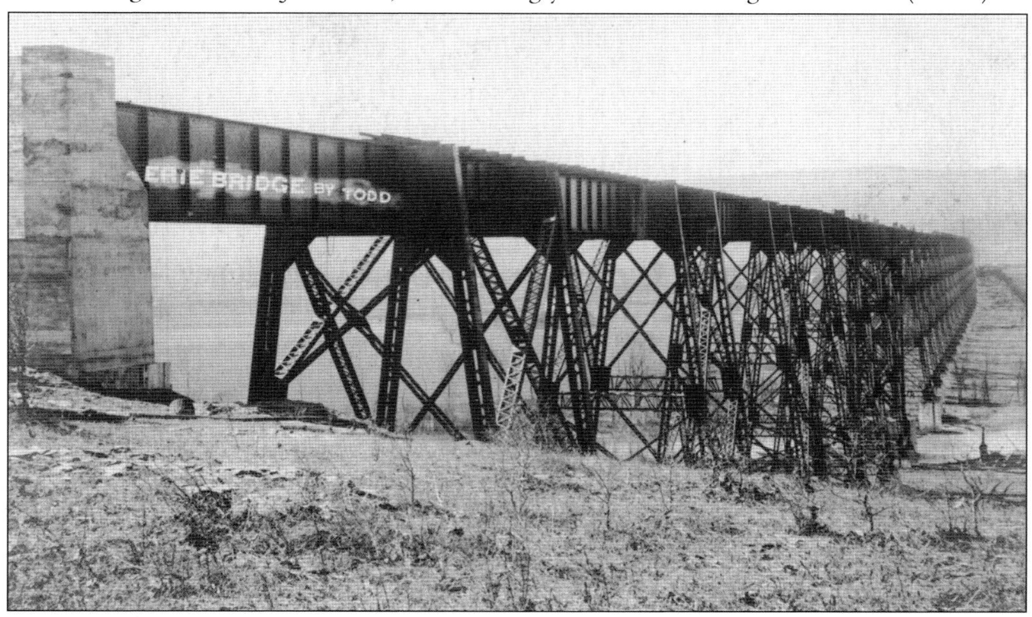

In March 1981, workers began dismantling the 72-year-old Belfast Bridge to be sold as scrap. Despite protestors who wanted to preserve the no longer used structure as a historic landmark, the trestle soon was just a memory. In spite of their efforts, this miracle of engineering and beauty was gone by August 1981. Today, in a marshy field alongside the river, the concrete pillars are all that remain except for memories and photographs like these. (CRB.)

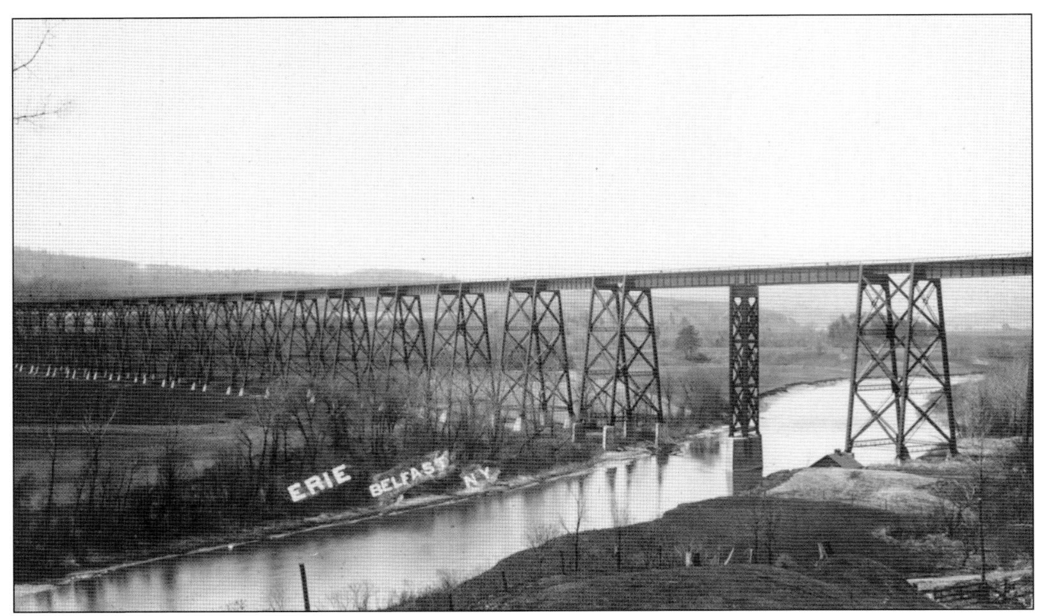

Construction on the Belfast Trestle began in 1906 with the pouring of concrete pedestals. By 1907, the steel construction began. This viaduct spanning the Genesee River Valley was completed in 1908 at a cost of $464,000. The railroad bridge was comprised of 4,089 tons of steel hauled to the site by teams of horses; 500 construction men worked for two years to complete the project. The bridge was 3,120 feet long and 140 feet high. There were 24 tower spans that were 40 feet long, 24 intermediate spans that were 80 feet long, and two river spans that were 120 feet long. Piers and abutments contained 11,600 cubic yards of concrete. The foundations rested on 10,819 lineal feet of timber pilings. Below, a test train crosses the Belfast trestle. (CRB.)

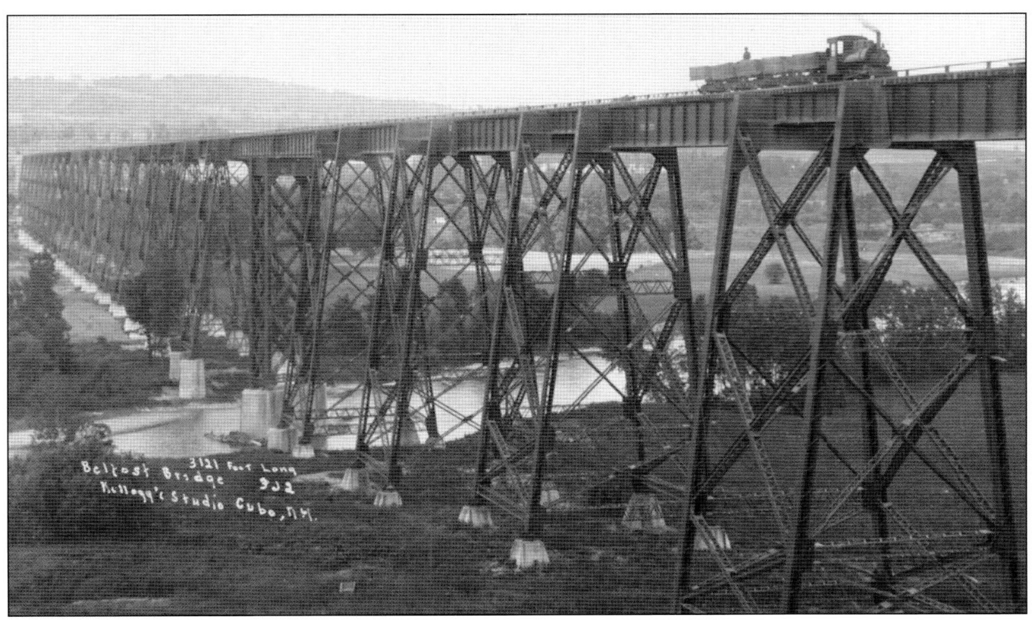

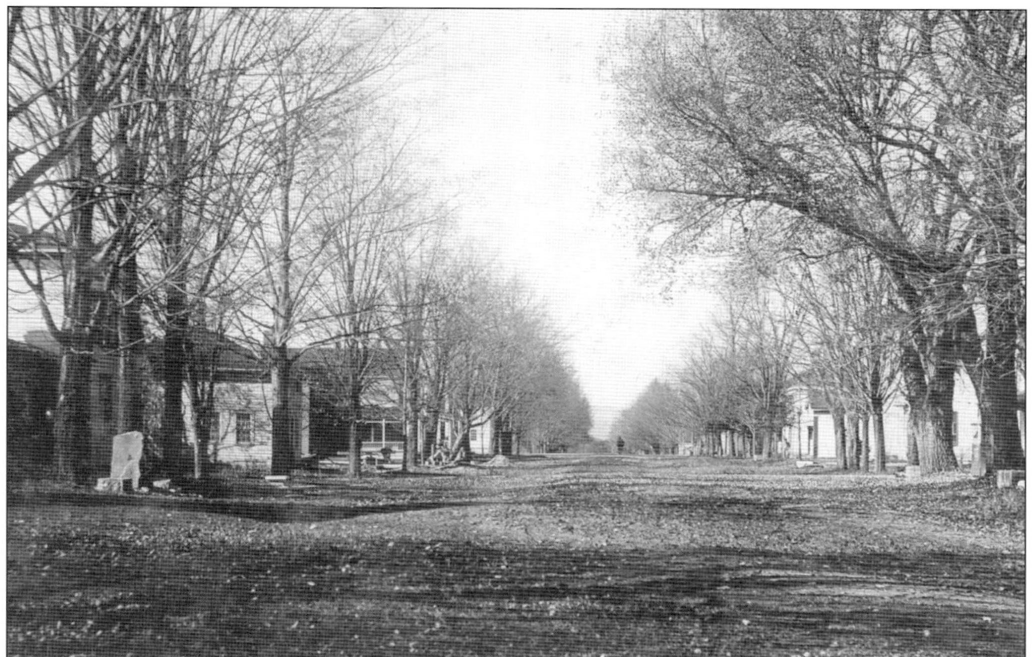

The hamlet of Oramel is located on Route 19 just northeast of Belfast. It was incorporated as a village in 1856 but later abandoned that status. The community owes its existence in great part to the Genesee Valley Canal. (CRB.)

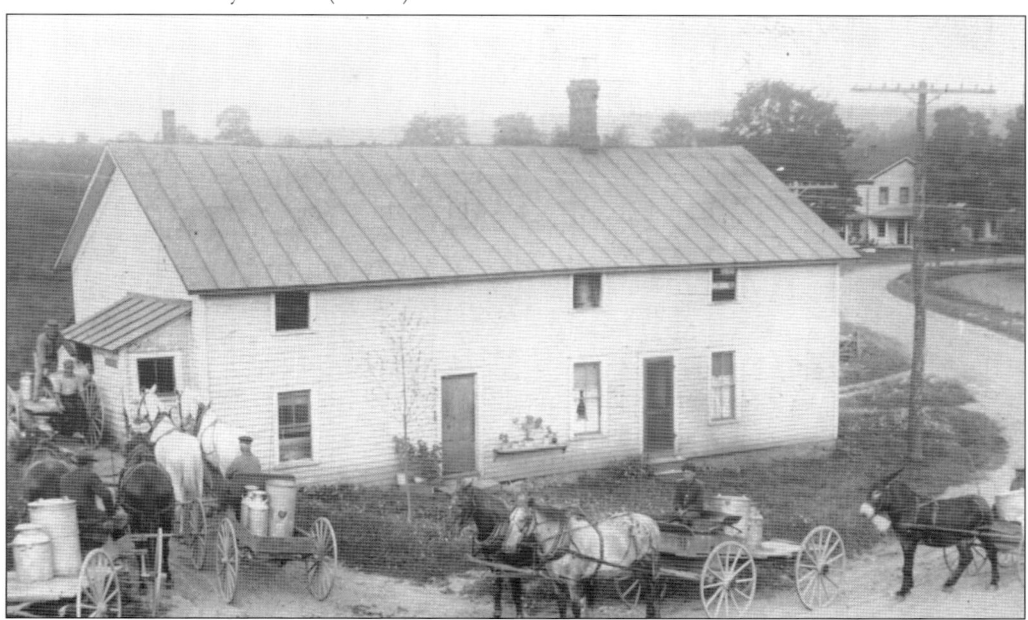

Here is an early-1900s photograph of a milk processing plant (cheese factory) in the hamlet. Today, officials are concerned as the Genesee River is swinging toward Oramel, widening a bend in the river, carrying away valuable topsoil, and threatening a cemetery nearby. State and county Department of Transportation workers are attempting to change the course back to its former channel. (CRB.)

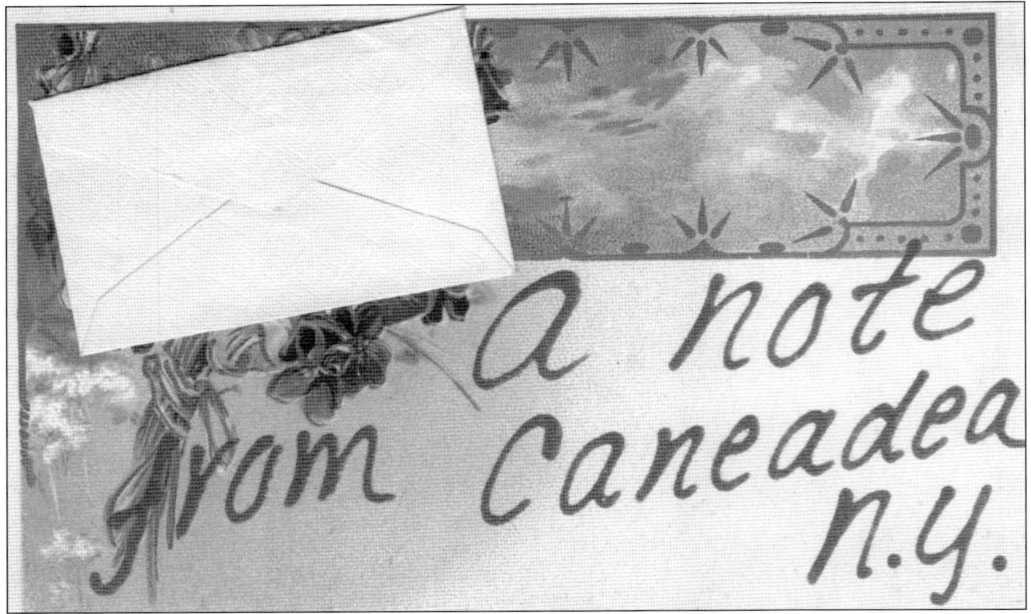

The Town of Caneadea contains three hamlets, including Oramel, Caneadea, and Houghton, and no villages. Many small mom-and-pop stores sold generic postcards like this that had the community's name printed on the front by a local printer.

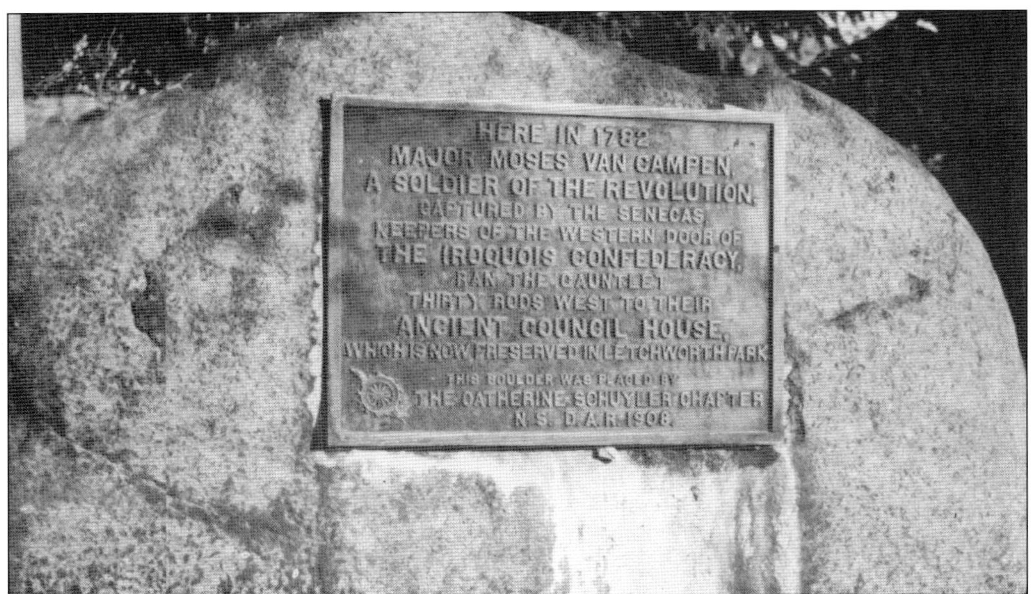

A boulder on Council House Road marks the spot along the river that played an important role in the area's settlement. It reads, "Here in 1782, Maj. Moses Van Campen, a soldier of the Revolution, captured by the Senecas, keeper of the western door of the Iroquois Confederacy, ran the gauntlet 30 rods west to their ancient Council House, which is now preserved in Letchworth State Park." (JSB.)

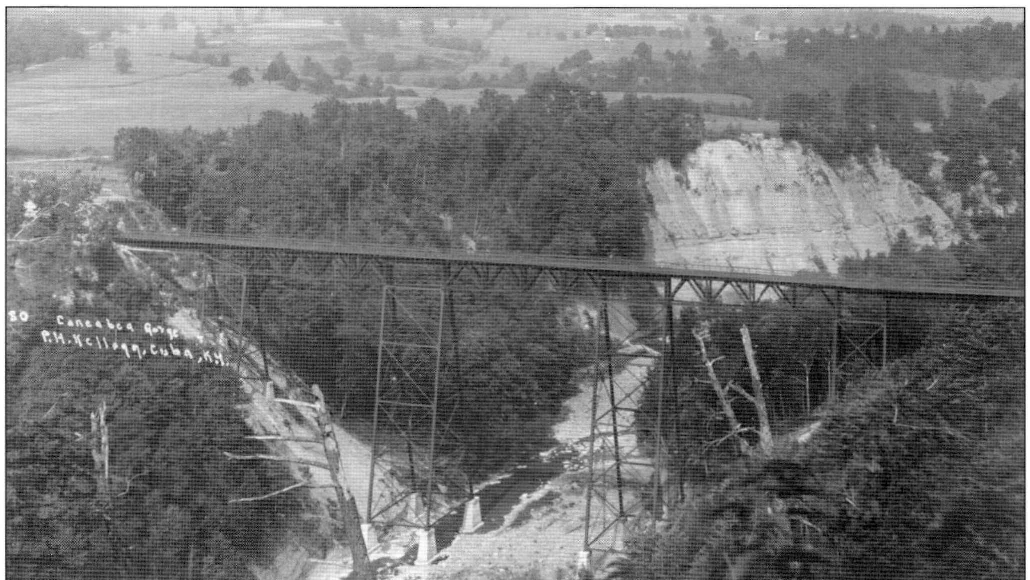

This Kellogg postcard shows the Buffalo & Susquehanna Railroad Bridge crossing the gorge of Caneadea Creek. The 175-foot-high steel bridge was 754 feet long and was an added tourist attraction for people who just came to see the spectacular gorge. In 1916 and 1917, the bridge was torn down and the scrap metal sent to England for the war effort. (JSB.)

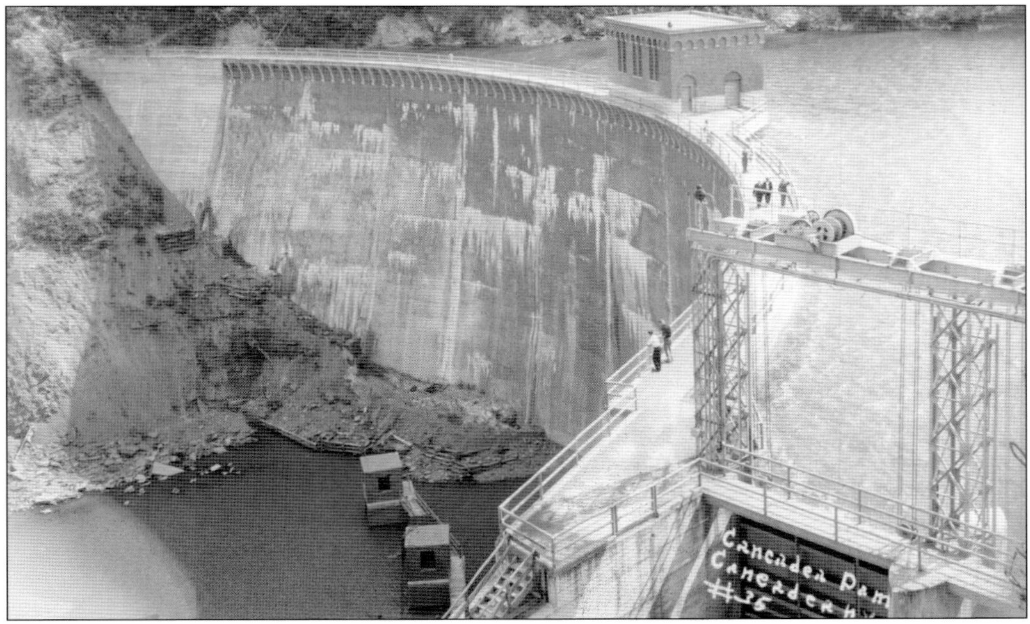

The initial purpose in constructing the Caneadea Dam across Caneadea Creek was to augment the flow of the Genesee River in time of low water levels and increase the ability of Rochester Gas and Electric to generate electricity at its hydroelectric plant in both Mount Morris and Rochester. The dam was built during 1927 and was completed in the spring of 1928. It is an arch shaped concrete dam at 140 feet high and 600 feet wide. A lake with over 550 acres of surface area formed almost immediately and was called Rushford Lake. (JSB.)

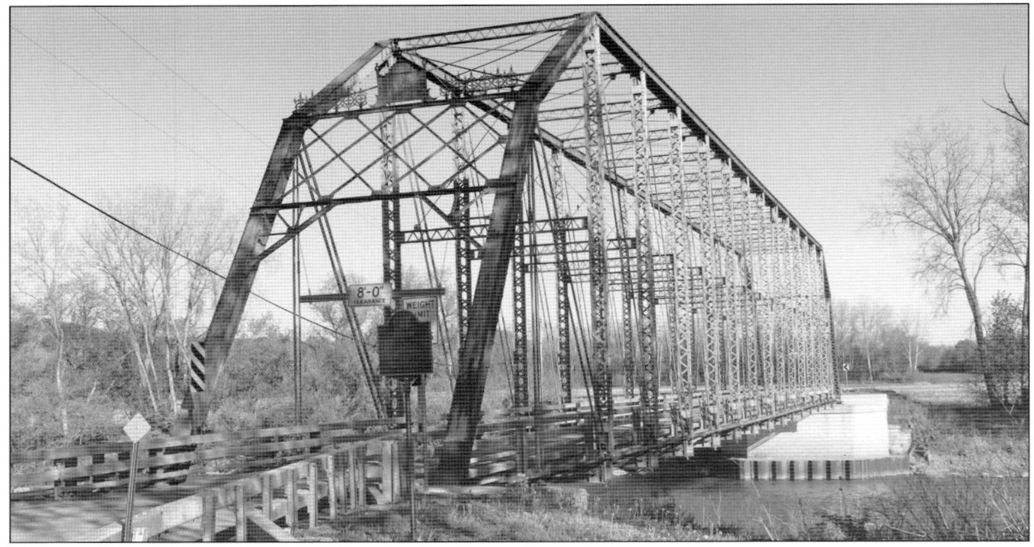

Both photographs on this page show the historic Caneadea camelback bridge, a single-lane span across the Genesee River on East Hill Road. This rare Parker truss iron bridge was constructed in 1903 with the names of the elected officials on the metal sign above the supports. In recent years, the structure has undergone extensive repairs and was finally reopened and rededicated on May 5, 2007. Sadly, however, it was recently found to be structurally unsound and has been closed. (JSB.)

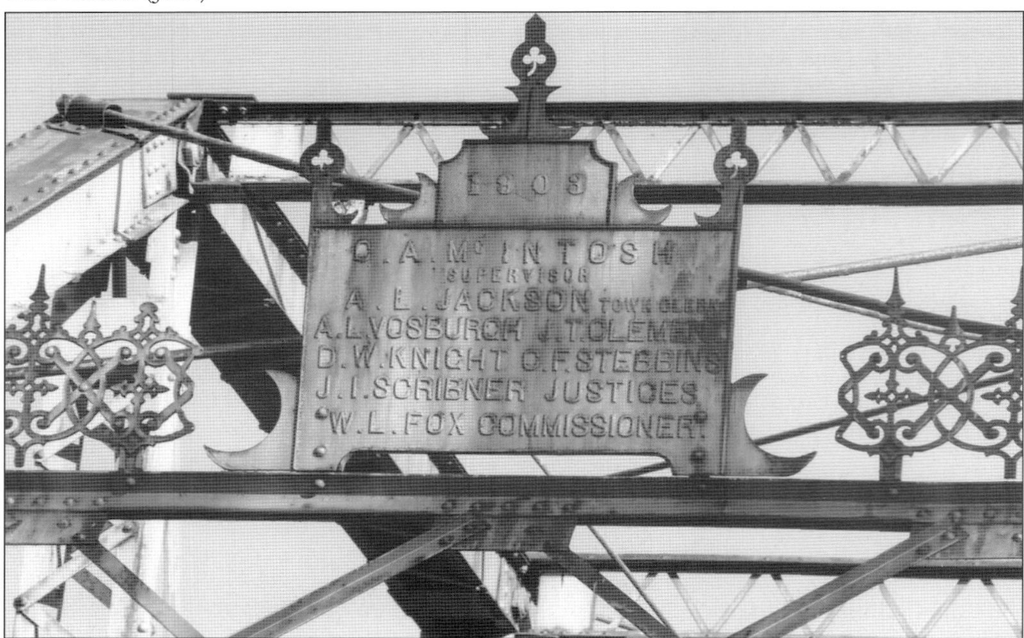

This bridge made history from September 1989 to April 1990 as the site of a nuclear waste dump protest. "Grandparents of the Future" first marched and then chained themselves to the bridge. After widespread media attention was focused on the county protesters, state officials retreated. In 1998, the bridge was placed in the New York State and National Register of Historic Places. (JSB.)

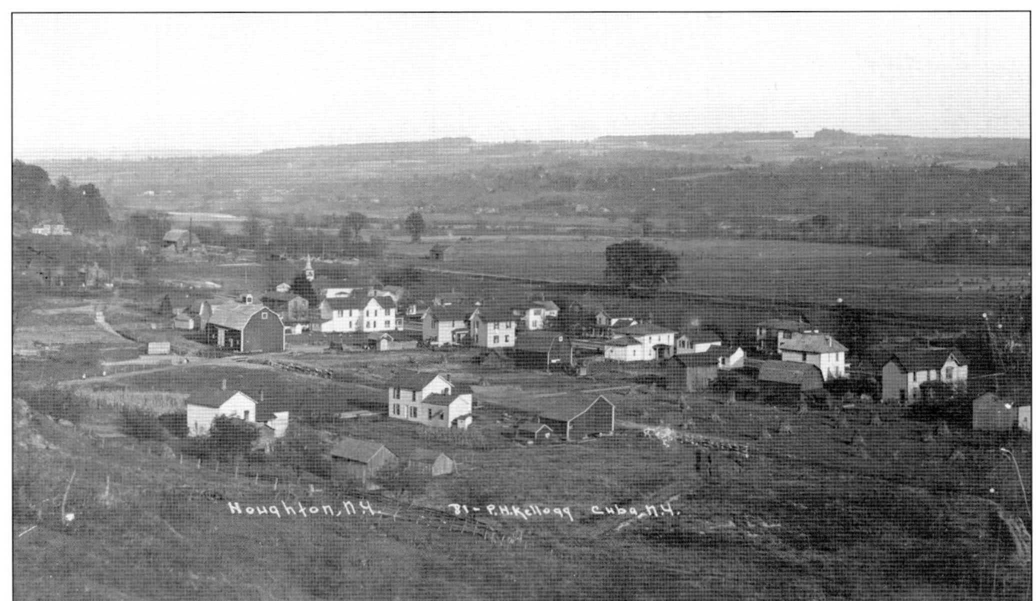

Willard Houghton, whose ancestors were among the first to settle here, was a prosperous farmer who became increasingly active in the Wesleyan Methodist Church. In 1883, with the encouragement of church officials, he founded Houghton Seminary to provide a Christian education for high school graduates. Houghton started out as a hamlet on the west bank of the Genesee. (CRB.)

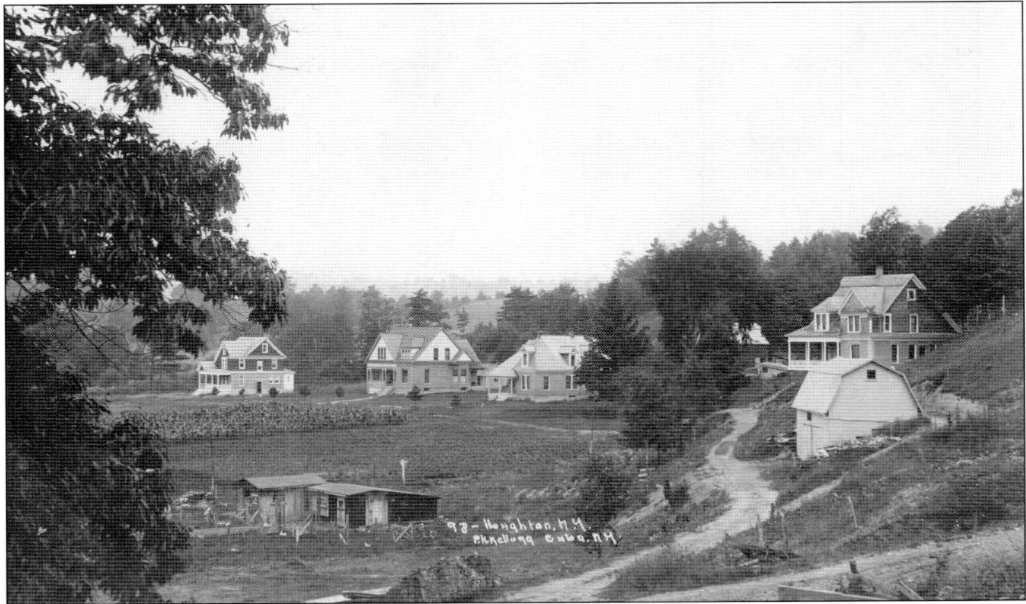

In 1896, John S. Minard, a noted Allegany County historian, wrote that "Houghton never in canal days aspired to be a village, but since the advent of the railroad and the seminary, it has made a healthy growth and is a very pleasant, clean, and tidy village." By June 16, 1937, the last passenger train had passed through Houghton. On February 16, 1963, the final freight train went through. (CRB.)

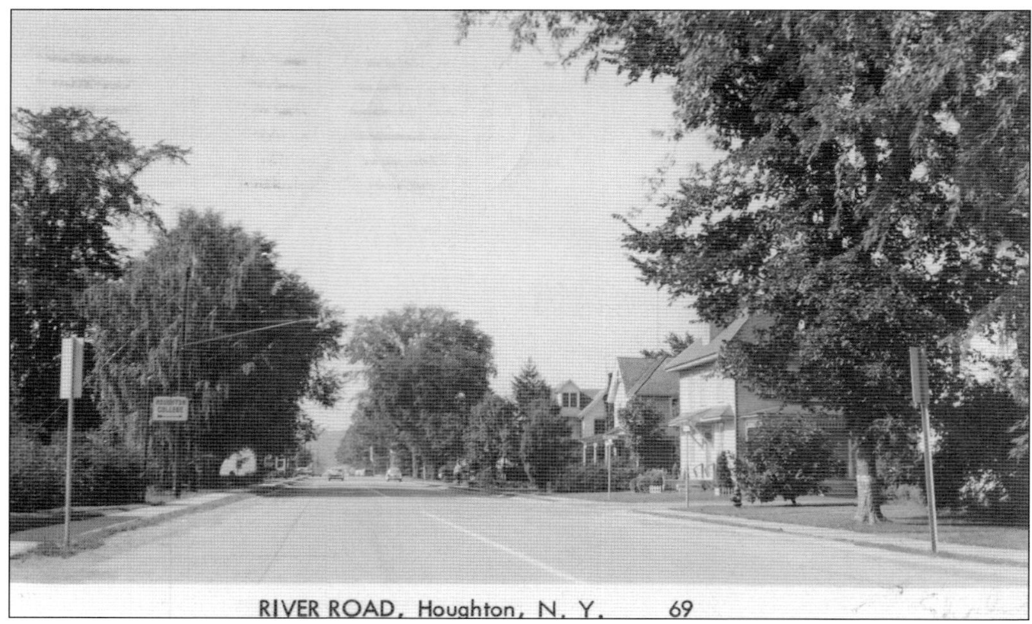

The River Road, now State Route 19 in Houghton, was so named for the Genesee River, which it parallels. On June 22, 1972, the village was flooded as the Genesee overflowed its banks from the heavy rains of Hurricane Agnes. (CRB.)

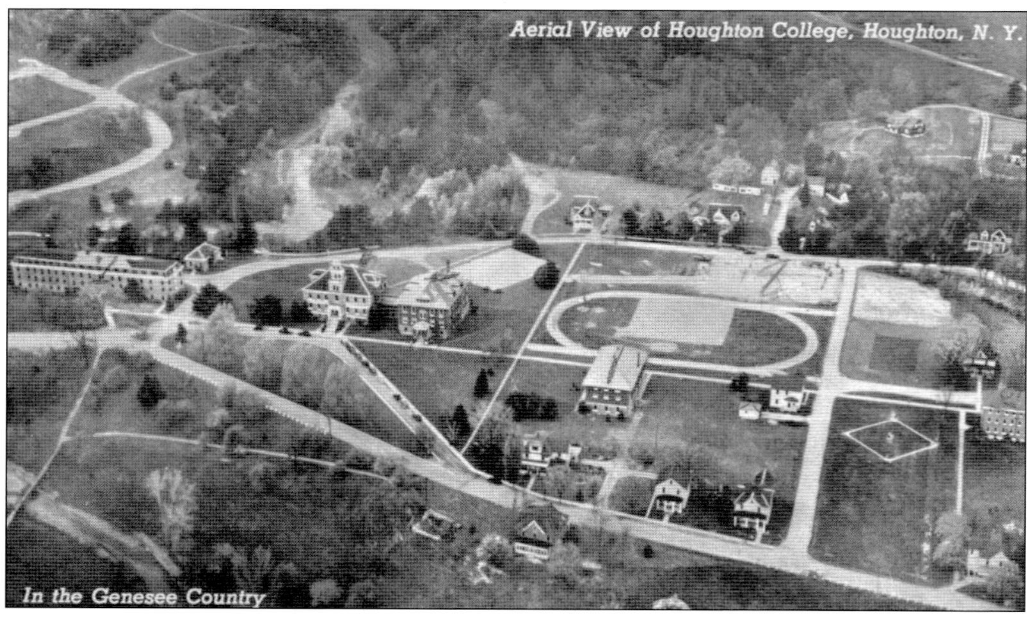

This aerial view was taken around 1940. Houghton College is a private Christian liberal arts college that began in 1883 under the Wesleyan Methodist Church. In 1908, James Luckey became the first academically trained president. In 1923, Houghton Seminary received its provisional charter and made application to the board of regents for a college charter. It was granted. (CRB.)

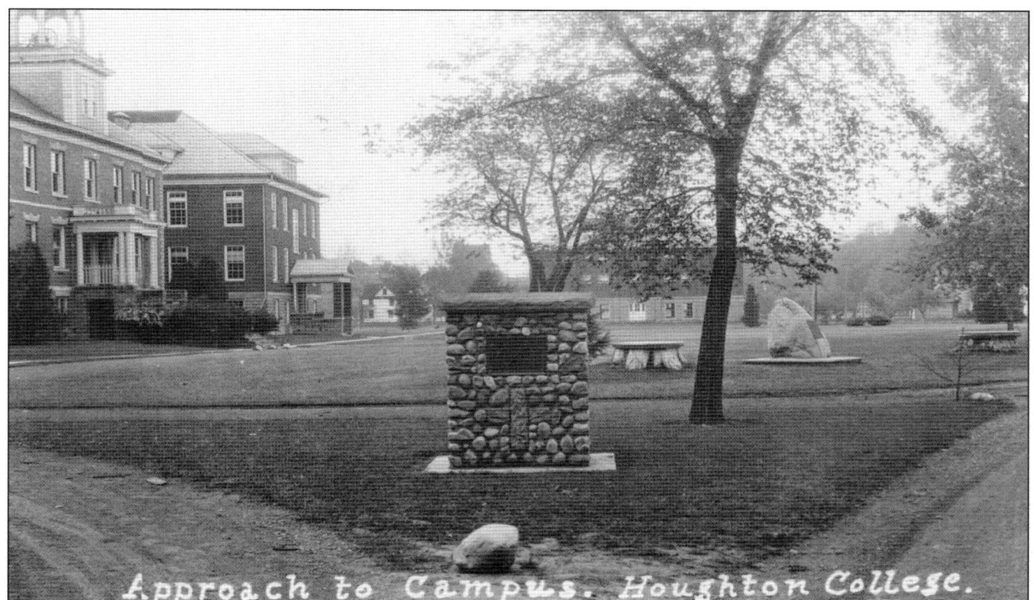

At the entrance to the college stands this monument erected by the class of 1925, the first graduates from Houghton College. The monument honors founder Willard Houghton and his faithfulness to the dream of Christian higher education. (CRB.)

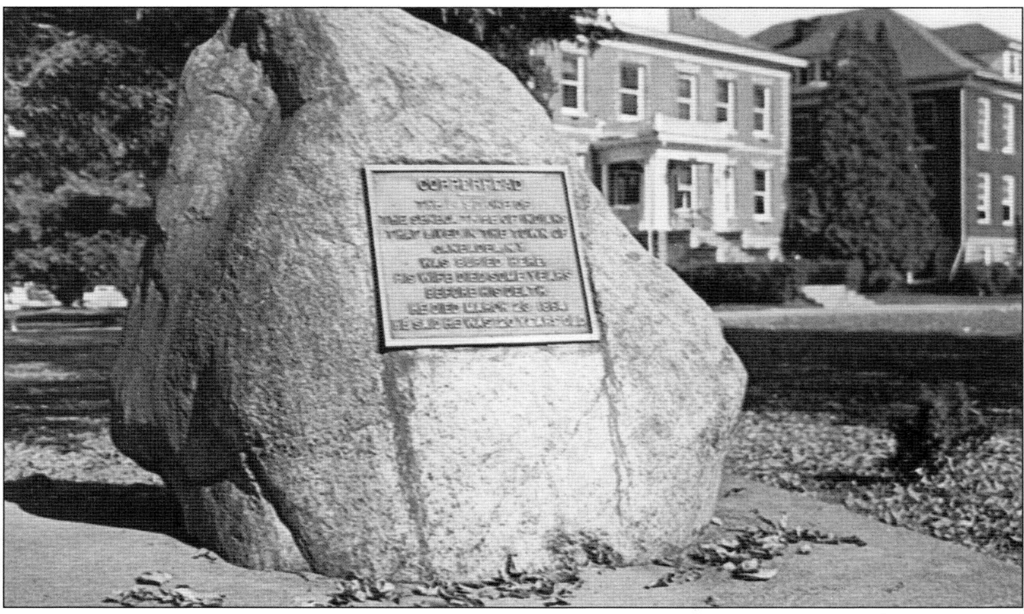

The hills surrounding Houghton are rich in Native American history. This boulder near the entrance to campus commemorates Copperhead, the last of the Senecas to reside in the valley. On June 10, 1914, supposedly at age 126 years, Copperhead's remains were interred beneath the campus boulder. (CRB.)

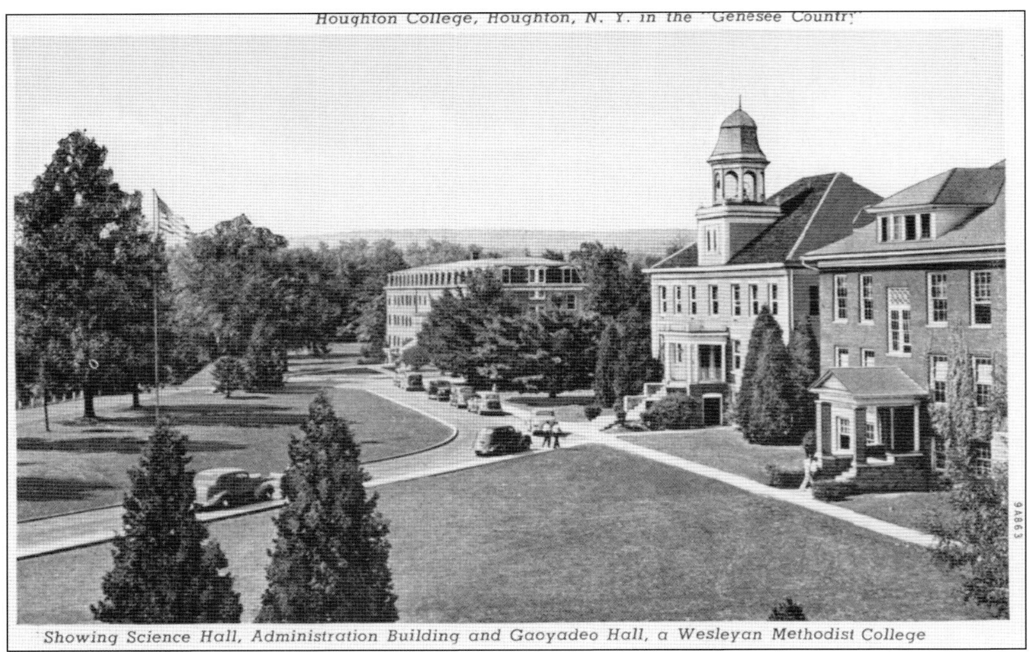

In 1906, the campus was moved to its present location, the site of the former Caneadea Indian reservation. The postcard shows the first three buildings of the new college: the science hall, administration building, and Gaoyadeo Hall. (CRB.)

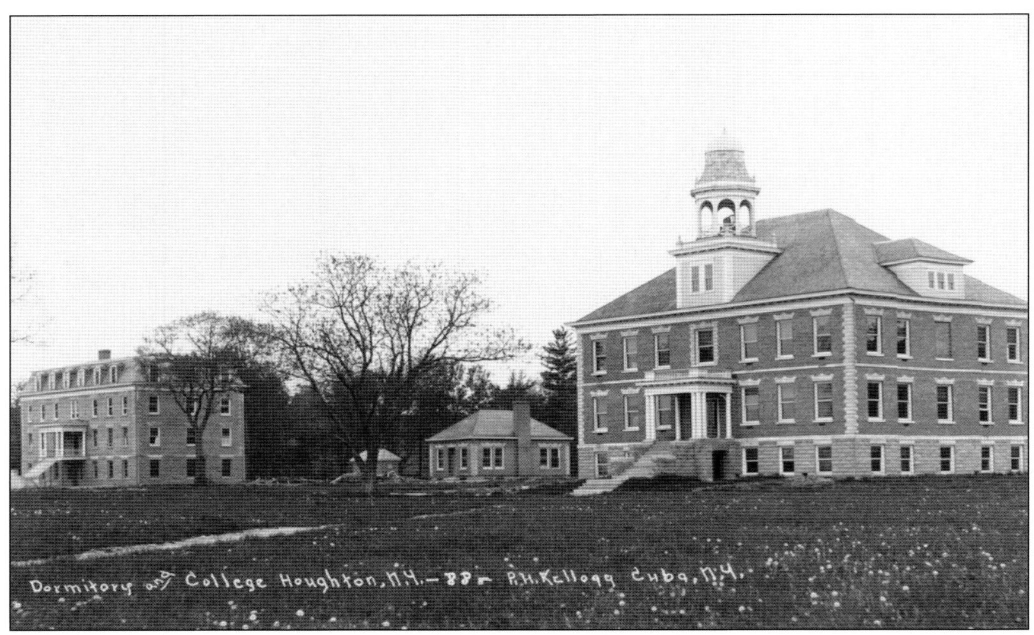

This view of the campus shows Gaoyadeo, the girls' dormitory and dining hall; the heating plant in the background; and science hall. (CRB.)

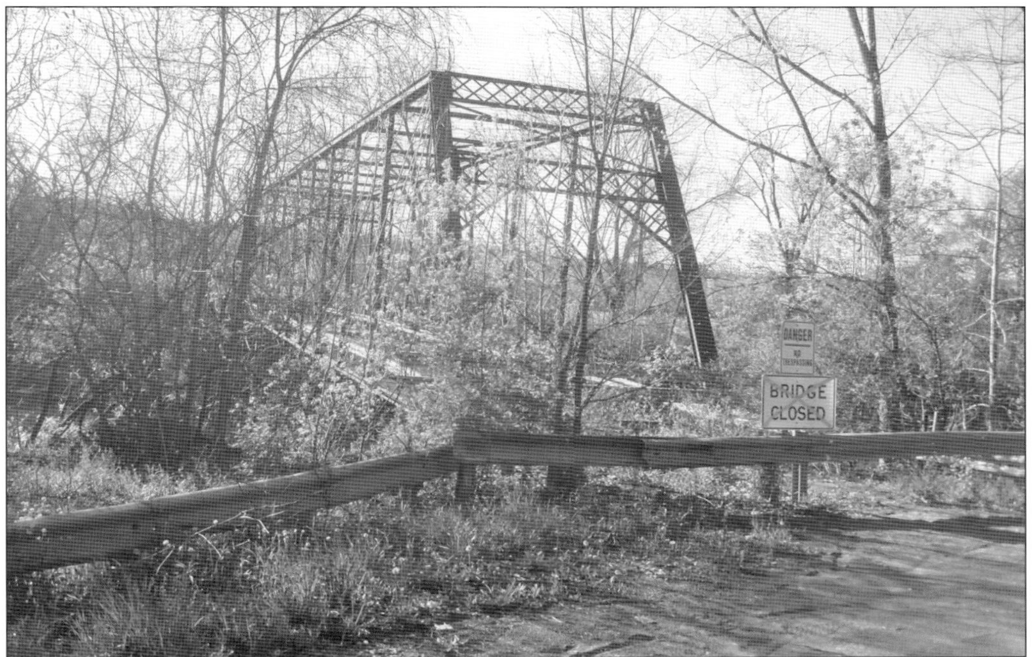

Here are two scenes of Lattice Bridge, which crosses the Genesee a mile south of Fillmore, New York. In its day this was a vital link to area residents that needed to cross the Genesee, but today the wooden plank flooring has rotted away and the metal framework weakened to the point where the bridge became unsafe and had to be closed. The name "lattice" comes from the design that uses a large number of small and closely spaced diagonal elements that form a lattice. (JSB.)

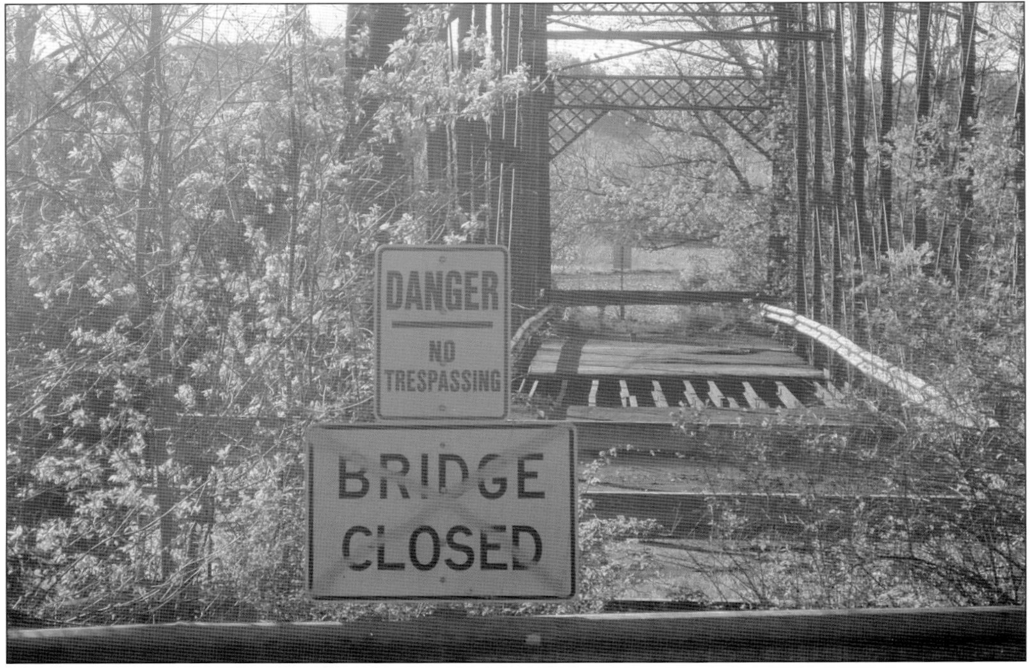

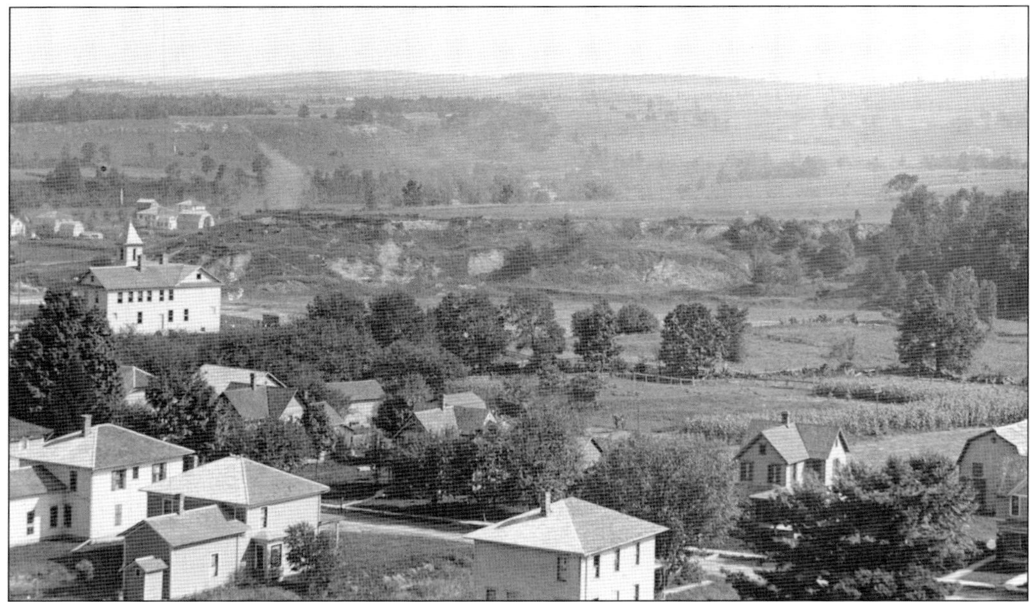

Fillmore is a hamlet in Allegany County that was named after Pres. Millard Fillmore. It was first settled by John Whiting who built a sawmill in 1835 and started clearing the dense stands of timber. Fillmore's first merchant set up shop with a small stock of goods in 1839, and in 1850, the first post office opened. By the late 1800s, Fillmore was well-established with a hotel, two stores, one cheese factory, two blacksmiths, a wagon shop, and two millinery stores. (JSB.)

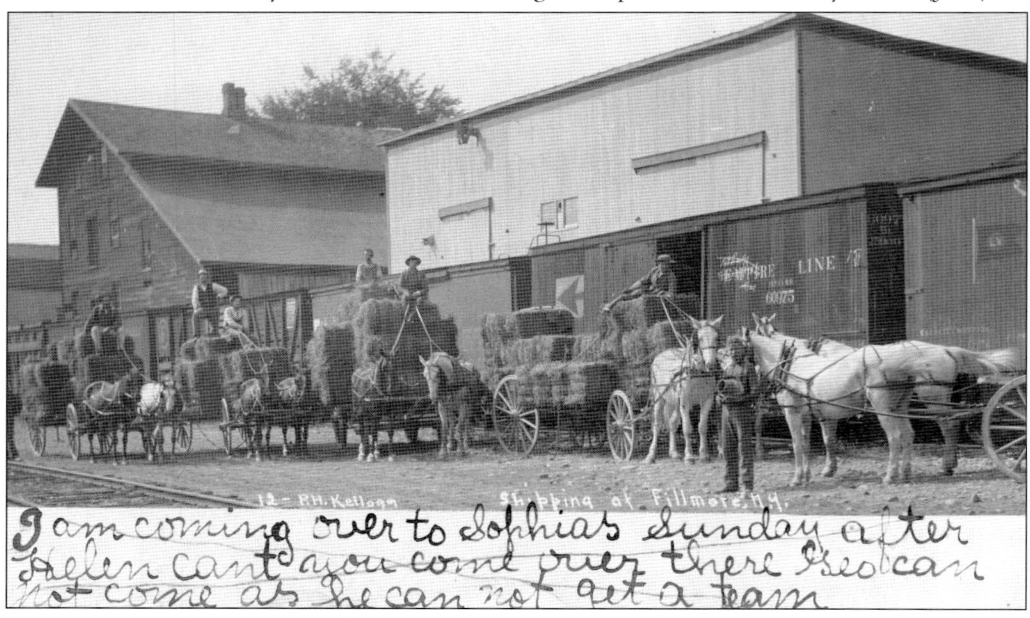

In May 1888, Judson Howden first began publishing the *Northern Allegany Observer* in Fillmore. His son Melvin carried on the tradition as the next editor and publisher. The Town of Hume Museum now has a collection of the *Northern Allegany Observer* newspapers in its archives and is in the process of printing copies and also of scanning them into the computer for public access and research. (CRB.)

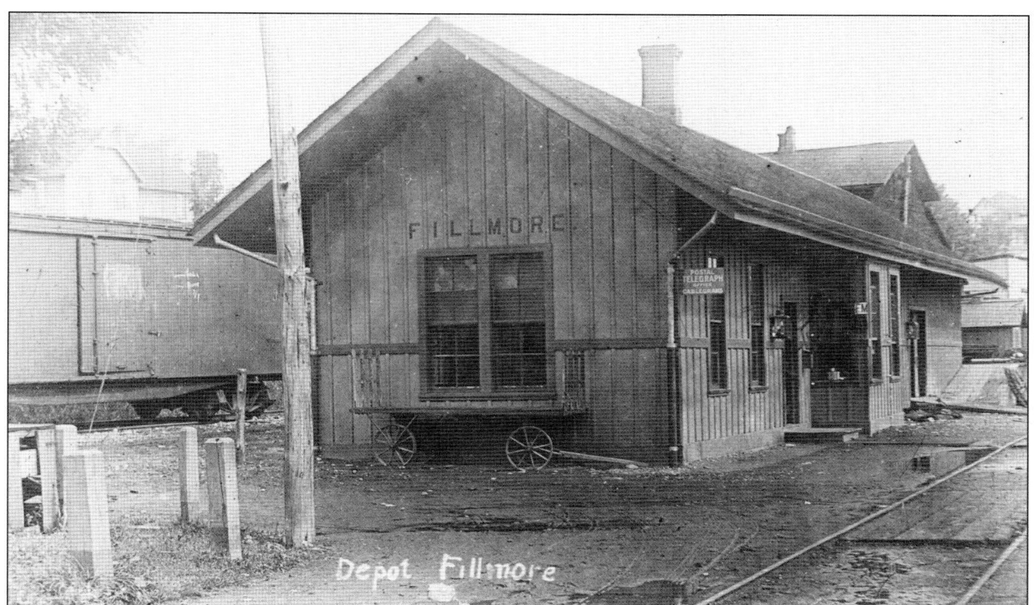

In 1882, Fillmore's first railroad was the Rochester division of the Buffalo, New York & Philadelphia Railroad. It snaked through the valley following the Genesee River. Shown here is the Pennsylvania Railroad depot. As the usefulness of the Genesee Valley Canal faded, the railroad tracks replaced the canal towpath with the depot built across the street from the old Agway building. The depot was torn down in the late 1950s. (CRB.)

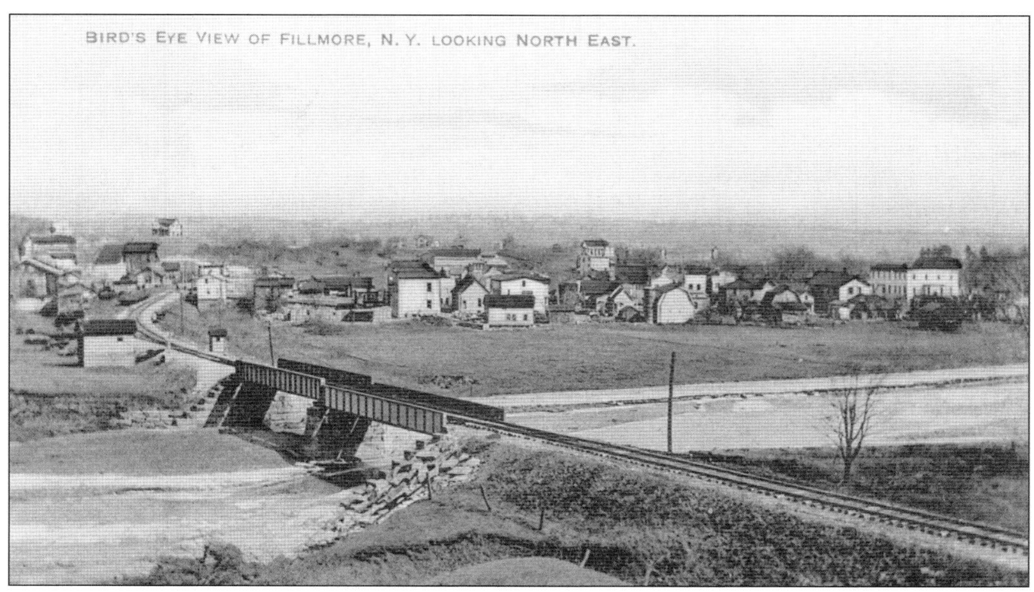

Known once as "the mouth of the creek" because it sits at the outlet of Cold Creek, Fillmore is shown here lying closely along the river. Today, the wide and shallow area of the river under and west of the bridge makes for some fine swimming places. However, at numerous times, the scene has not been peaceful, but one of raging torrents of water, washing away livestock and crops, houses, and barns. (JSB.)

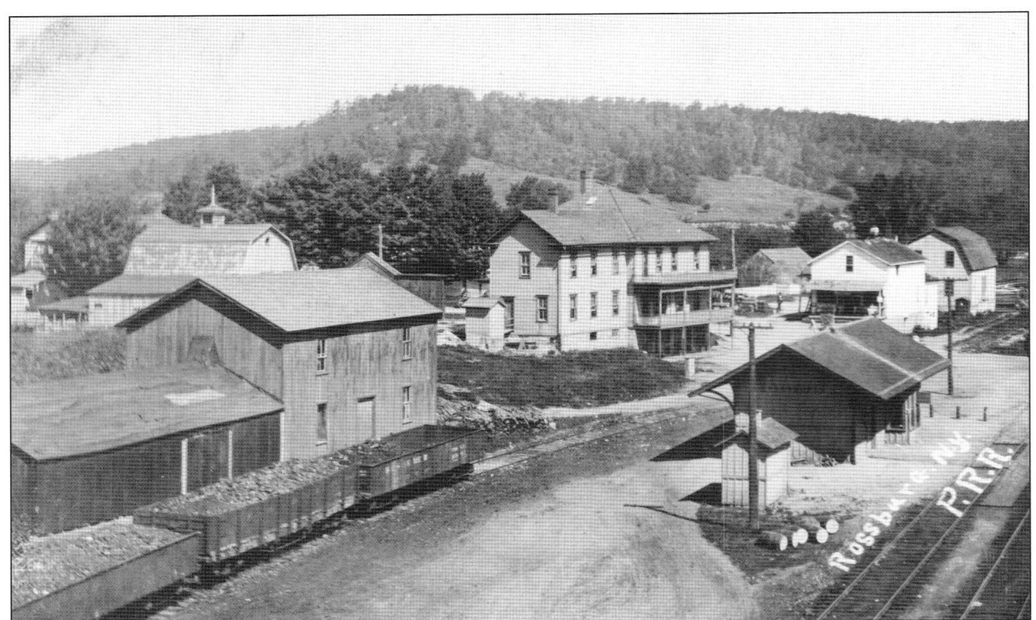

Rossburg is a hamlet located in the Town of Hume northeast of Fillmore on Route 19A. The hamlet was settled in the early 1800s and named for early settler Ross. Its heyday was during the days of the Genesee Valley Canal operations and later during the days of the Pennsylvania Railroad. A large hotel and railroad depot were the focus of the community. Several houses stand today in the hamlet that face the old canal bed. (CRB.)

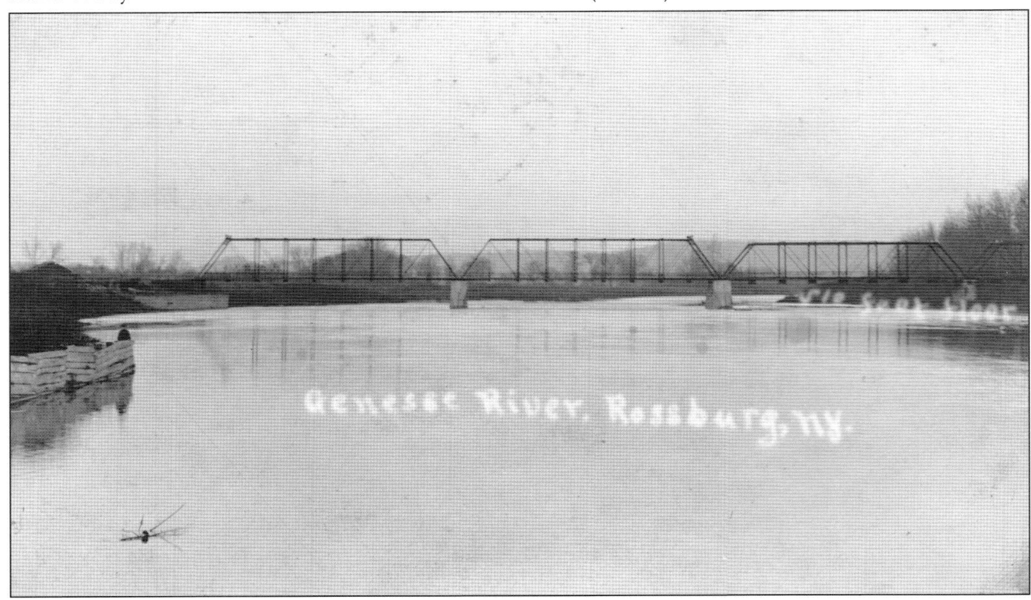

This postcard view shows a triple span bridge crossing the Genesee. The photograph was taken from the river level. The floor of this bridge measures 510 feet. This is a great example of a beam bridge where the horizontal beams are supported at each end by abutments. Where there is more than one span in this image, the intermediate supports are known as piers. Usually made of concrete, these are vital supports in the middle of the bridge. (CRB.)

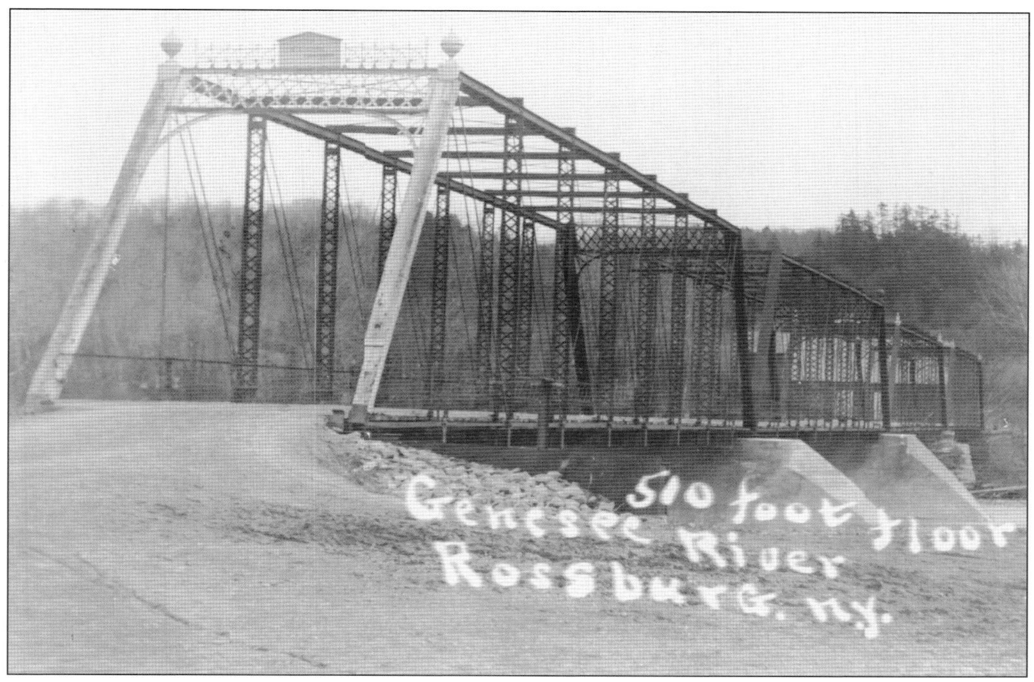

This postcard view again shows the three sections of the bridge from a different angle. The floor of this bridge measures 510 feet. From the image, one can see that it was made up of three individual beam bridges supported by concrete piers. This was one of the longer span bridges that crossed the river. (CRB.)

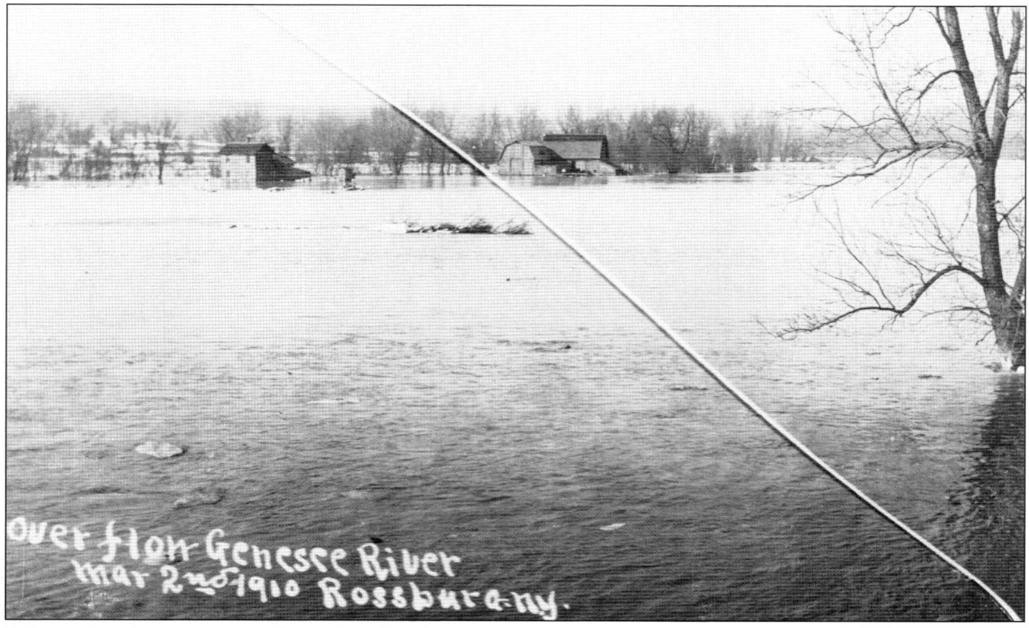

When the Genesee overflowed its banks on May 2, 1910, it meant disaster for tiny Rossburg. Both images on this page were made from glass plates. The river scene has a crack running diagonally across the glass plate that the image was printed from. (CRB.)

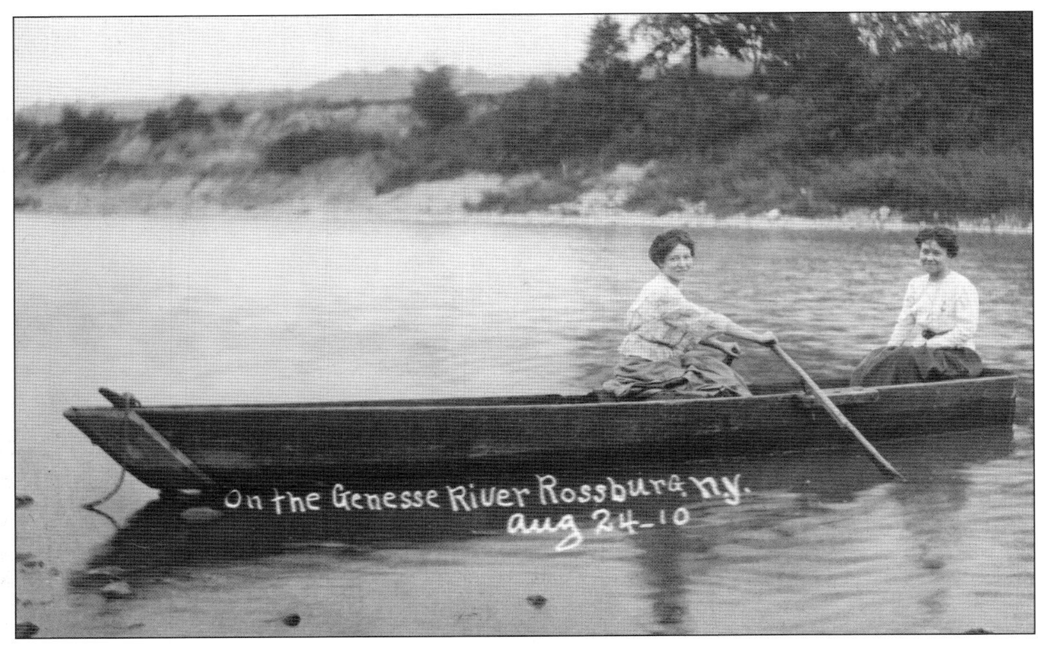

"Romancing the River" took many forms: swimming, picnicking, and boating. These spectacularly preserved photo postcards, dated August 24, 1910, show young and old enjoying time on the river near Rossburg, New York. (CRB.)

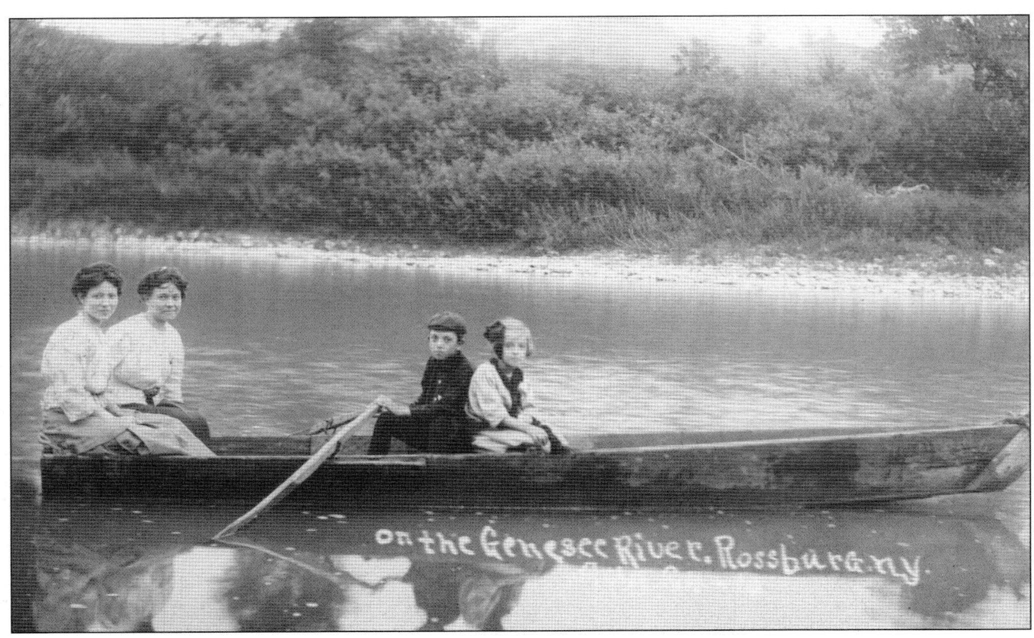

Three

Wyoming and Livingston Counties "Grand Canyon of the East"

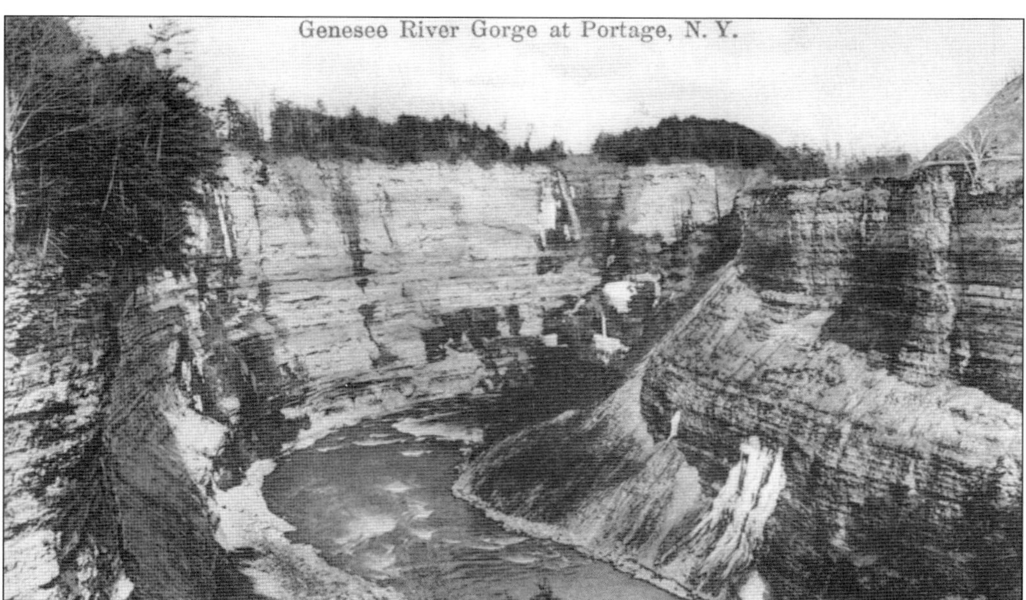

As the Genesee reaches Portageville, "nature touches the river with a magic wand and like Cinderella at the stroke of midnight, throws off its drab and dons robes of dazzling splendor." Through Letchworth State Park, the Genesee River has cut a 17-mile-long channel that is 550 feet at its deepest point, creating a magnificent river gorge. The Genesee falls over three natural cataracts. Its natural beauty has earned it the name "Grand Canyon of the East." The park was named after William Pryor Letchworth, who in 1906 left the park to the people of New York State. (JSB.)

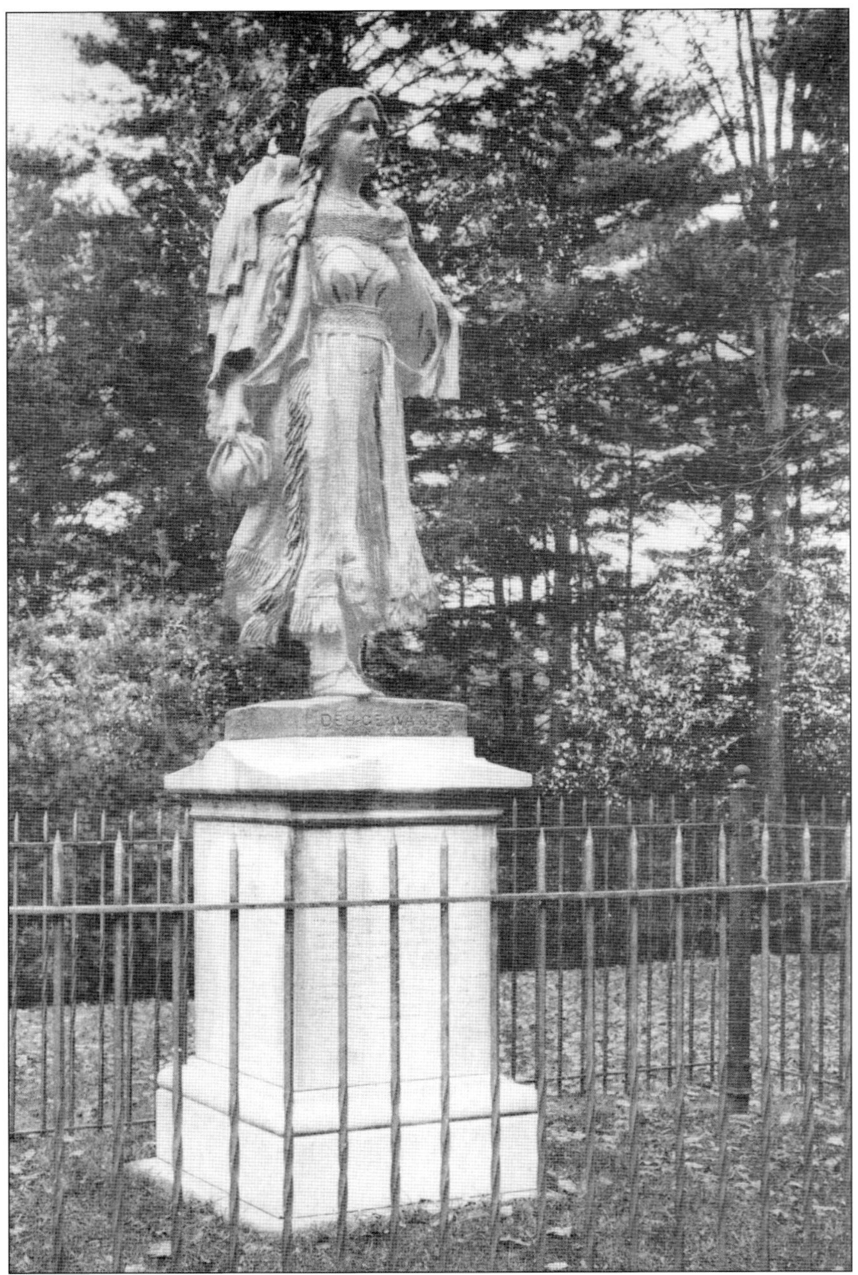

The White Woman of the Genesee was born on the ocean in 1742. Taken captive at Marsh Creek, Pennsylvania, in 1775, she was adopted into an Indian family in Ohio. In 1759, she was removed to the Genesee country. She died on September 19, 1833. The story of Mary Jemison is one of a stubborn little woman who squatted on the banks of a stubborn river, determined to trust her luck with the people of a savage race. She lived with the Seneca Indians for more than 70 years, outliving two husbands. Her close connection with the history of the Genesee River Valley caused her to be known as "Mary Jemison, the White Woman of the Genesee." This monument in Letchworth State Park was erected by the Hon. W. P. Letchworth. (JS.)

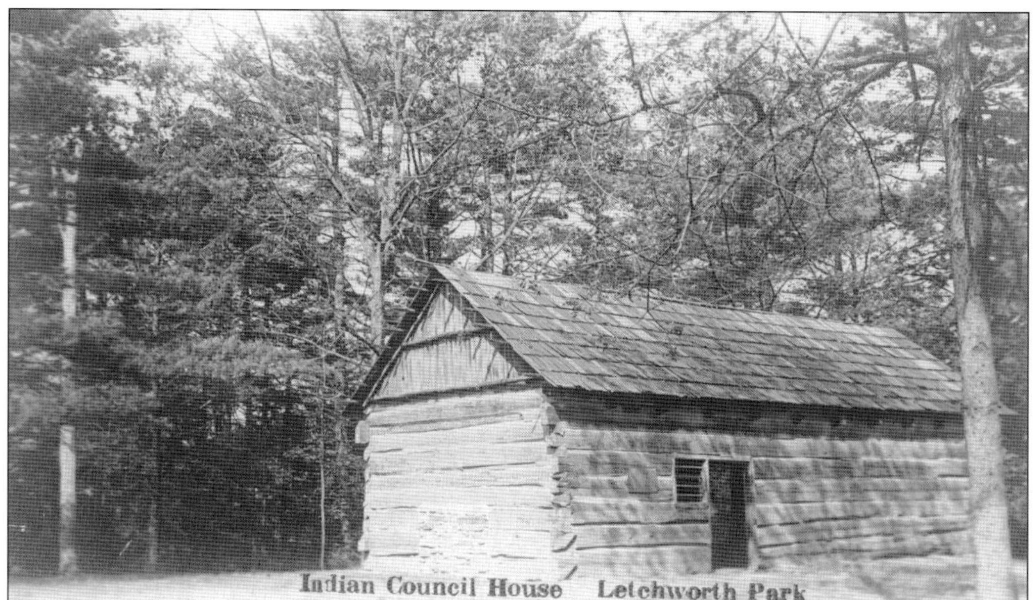

In 1871, at the request of John S. Minard, noted historian and writer William Pryor Letchworth went to Hume where Minard was living and together they visited the Indian Council House at Caneadea. The historic building was over 100 years old and falling apart. Letchworth commissioned Minard to purchase the Indian Council House. After its purchase, the Indian Council House was moved to his Letchworth Estate and restored. A statue of Mary Jemison was erected at the site. (JSB.)

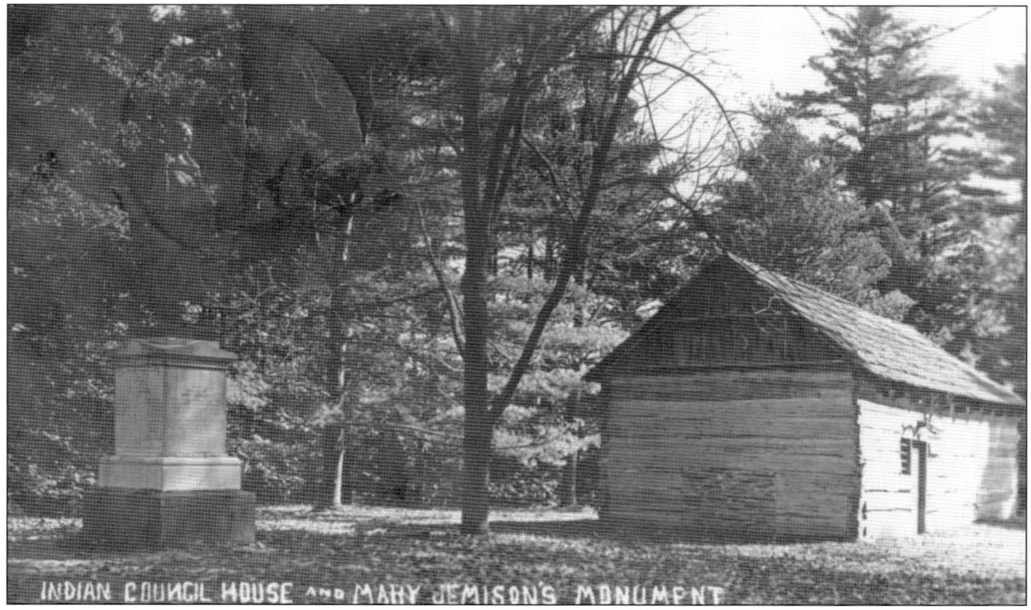

The Indian Council House is one of the oldest buildings in western New York, dating back to the mid-1700s. The Indian Council House was made of hand-hewn logs that were a foot or so thick and were neatly dovetailed at the corners and their crevasses filled with clay.

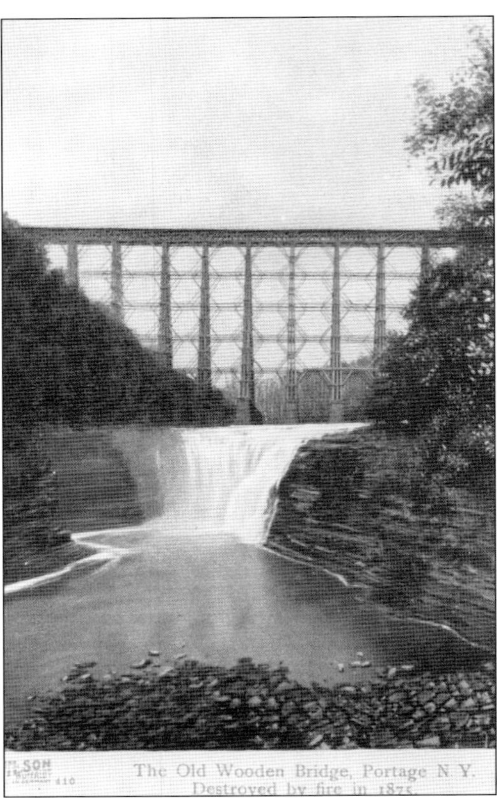

In 1852, a wooden railroad bridge was built for the Erie Railroad over a narrow part of the Letchworth Gorge. It was the longest and tallest wooden bridge in the world at this time. The bridge was 800 feet long, 234 feet high, and contained 1.6 million feet of timber and 106,829 pounds of iron. Its unique lattice-like structure allowed individual timbers to be replaced as needed. In the early morning hours of May 6, 1875, the bridge was destroyed by fire from the sparks of a passing locomotive. (JSB.)

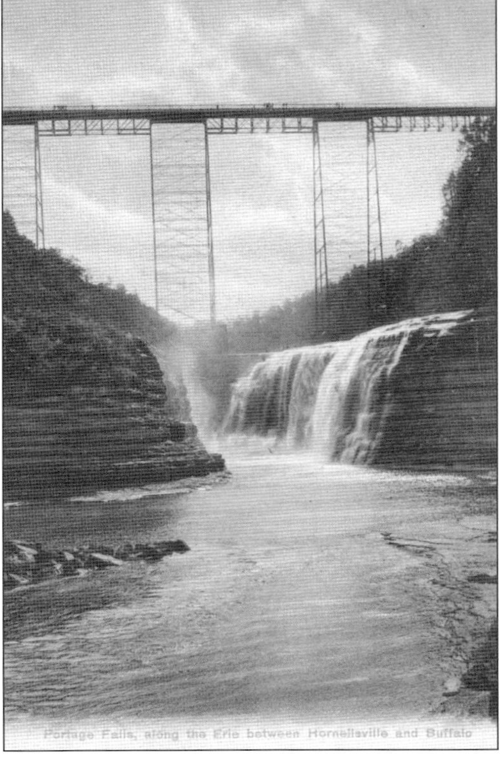

In anticipation of just such an event, plans had been made to replace it with an iron bridge. Four days after the fire, materials began arriving for a new bridge. The bridge was completed in just three months. The bridge spanning the Genesee connects Livingston and Wyoming Counties. (JSB.)

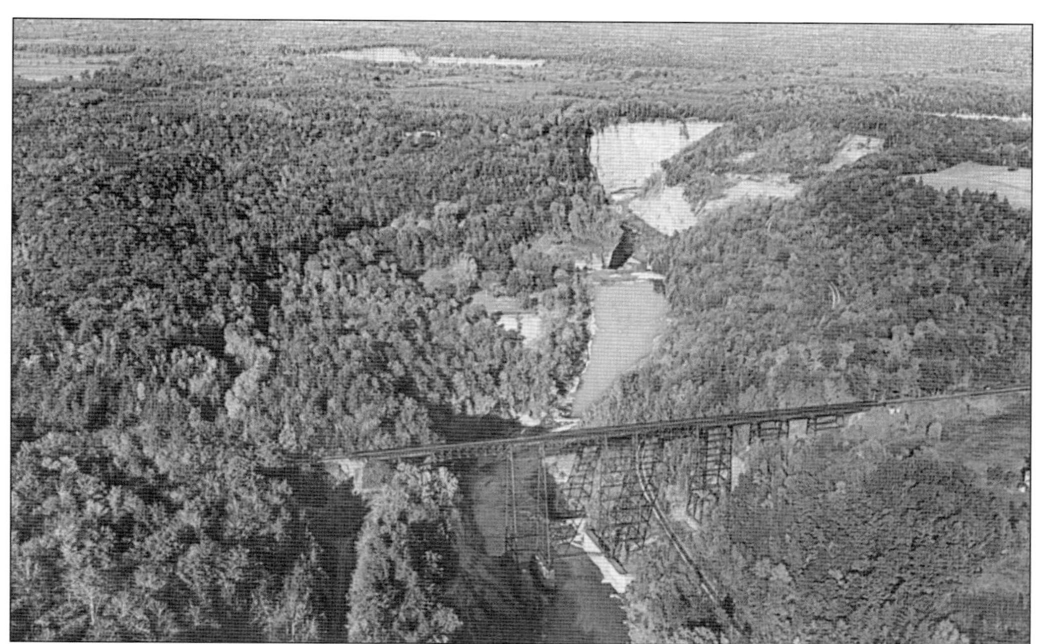

Letchworth State Park comprises 14,350 acres of scenic beauty along the Genesee River. The magnificent walls of the Genesee Gorge, the winding river below, the dramatic waterfalls, and the lush forests all contribute to make it one of the finest scenic parks in the east. Long before the coming of white man, the Indians roamed the area and called it Seh-ga-hun-da, which meant the "vale of the three falls." Railroads have always been a part of the park. In the early days, trains brought visitors to the park. Today, the railroad trestle offers breathtaking views of the gorge and falls. (JS.)

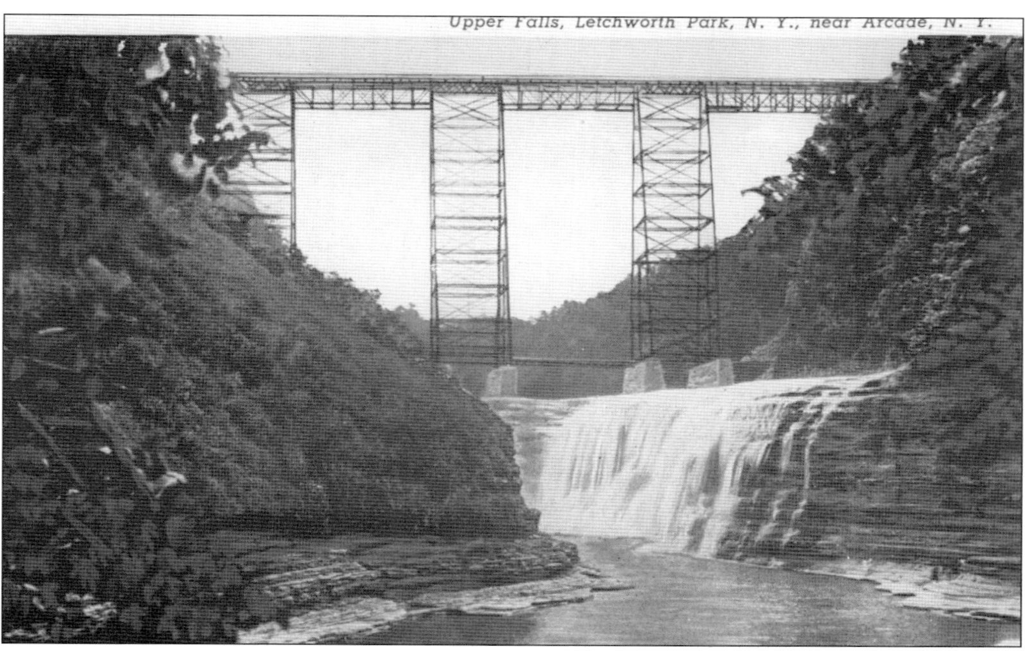

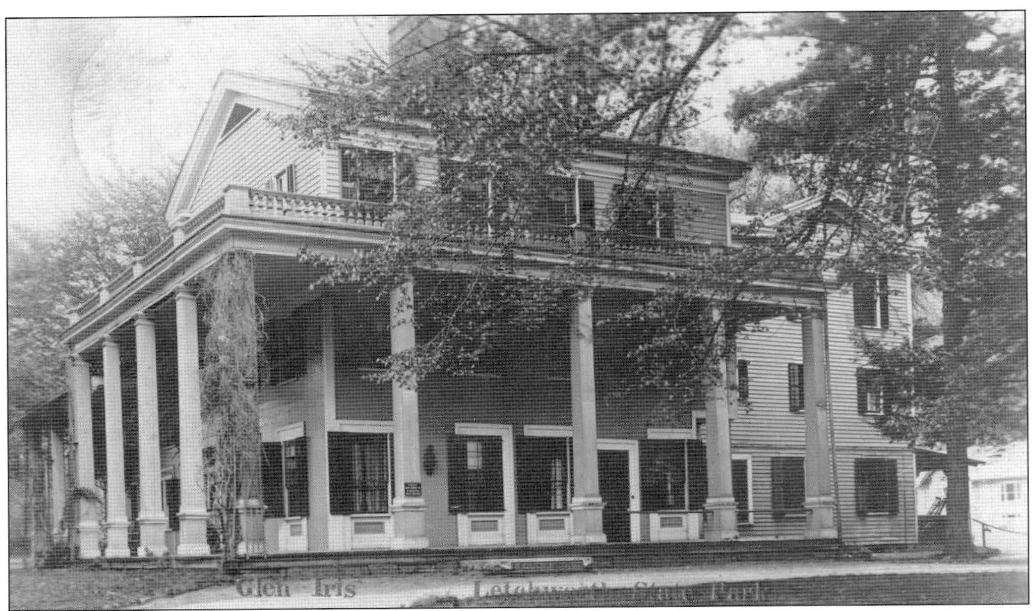

In the spring of 1858, William Letchworth arrived in the Genesee River Valley. He was touched by the natural beauty of the area. Letchworth acquired property in February 1859 and began renovations. He built a beautiful home on the banks of the Middle Falls. Before his death in 1910, he gifted the property to the people of New York State to be used as a permanent place for all to enjoy. (TC.)

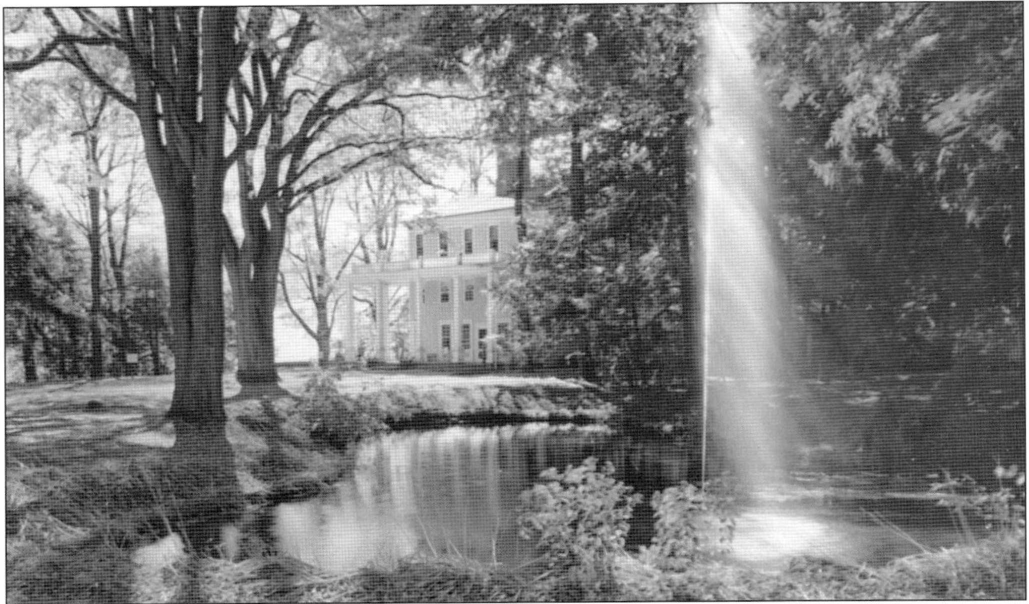

Today, the Glen Iris Inn and Restaurant is open to the public. Letchworth's home is open daily serving breakfast, lunch, and dinner from Easter until early November. During the summer months, it is a popular place for outdoor weddings and receptions. The restaurant has achieved widespread acclaim for its cuisine and outstanding service. (LCoHO.)

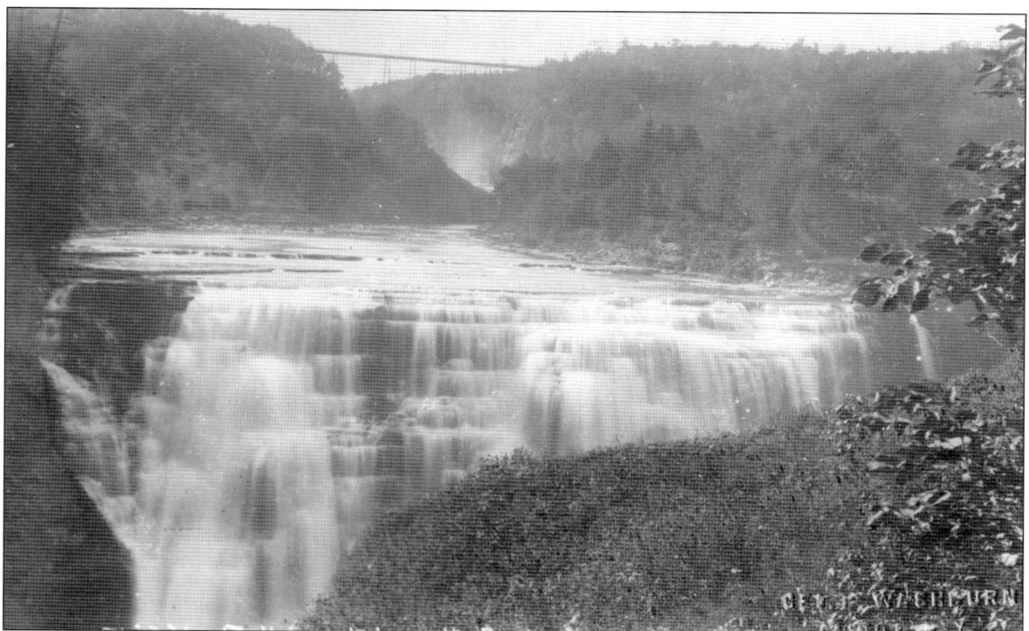

The Middle Falls is one of the favorite spots for visitors. Its easy access by car and foot provides spectacular views. The falls are 107 feet high. The Seneca Indians called the falls Ska-ga-dee, and believed that the sun stopped at midday to gaze in awe at its great beauty.

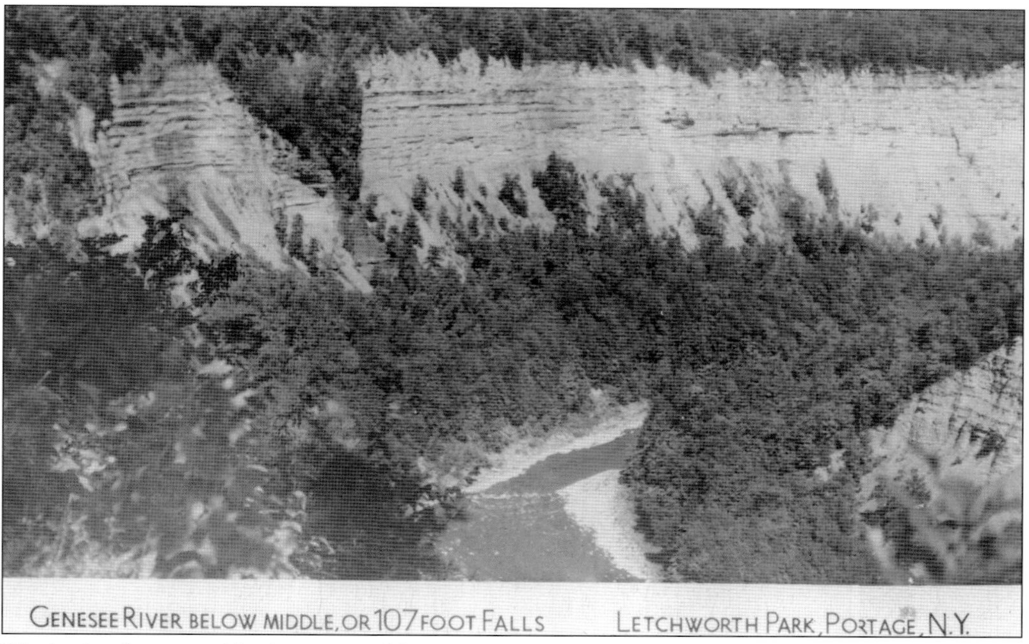

The bedrock exposed in the gorge of the Genesee River is of the Devonian and Silurian Geologic time periods and consists of shales and limestone rock layers that were part of an ancient seabed laid down millions of years ago. Many marine fossils can be found in the rock layers.

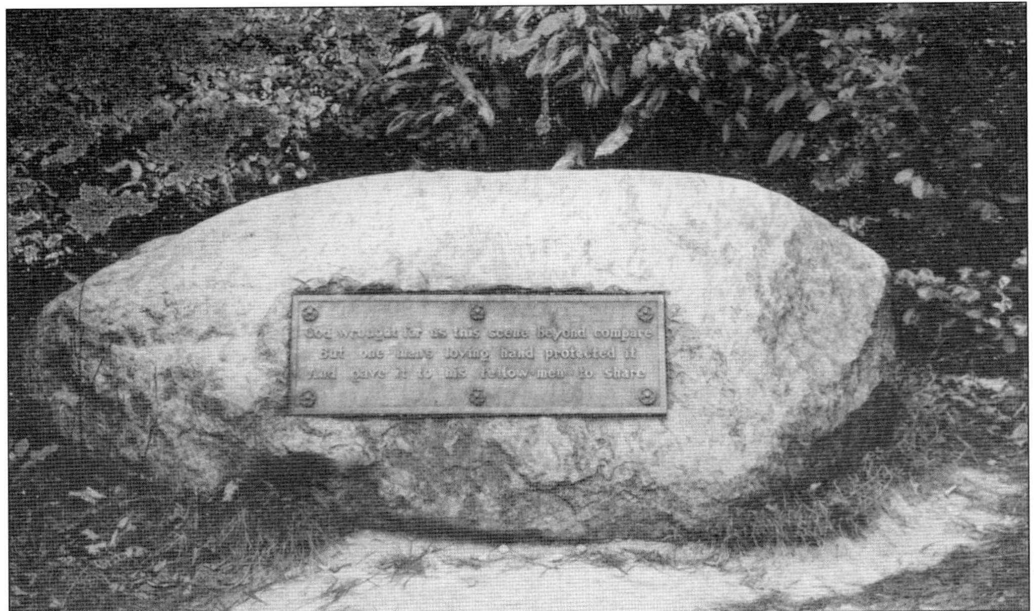

This special memorial boulder is near Inspiration Point. On the boulder is a verse from a poem titled "Inspiration Point, Letchworth Park" written on June 8, 1909, by Sara Evens Letchworth: "God wrought for us the scene beyond compare, but one man's loving hand protected it and gave it to his fellow man to share." She wrote this as a tribute to her uncle, William Pryor Letchworth, the park's benefactor. Near this boulder is probably the most spectacular view of the river gorge. (LCoHO.)

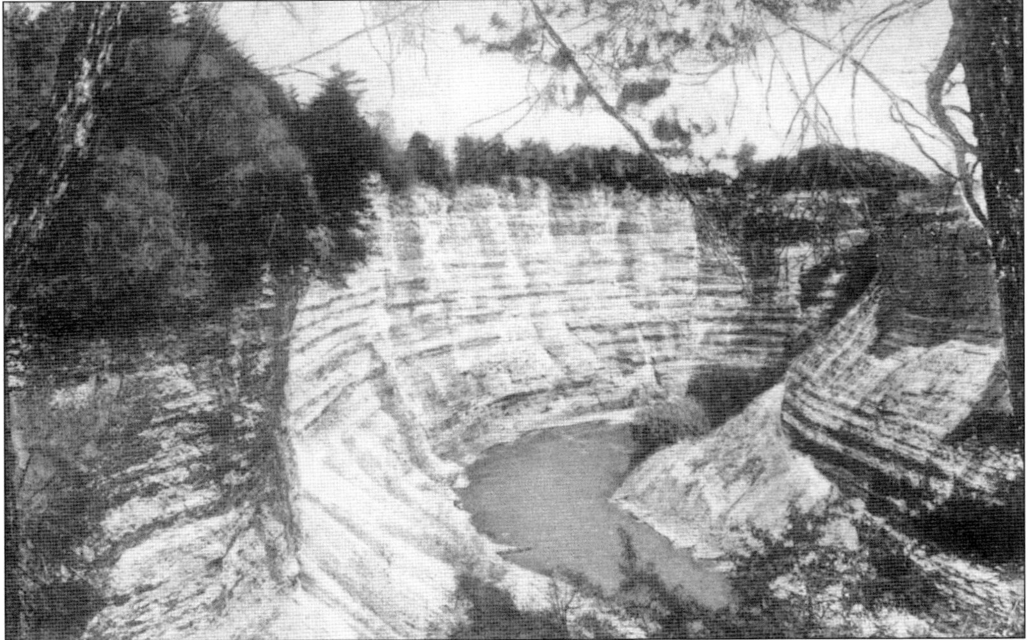

In its 10,000 years since the last ice age, the Genesee River has carved out a spectacular gorge in this 17-mile stretch of the park. (LCoHO.)

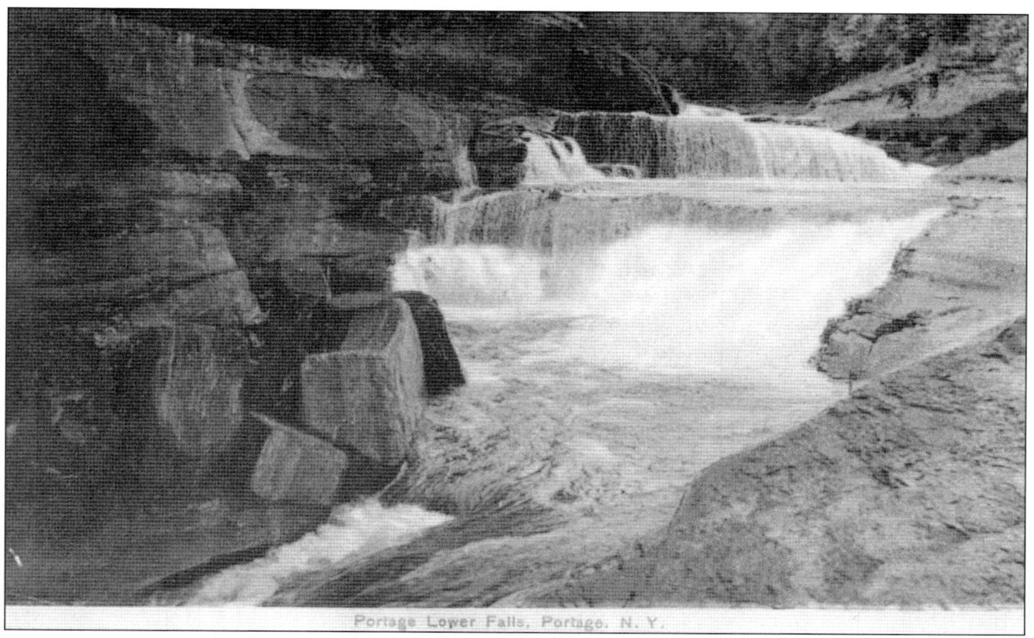

Portage Lower Falls, Portage. N. Y.

The Lower Falls of the park are less dramatic and require a short hike to get to them. The Lower Falls consist of two distinct falls, with a lower section dropping about 30 feet and an upper section dropping about 40 feet, with about 350 feet separating them. A stone footbridge crosses the gorge below the falls and connects to a hiking trail along the east side of the park. (Above, AHS; below, LCoHo.)

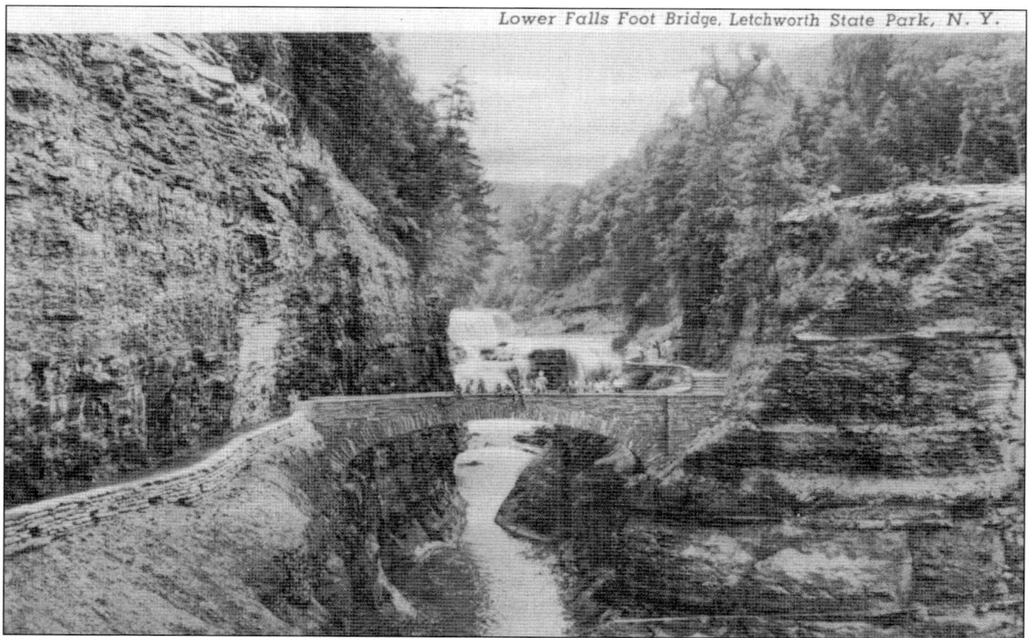

Lower Falls Foot Bridge, Letchworth State Park, N. Y.

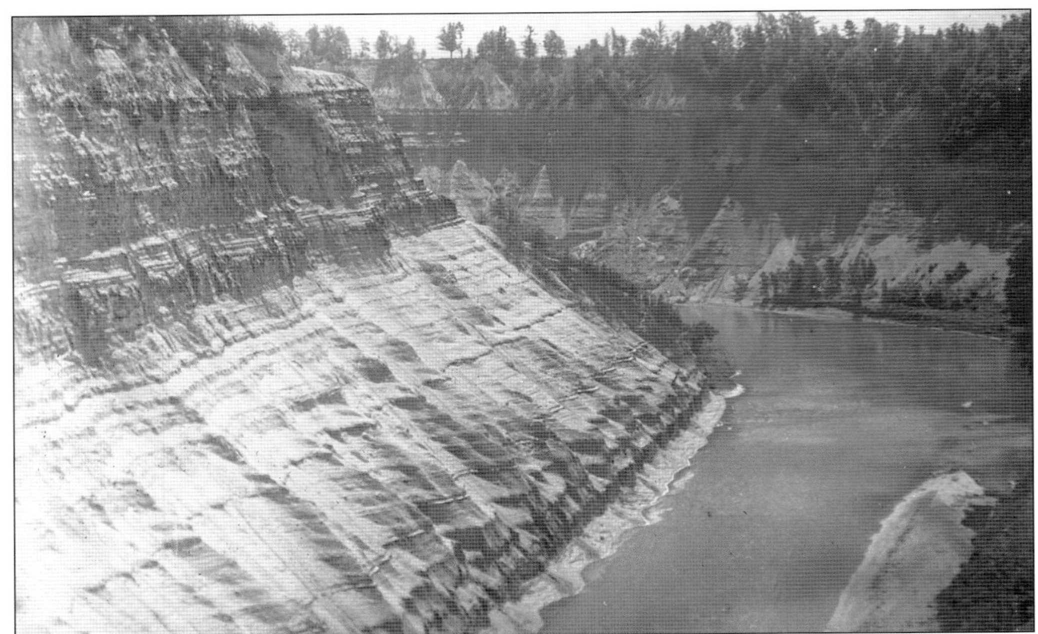

These spectacular images were produced from four-inch-by-six-inch glass plates. Their time frame puts them in the early 1900s. The following information was recorded on the glass plate sleeve: "subject: High Banks of Genesee at Letchworth; date: July 18; time: 1:00 p.m.; sun: bright; f-stop: 64; and exposure: 1.5 seconds." Glass plate photography was a highly skilled operation in the early days. A photographer would have to transport a great deal of equipment to the scene. Then he would set up a portable darkroom, coat his glass plates, do the required exposure, and process the plate immediately. It took many tries in the early days to get a correct exposure. (NA.)

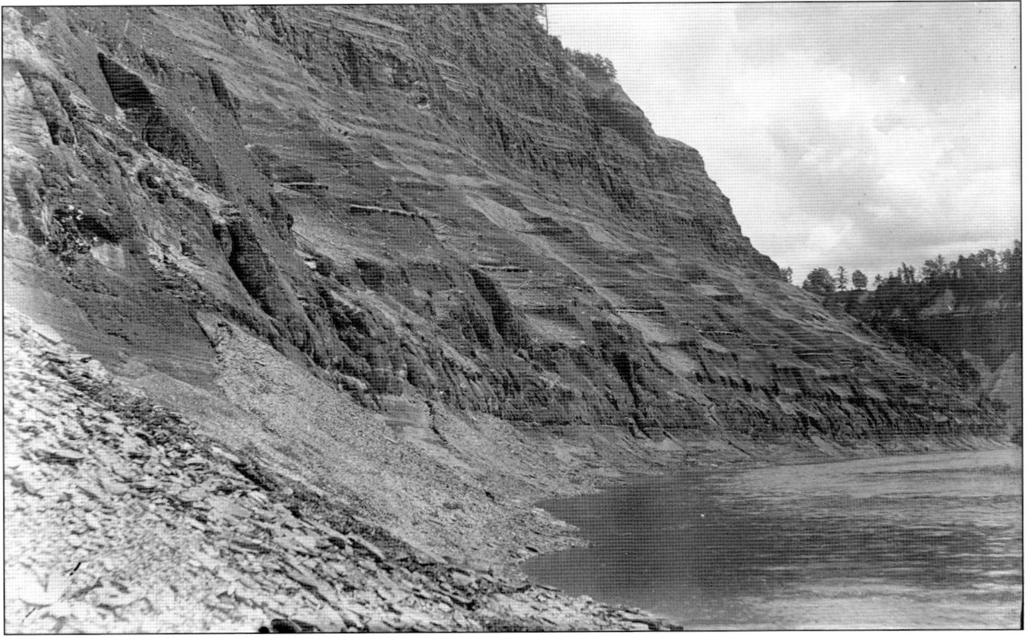

On May 6, 1836, an act was passed in the New York Legislature authorizing the construction of the Genesee Valley Canal. It was to run from the Erie Canal on the south side of Rochester, south-southwest along the Genesee River Valley to Mount Morris, Portageville, and Belfast, and then cross-country to the Allegheny River at Olean, with a branch from Mount Morris paralleling the Canaseraga Creek to Dansville. The most difficult section to build was the bypass around the gorge and falls at present-day Letchworth State Park. The canal followed the old Native American portage route. On June 4, 1877, the legislature approved an abandonment of the canal on or after September 30, 1878. The canal was sold on November 6, 1880, to the Genesee Valley Canal Railroad, which had been chartered on July 15 of that year. (Right LCoHo; below, JS.)

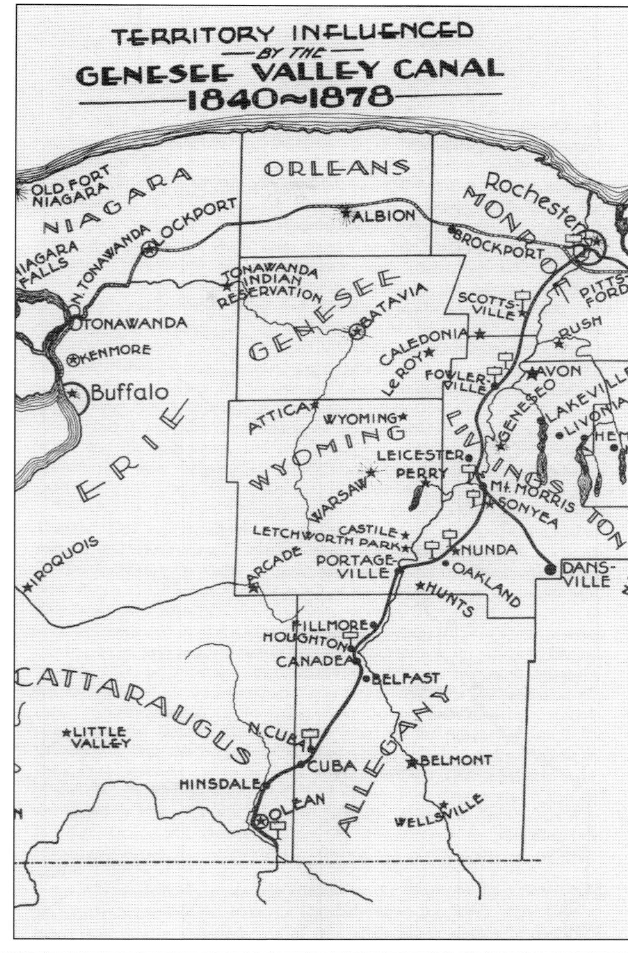

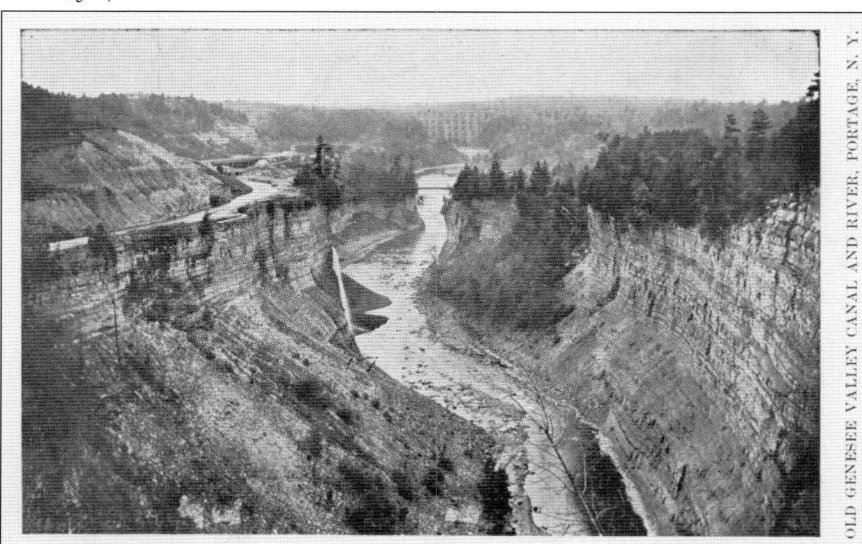

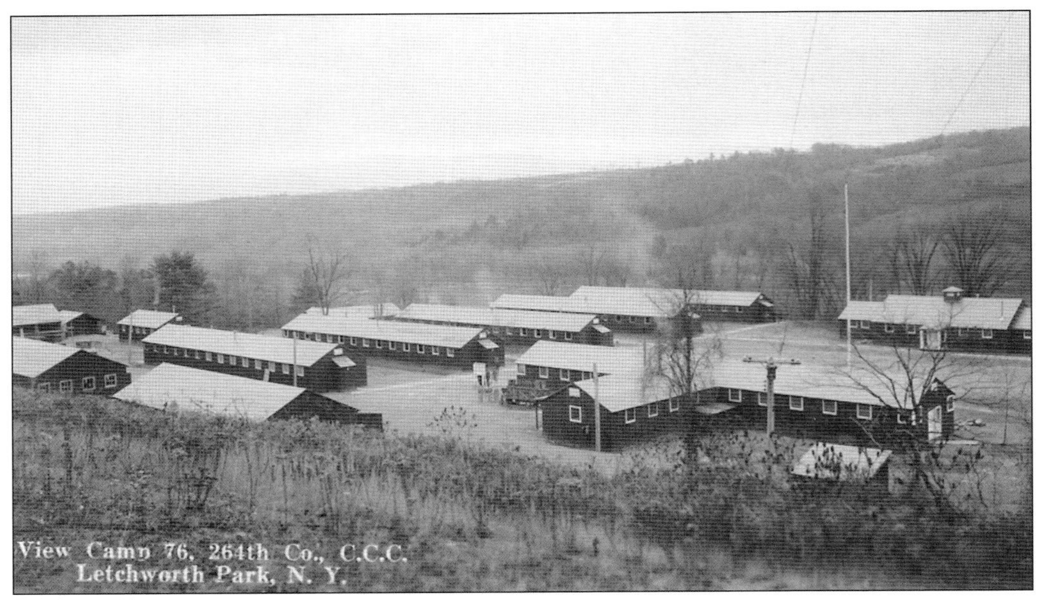

During the Great Depression, Letchworth State Park was the site of four Civilian Conservation Corps camps. The camps were built during the summer of 1933 to house a group of young, unemployed men from the cities that were being hired by the government to do work in the park. The complex included dormitory housing, recreation buildings, a hospital, and a mess hall. Most camps had a military layout and were supervised by the Army. (JS.)

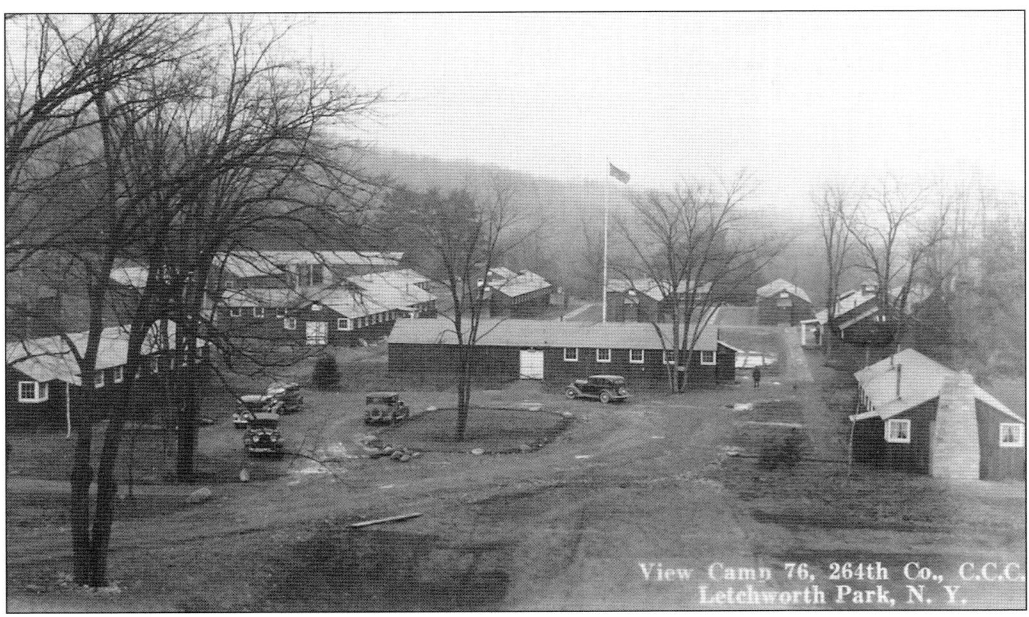

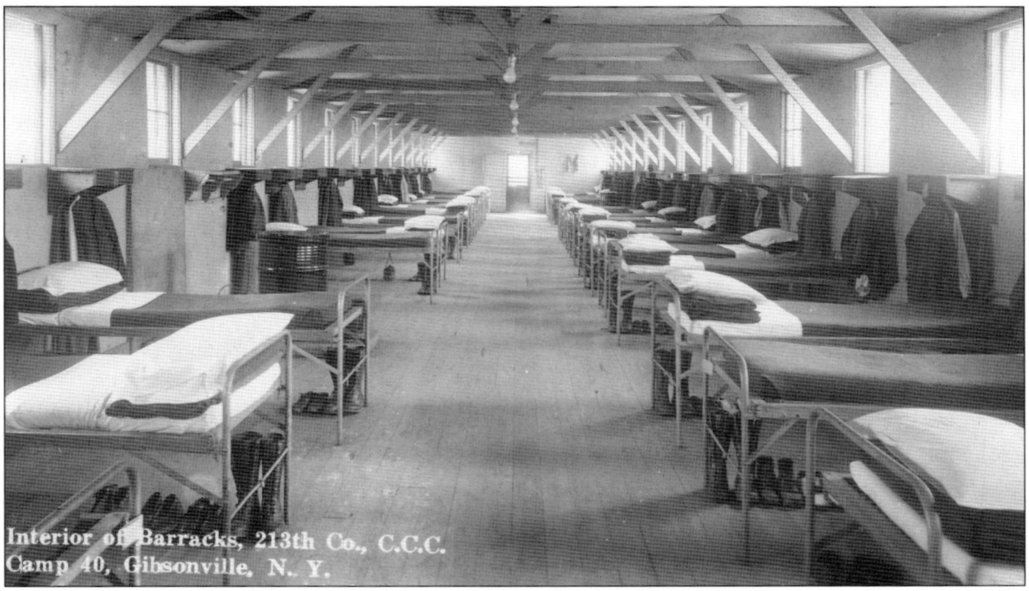

These spectacular cards show the military influence that the camp was operated by. From 1933 to 1941, over 3,000 men were employed. The work done by this enthusiastic and skilled group is still evident today in many New York State parks. The men established roads through the parks; built beautiful stone bridges and walls, cabins, and restrooms; provided forest improvements; and laid the ground work for water and electric lines. (JS.)

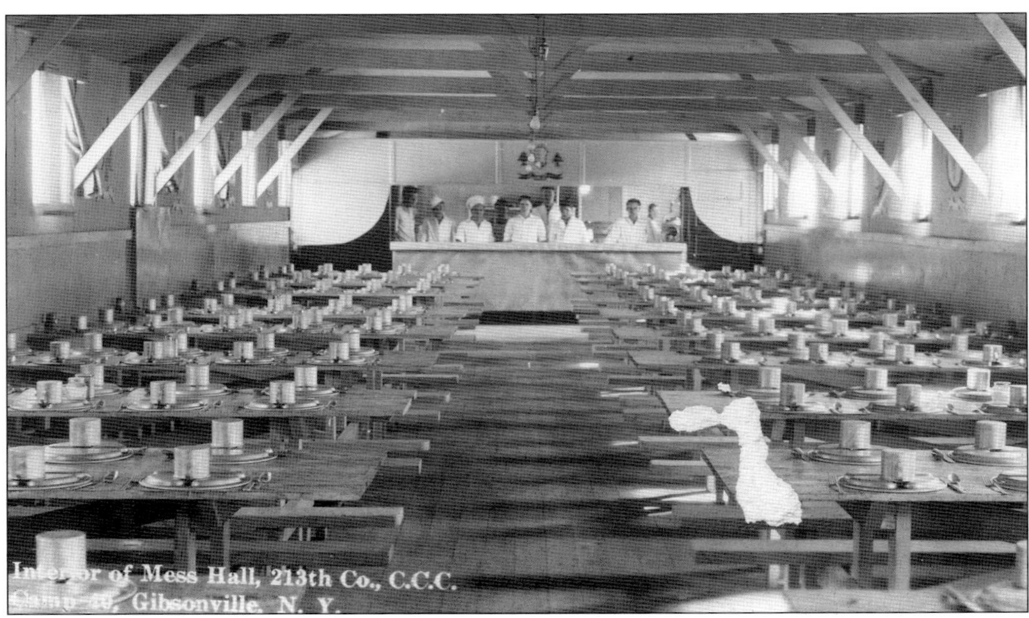

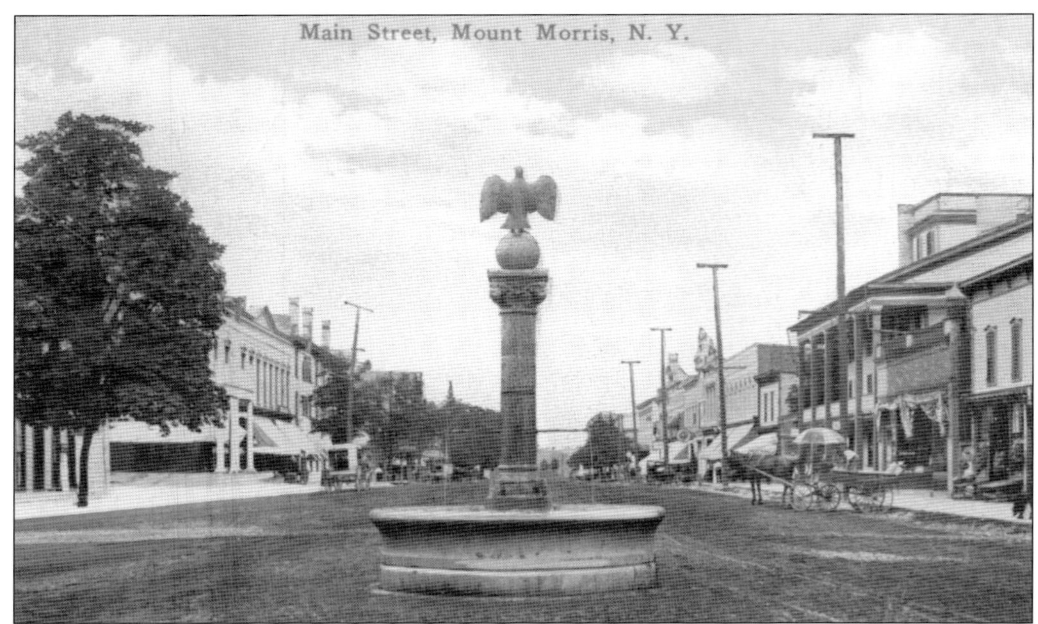

Mount Morris is a village at the northeastern entrance to Letchworth State Park. It was incorporated as a village in 1835 and was named after Robert Morris, a financier during the American Revolution. (LCoHo.)

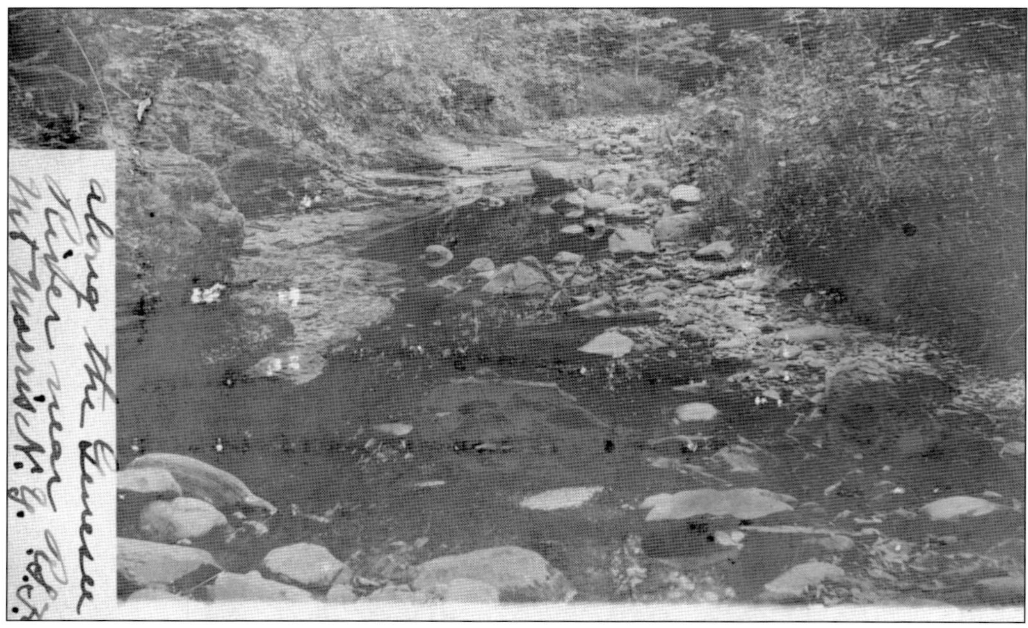

A spectacular photo postcard of a scene along the Genesee River near Mount Morris is seen here. The view shows a very small Genesee River passing through the village in the early 1900s. These postcards are one-of-a-kind images, as they were individually created by the photographer. (CRB.)

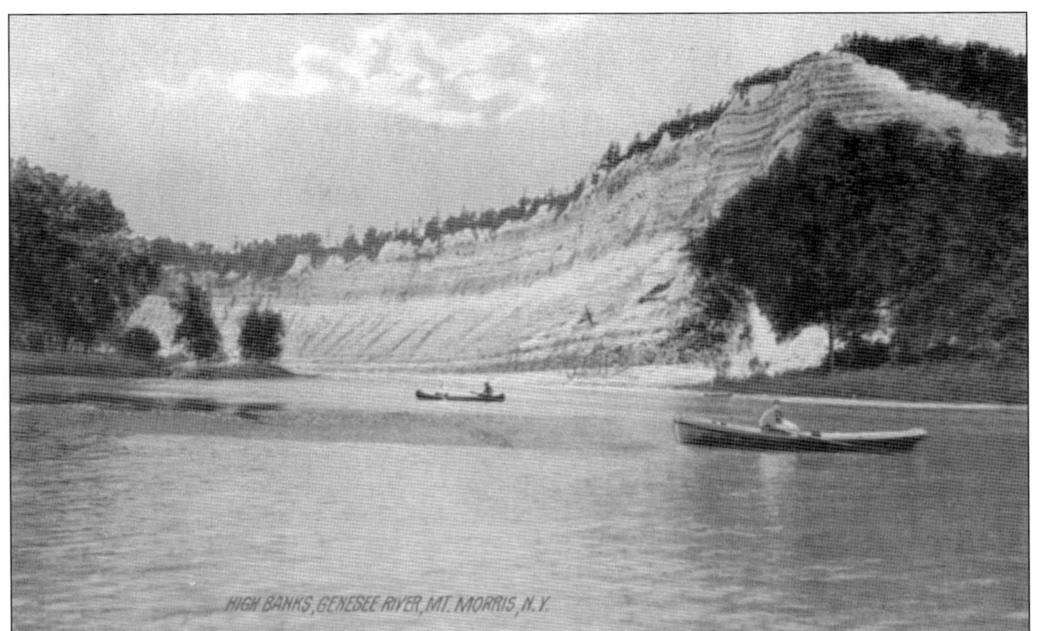

The Mount Morris High Banks of the Genesee are shown here. The pre-glacial eastern branch of the Genesee ran south of Mount Morris and, in its early days, was completely diverted by extensive terminal moraines south of the village. Today, the canyon walls are some 300 feet high above the river. (LCoHO.)

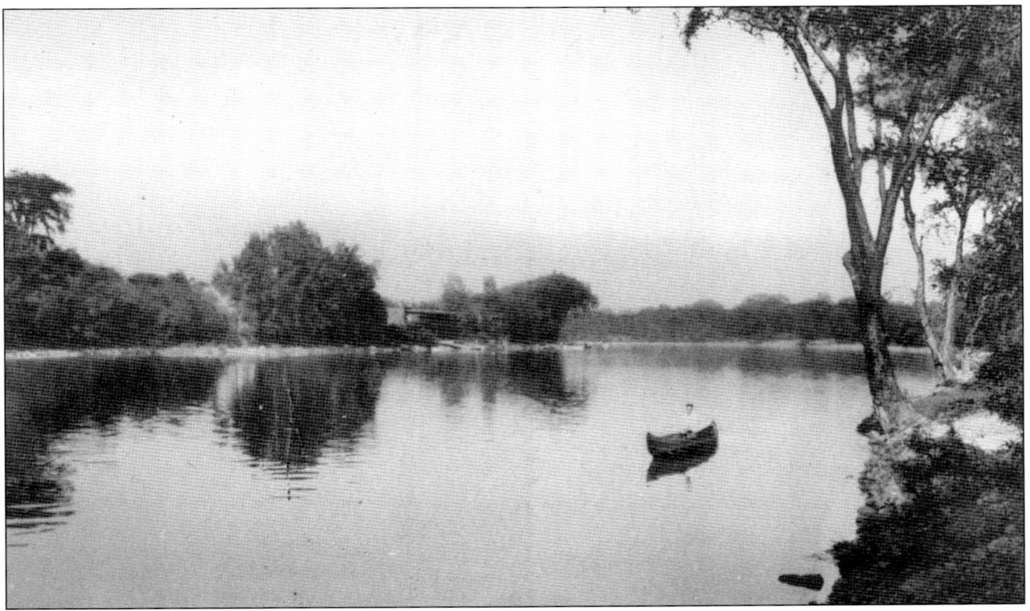

Today, only a small creek flows in what is left of this large valley. The natural beauty of this area has drawn visitors since the early days. The Indians built their villages upon the cliffs and farmed the fertile lands along the gorge. Later, early settlers called the High Banks their home. Today, the High Banks has become a recreational area with ball fields, a swimming pool, and picnic areas. (RPL.)

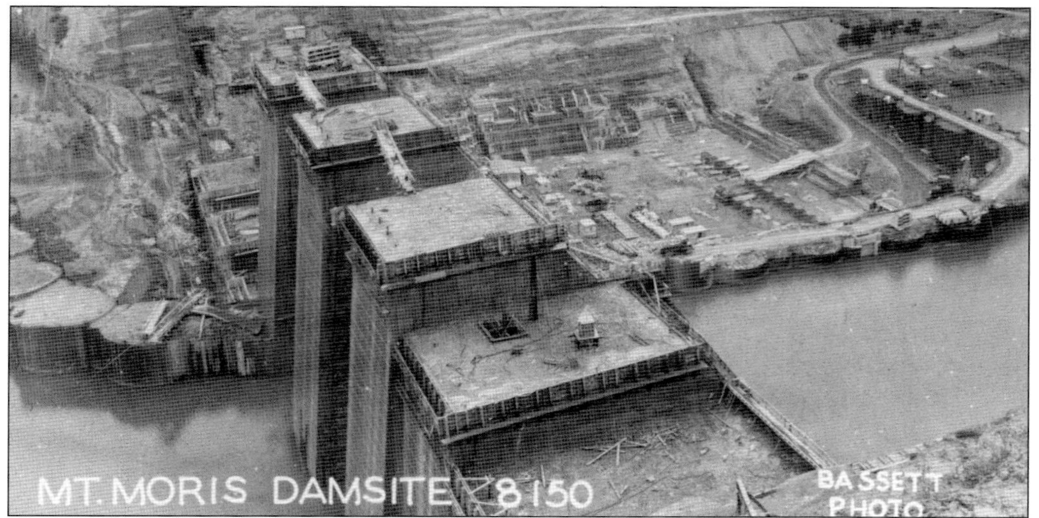

The Buffalo District Office of the US Army Corps of Engineers oversaw the construction of the Mount Morris dam from 1948 to 1952. The project was authorized by Congress in the Flood Control Act of 1944 at a cost of $25 million. The dam was constructed deep in a gorge of the Genesee River, 40 miles upstream from the city of Rochester, New York. Work began in early 1948 as cofferdams were constructed to divert the Genesee so preparations could be started on the gorge walls and riverbed. (CRB.)

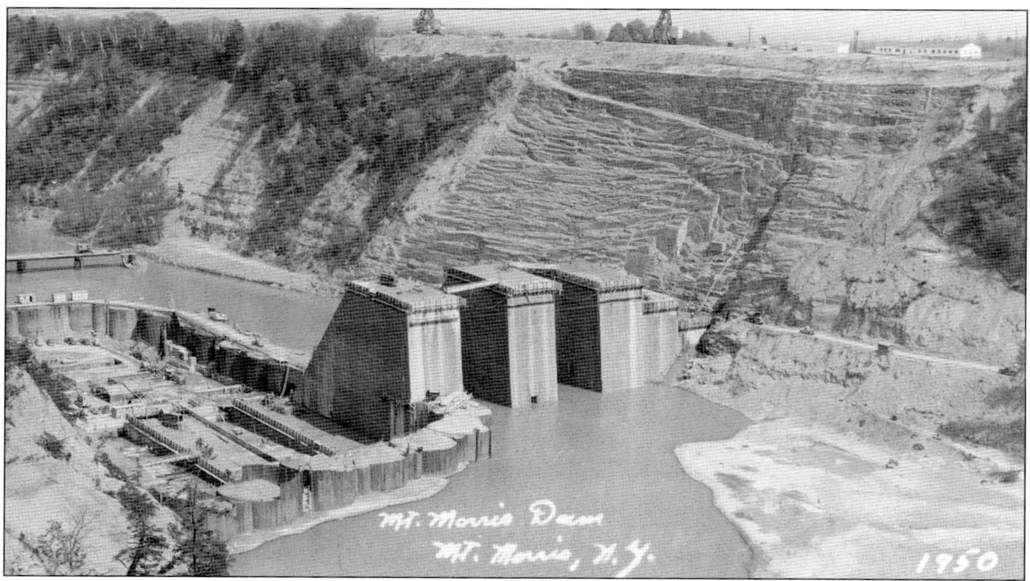

Work was dangerous as men scaled wooden ladders setting off blasting caps. From May 1949 to November 1951, twenty-two tons of concrete were carried in eight cubic yard buckets every five minutes, day and night. The last bucket of concrete was poured on Halloween. By the time the project was completed, over 750,000 cubic feet of concrete was poured. Any project of this magnitude had injuries or deaths. Eight men were killed when a giant bucket of concrete fell. One worker was killed in a fall. The construction was one of the biggest public works projects in western New York since the building of the Erie Canal. In four years of construction, 470 workers were involved. (LCoHO.)

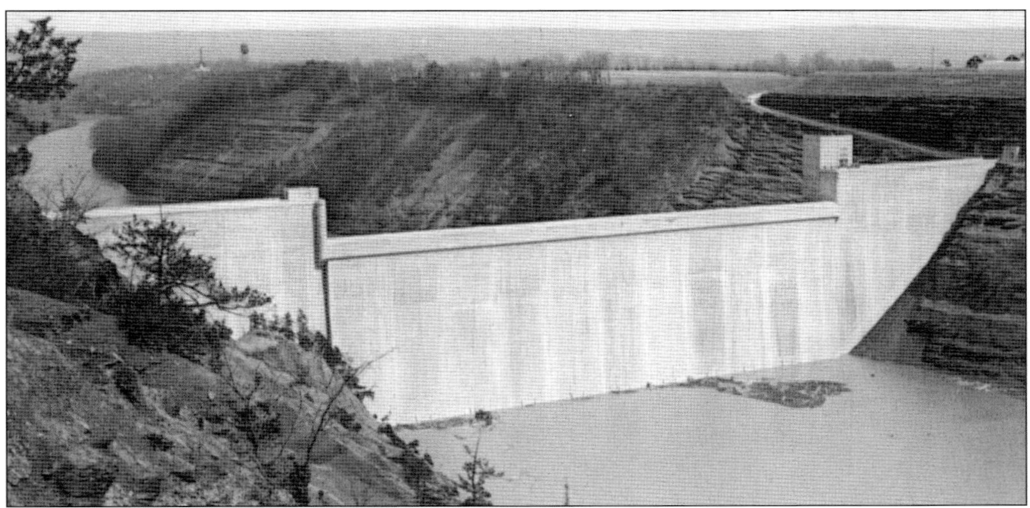

The Mount Morris Dam received its name from the small community located near its site. It is the largest concrete dam east of the Mississippi. It spans 1,028 feet across the valley. From a flat base of 213 feet, the dam rises 245 feet, tapering at a 20-foot walkway along the top. From 1865 to 1950, a major flood ravaged the Genesee River Valley on an average of every seven years. Completion of the project significantly reduced the risk of flood disaster, which formerly threatened the lower Genesee River Valley. The capacity of the reservoir in the river gorge is ample to protect the basin below from all but very infrequent floods. (LCoHO.)

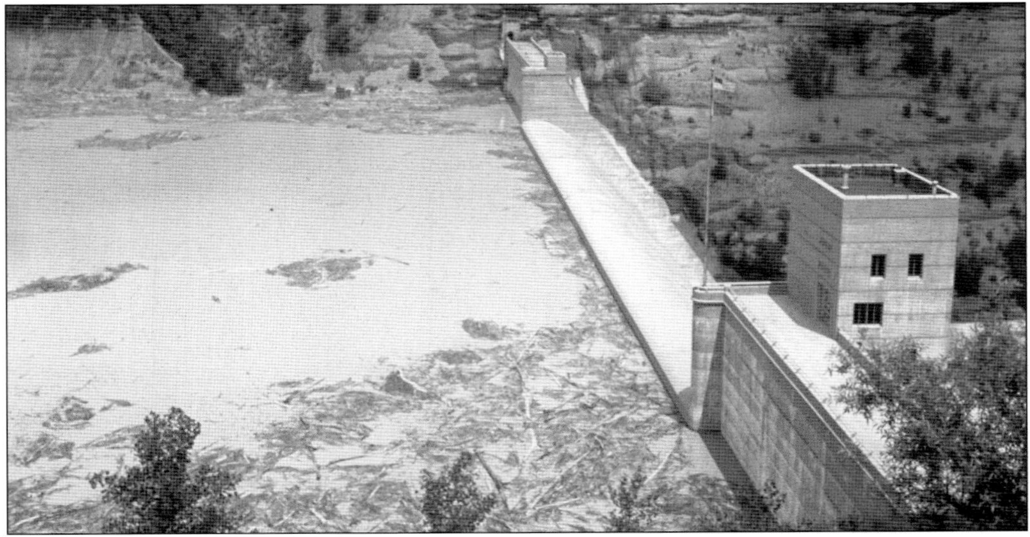

The United States Army Corps of Engineers states that, in the years since the completion of the dam, an estimated $1 billion in flooding damages have been prevented, and that during Hurricane Agnes in 1972, a total of $210 million in damages was prevented, primarily to the city of Rochester. The water inflow due to Hurricane Agnes exceeded the storage capacity of the reservoir, and it was necessary to release water through the gates of the dam, causing minor downstream flooding. These releases were made to prevent overtopping of the spillway. Had the spillway overtopped, accumulated debris in the reservoir would have passed downstream, causing logjams and additional damage. Inflows of this magnitude are only expected to happen an average of every 300 years. (ACE.)

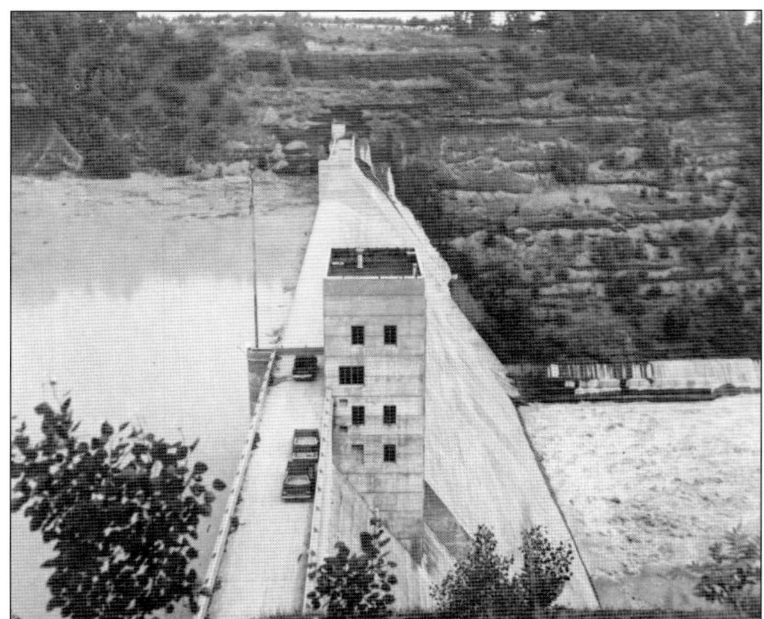

During the flood of 1972 (Tropical Storm Agnes), the dam was put to its test. A storm front stalled over the Genesee River Valley, dropping a record 13.72 inches of rain. The dam was filled to capacity, and millions of dollars worth of damage was prevented. The reservoir filled to within six feet of the top before the gates were opened to release pressure and prevent overflow. (ACE.)

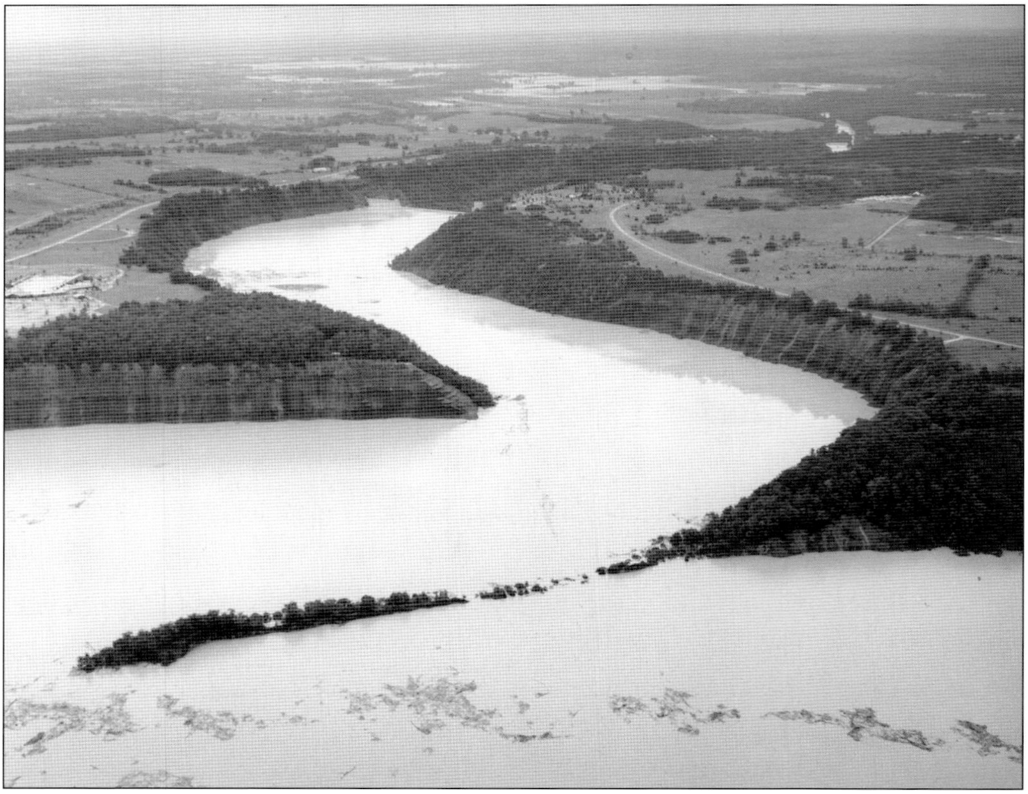

This view shows the Genesee River flowing through Letchworth State Park at the height of the flood. The water level in the gorge had reached a height that, between the foam and spray of the water, made it impossible to distinguish the falls. (ACE.)

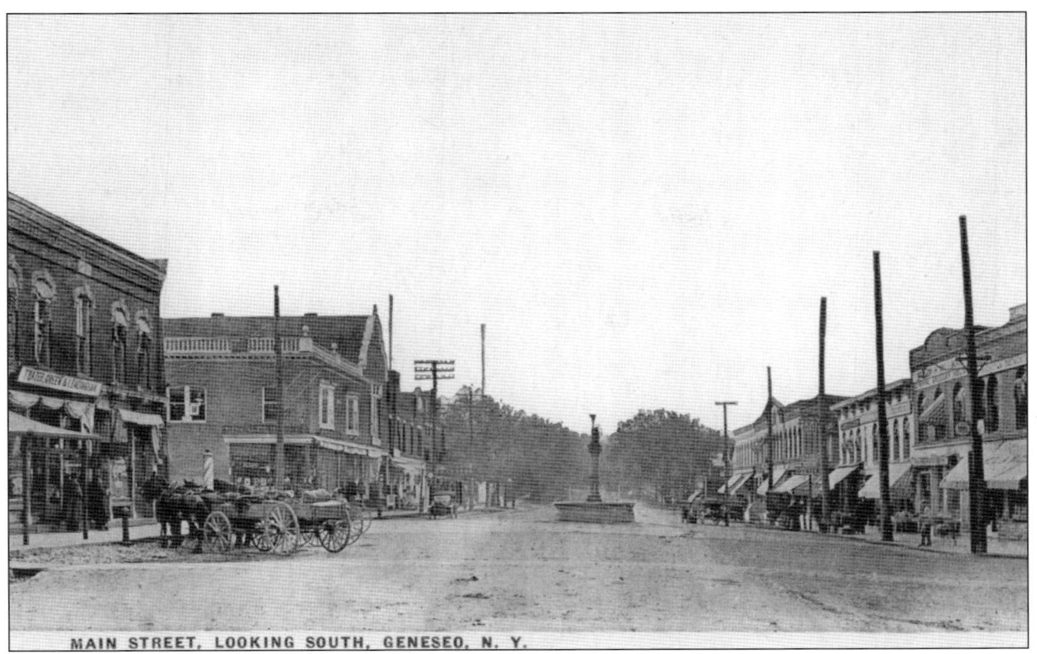

Geneseo was the site of the largest Seneca village in western New York. The English name "Geneseo" is a anglicization of the Iroquois name for Gen-nis-he-yo, which translates to "beautiful valley." The area surrounding the river here was flat and fertile, which made for great farming for the Indians and early explorers. (CRB.)

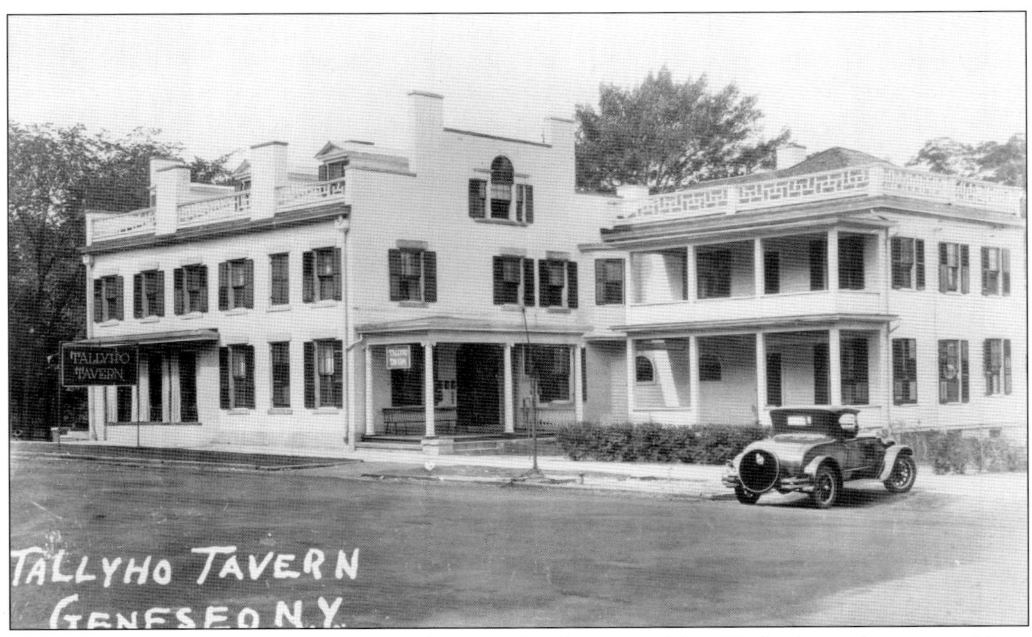

The Treaty of Big Tree in 1797 opened up much of western New York. As settlers moved into the region around early Geneseo, the TallyHo Tavern became a popular place to gather. This beautiful photo postcard is from the early 1940s. (CRB.)

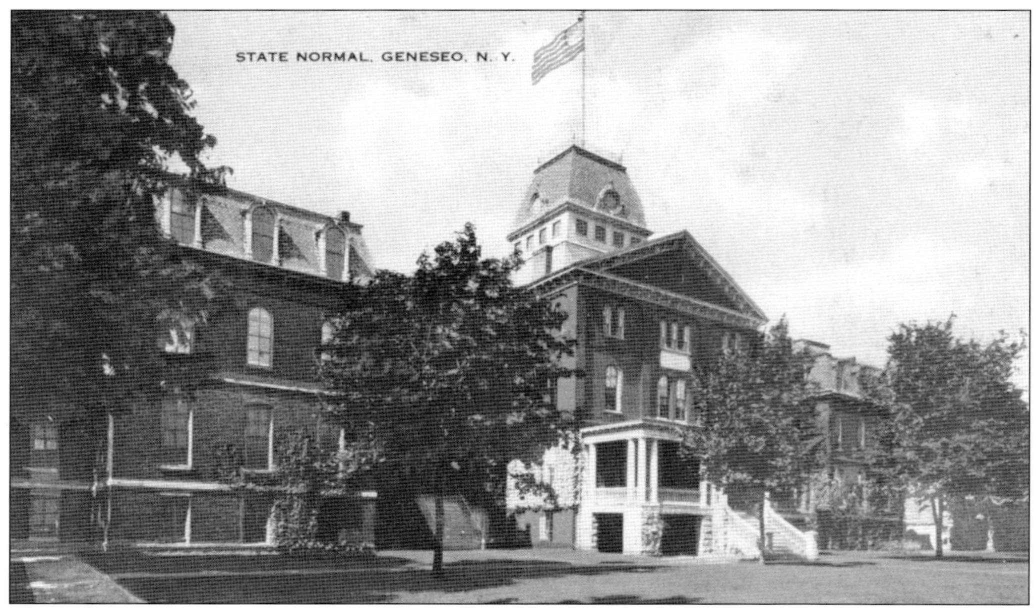

Early settler James Wadsworth's interest in public education planted the seeds of what would eventually become SUNY at Geneseo. In 1867, the Wadsworth Normal School was chartered by the New York State Legislature. In 1871, with 91 students, its name was changed to Geneseo Normal School, just one of nine name changes throughout the years. Today, SUNY Geneseo has an enrollment of over 50,000 students and is considered one of the highest-ranking teachers colleges. (CRB.)

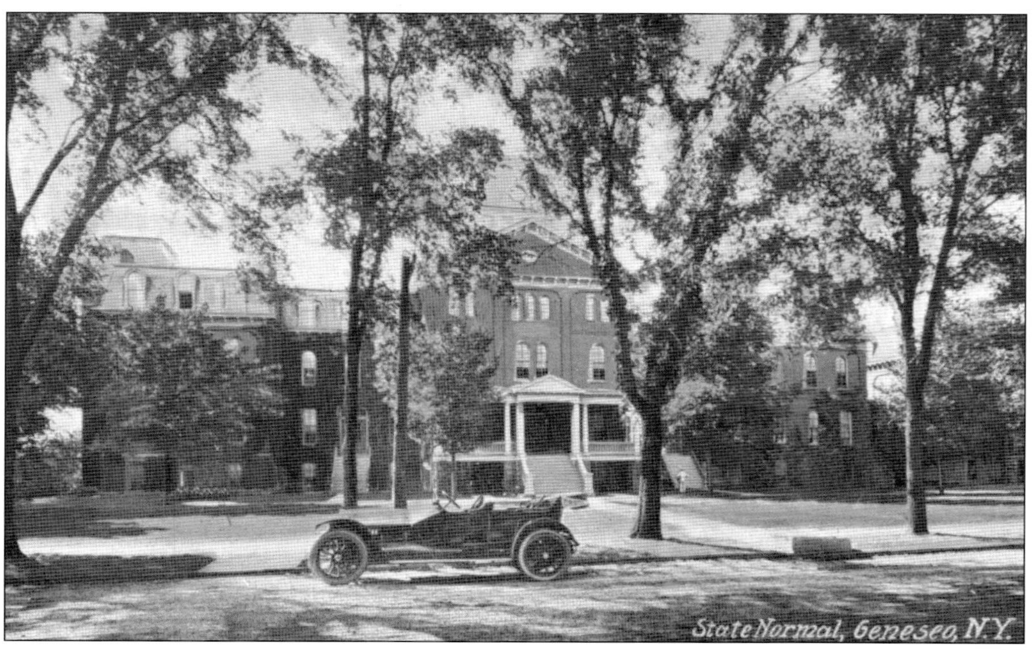

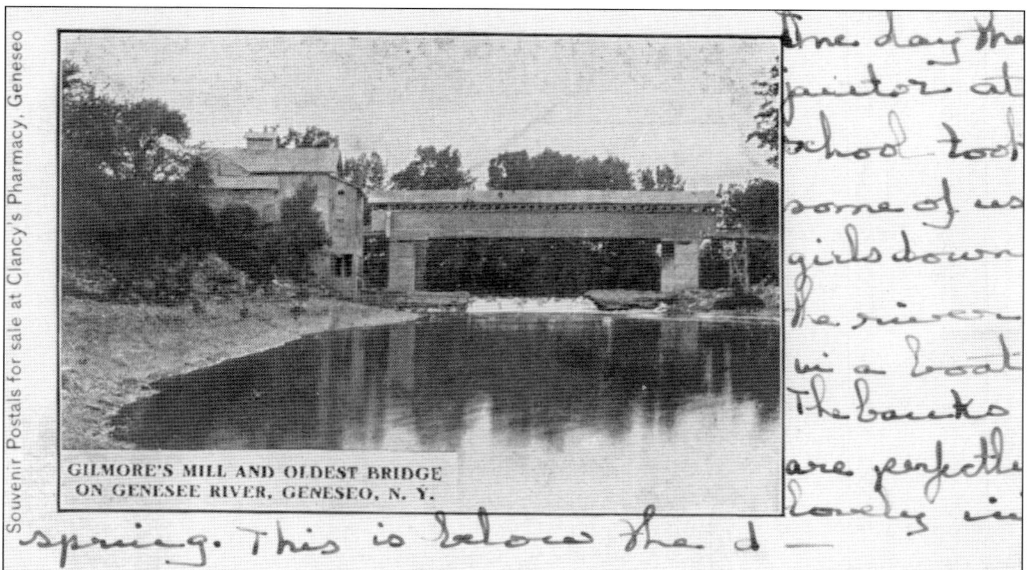

Pictured is Gilmore's Mill and supposedly the oldest bridge on the Genesee River. It was built around 1830 to replace an 1821 structure. It was recognized for its lattice pattern and was a remarkably long bridge. In 1913, it was seriously damaged by the crossing of a thresher and was replaced by a steel bridge. (CRB.)

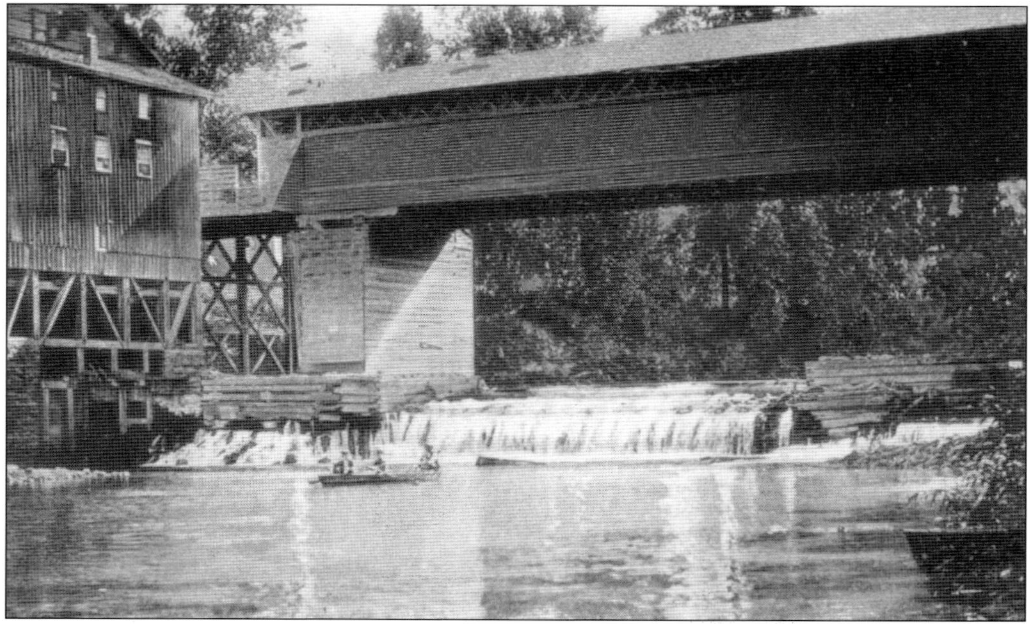

Covered bridges over the Genesee were common in the late 1800s. These bridges served as a place for people and canal animals to cross the river and be sheltered from storms. Oftentimes, these bridges would be washed out during high water. (LCoHO.)

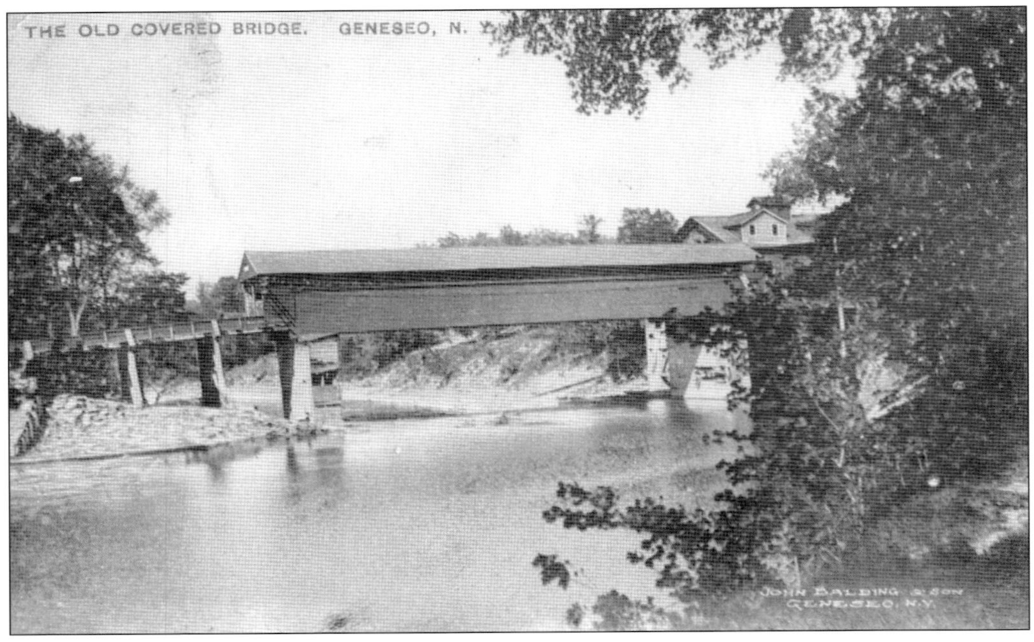

Today, Geneseo is still considered the "jewel of the Genesee." Its ingredients include scenic spots along the river, a rich Indian history, one of the top educational institutions, and many 19th-century buildings that can be found throughout the village. Geneseo is the home of the Livingston County Museum, which was once an old cobblestone school built on land donated by the Wadsworths. (LCoHO.)

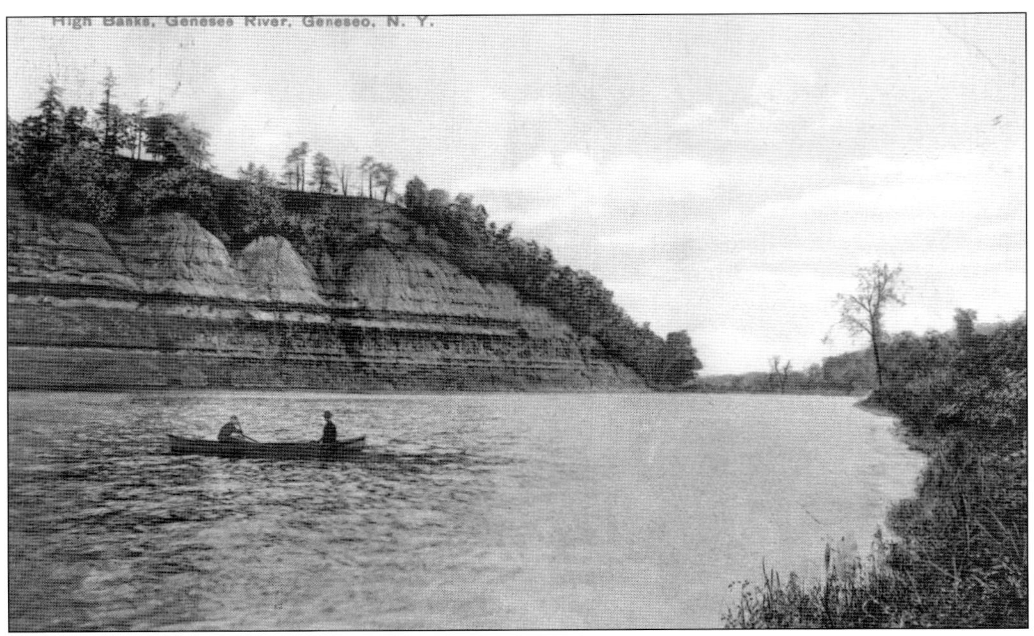

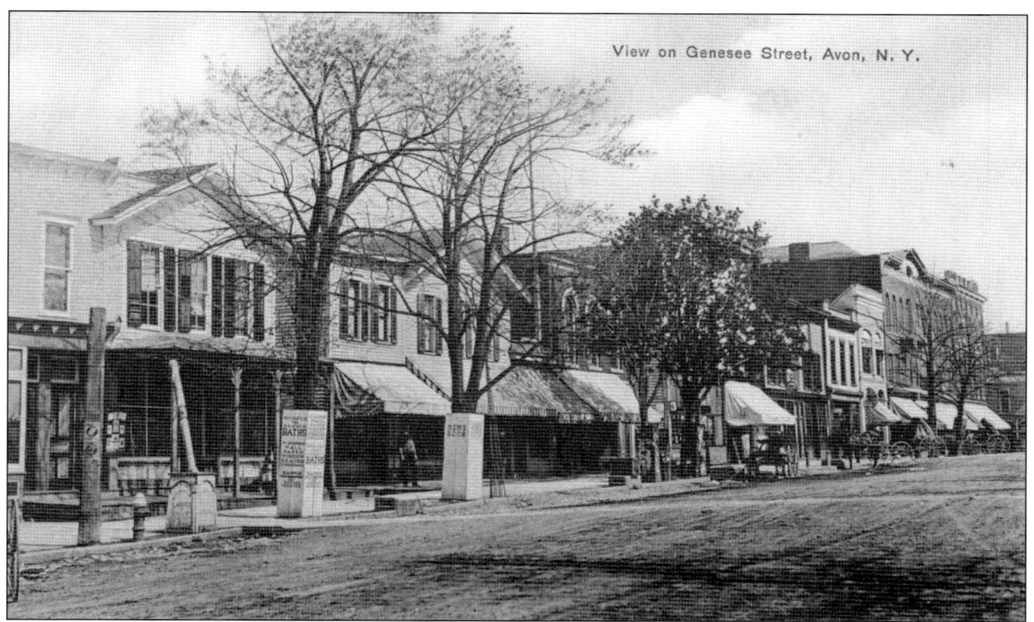

The town was formed in 1789 as Hartford, and the name was changed to Avon in 1808. Mineral springs were an important resource of the early town, and bathhouses were constructed for many visitors in the early 19th century. Avon was one of the places on the Genesee that the early settlers crossed on rafts. (RPL.)

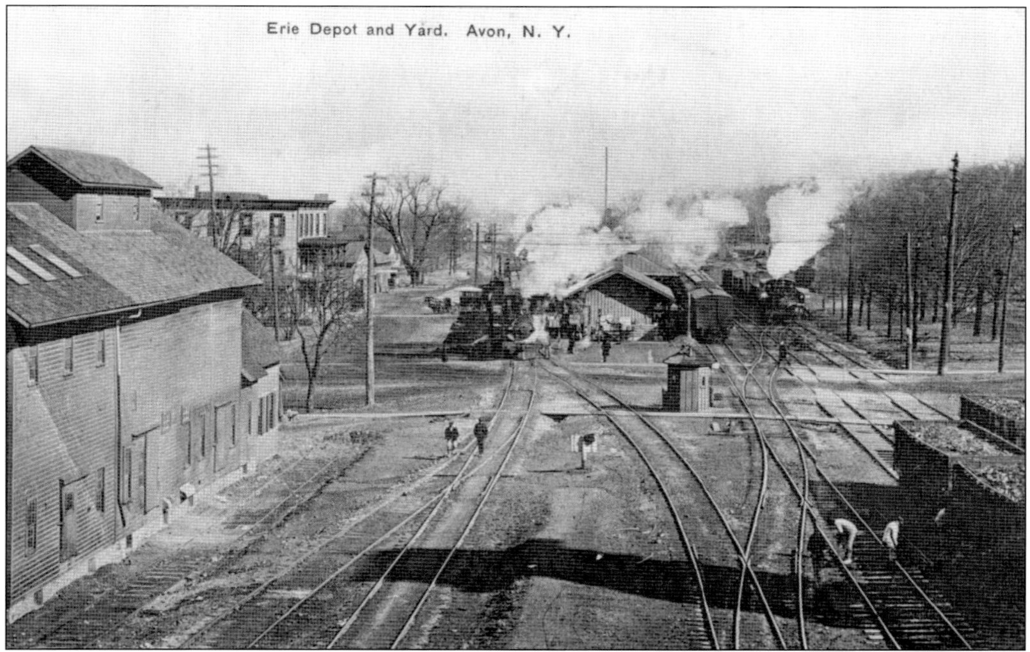

Like many early communities along the river, the railroad played an important role in its development. The railroad came to Avon in the mid-19th century when an 18-mile route was constructed from downtown Rochester. (CRB.)

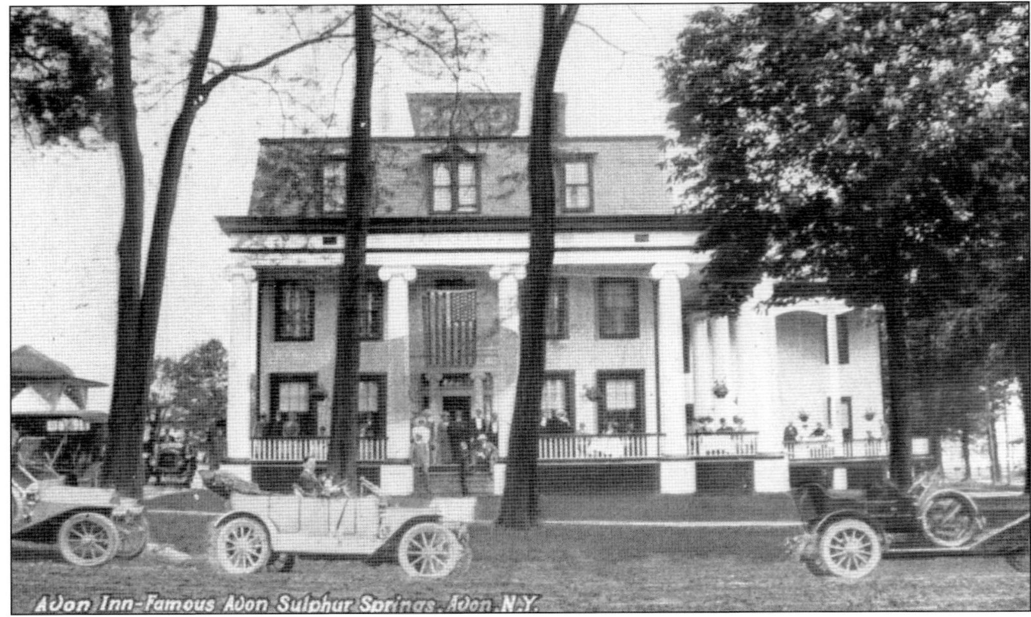

Built in 1820 and listed in the National Register of Historic Places, this beautiful Greek Revival mansion has carried on a century old tradition of dining and lodging. It began as the home of Jonathan H. Gerry, a prosperous farmer. It was next turned into a well-reputed health center where water from the nearby sulfur springs was used to treat common maladies of the day. The "Inn" was famous for having the first central heating system in the Genesee Valley, the first elevator in upstate New York, as well as housing the first bank and post office. (RPL.)

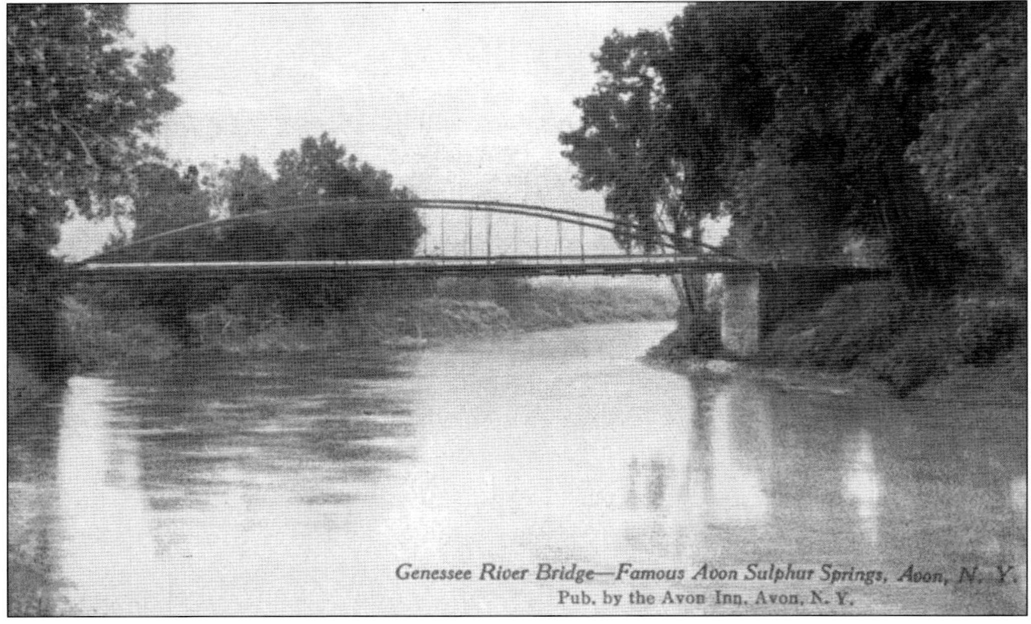

In its early days, Avon was a hub of activity. Large wooden hotels sprang up around Avon's famous sulphur springs. The resorts lingered on for over 30 years. Today, the area is a ghostly pasture where cows roam. (RPL.)

Four

Monroe County
Industrial Rochester

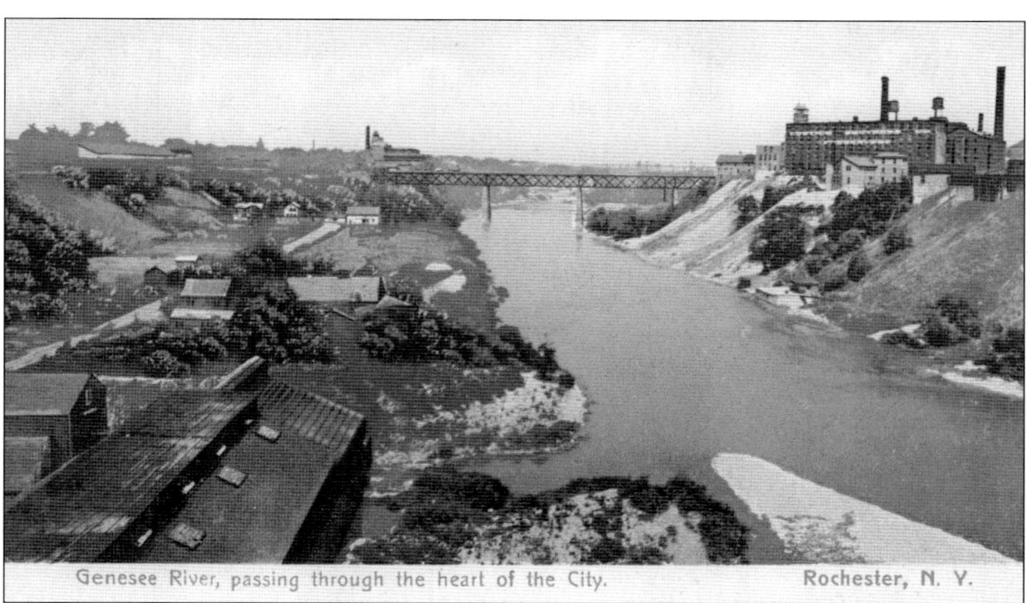

Genesee River, passing through the heart of the City. Rochester, N. Y.

In 1811, Nathaniel Rochester founded Rochesterville. Monroe County was formed from parts of Genesee and Ontario Counties in 1821. In 1834, the name was changed to Rochester. Rochester has had a colorful history, and it is home to nine colleges and universities as well as a number of international businesses, including Eastman Kodak, Bausch & Lomb, Paychex, and Pictometry International, all of which make Monroe County their world headquarters. Xerox, while no longer headquartered in Rochester, has its principal offices and manufacturing facilities in Monroe County. It is also home to regional businesses, such as Wegmans Food Markets. The Genesee River passes right through the heart of the city. In its early days, industries along the river were so intimately tied to its waters that it might not have existed at all without the river's presence. (JS.)

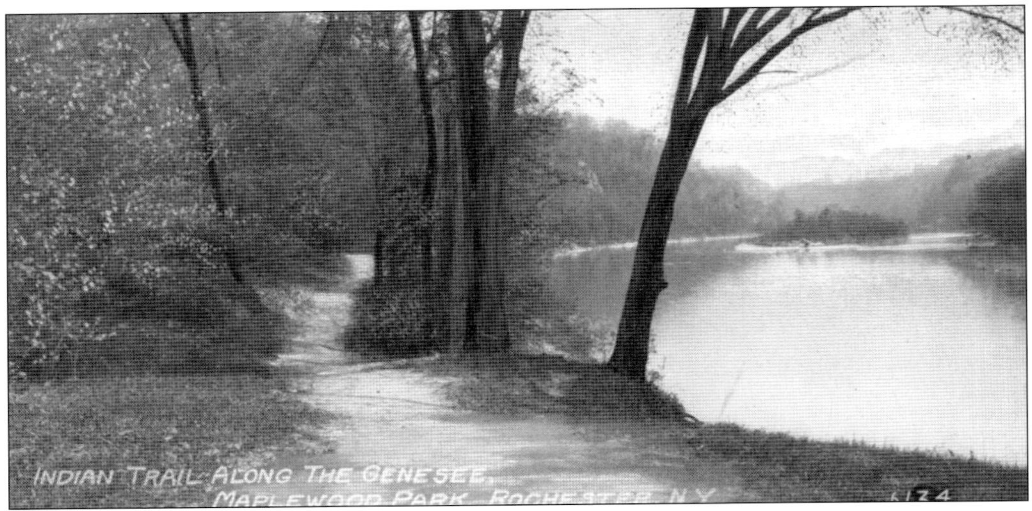

A well-worn footpath follows an old Indian trail along the banks of the Genesee. Today, the area is part of Maplewood Park. Maplewood Park, also known as Seneca Park West, is a landscaped public area in Rochester, New York, situated between Lake Avenue and the Genesee River. The two-mile park features many trails along the river gorge and the riverbank below, scenic views of two waterfalls, and a nationally accredited rose garden. The park was laid out by landscape architect Frederick Law Olmsted, who also designed nearby Highland Park. It was listed in the National Register of Historic Places in 2003. (JS.)

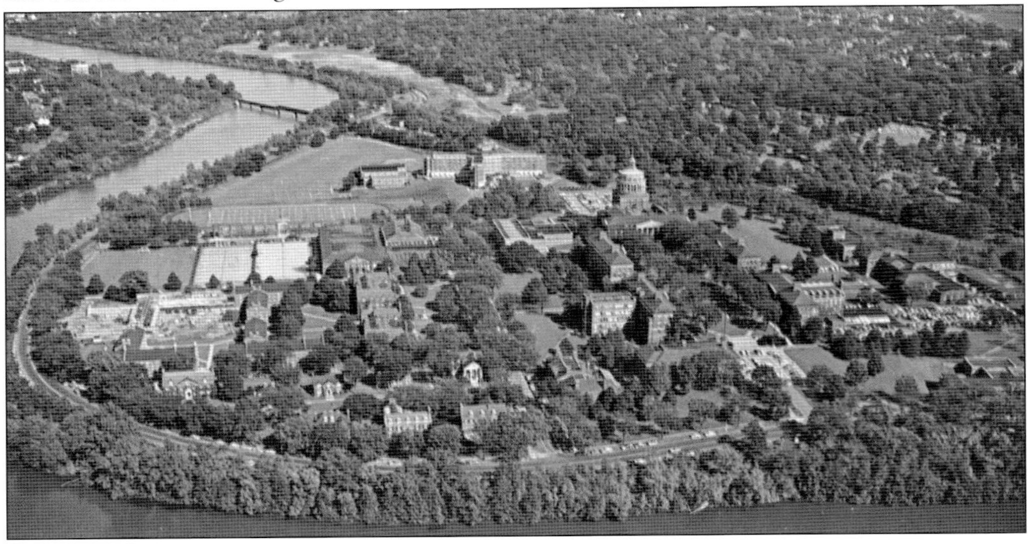

The University of Rochester (U of R, UR) is a private nonsectarian research university in Rochester, New York. The university grants undergraduate and graduate degrees, including doctoral and professional degrees. It has six schools and various interdisciplinary programs. The school is considered a "New Ivy." The University of Rochester is noted for its Eastman School of Music. The university is also home to the Institute of Optics, founded in 1929, the nation's first educational program devoted exclusively to optics. Rochester's Laboratory for Laser Energetics has the second most powerful fusion laser in the world. The University of Rochester, across all of its schools and campuses, enrolls approximately 5,600 undergraduates and 4,600 graduate students. (JS.)

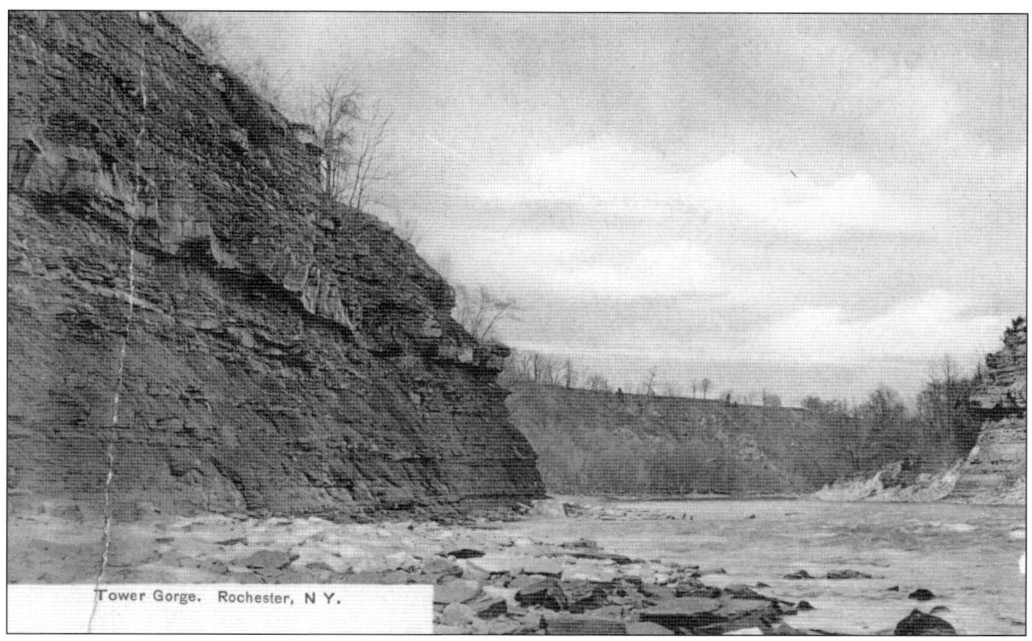

As the last ice age glacier retreated, vast amounts of glacial run off carved some deep gorges in the Rochester area. The carving was not continuous and simple down cutting by the Genesee River, as might be supposed. River erosion was opposed and hindered by the changing levels of the lake waters, which limited the river's flow of water. Today, the deep canyon that was carved beyond Charlotte and out into Lake Ontario has been partly filled in by river deposits of sand and silt. (RPL.)

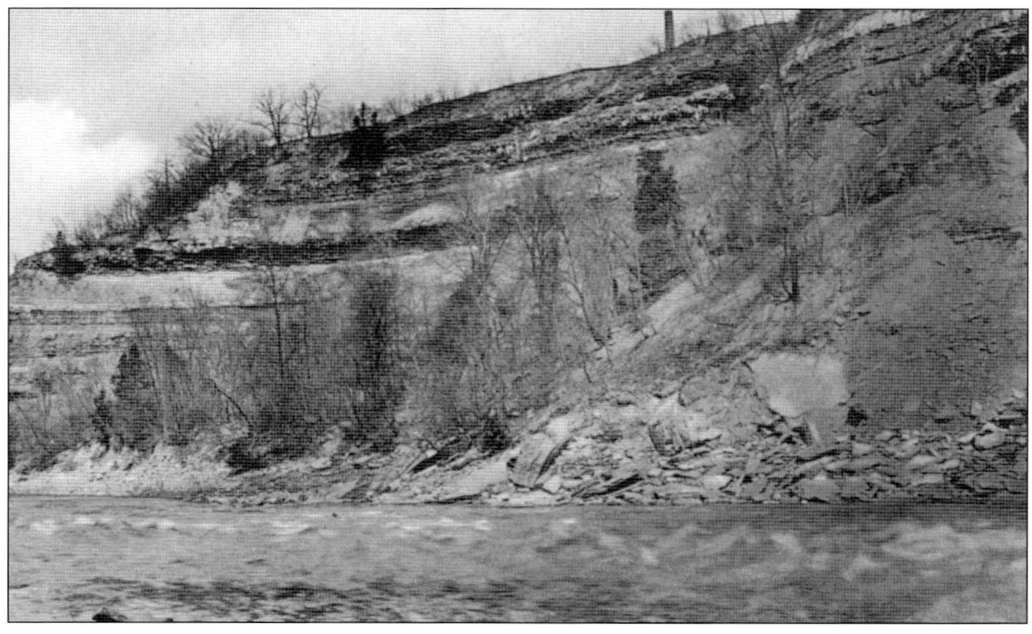

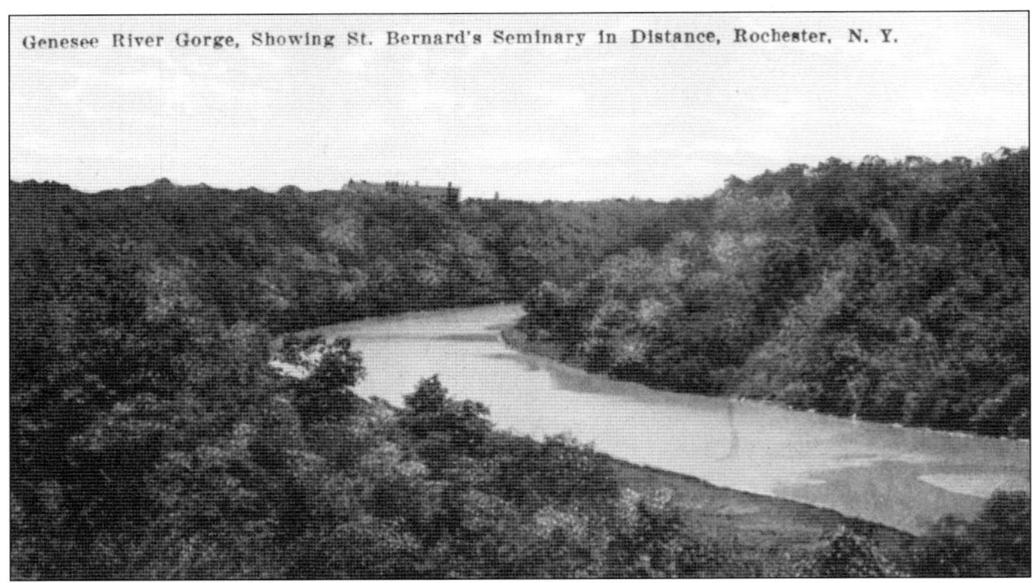

St. Bernard's Seminary is a historic Roman Catholic seminary complex located at Rochester on the banks of the Genesee. It is a group of four interconnected buildings designed by noted Rochester architect Andrew Jackson Warner and built between 1891 and 1908. The four structures are the center or main building (1891–1893), the Chapel (1891–1893), the South Building or Philosophy Hall (1900), and the North Building or Theology Hall (1908). All four buildings used Medina sandstone in their construction and share a Victorian Gothic style of architecture with stone walls and brick trim. The seminary was listed in the National Register of Historic Places in 1996. Today, the seminary offers three masters degrees in theology and a range of continuing education opportunities for those looking for further education in their profession as well as for those seeking personal enrichment and deeper understanding of the convictions of faith. (RPL.)

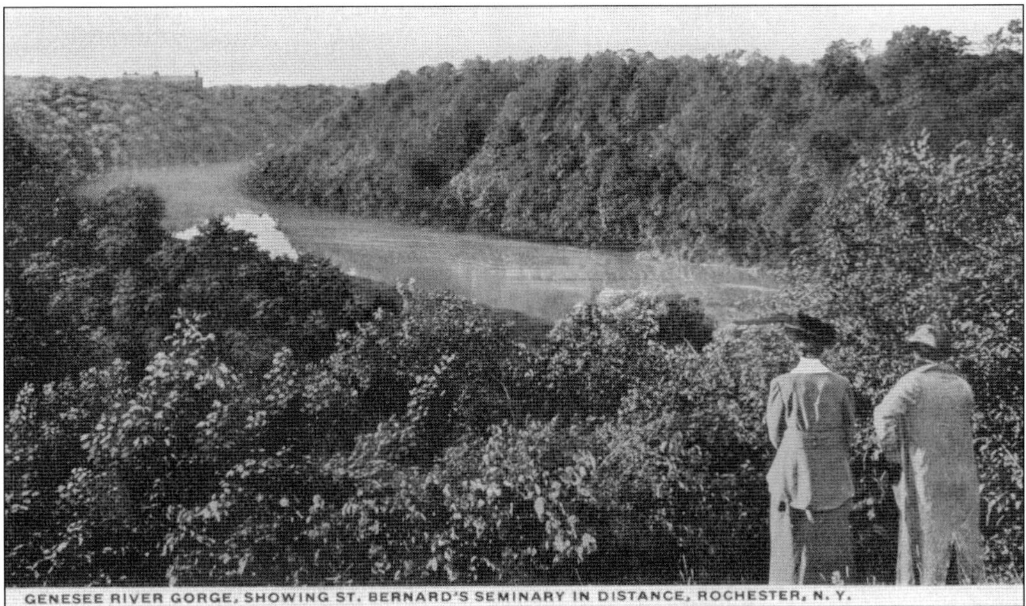

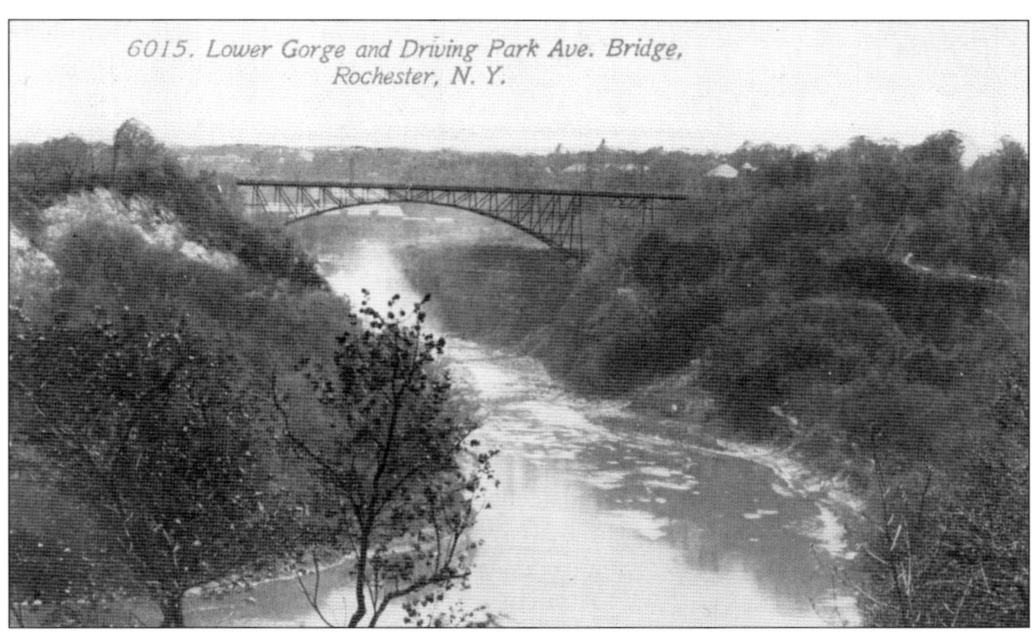

Driving Park Bridge was named after the Rochester Driving Park, a 19th-century racetrack for trotters. The original Driving Park Bridge (also known as Seneca Park Bridge) was built from 1889 to 1890 with an eight-ton load limit. It was 717 feet long and 220 feet from the bottom of the Genesee River Gorge and was considered to be the first spandrel-braced arch truss bridge built in the United States. It was one of the last wrought-iron bridges constructed, as steel was beginning to come into use. (RPL.)

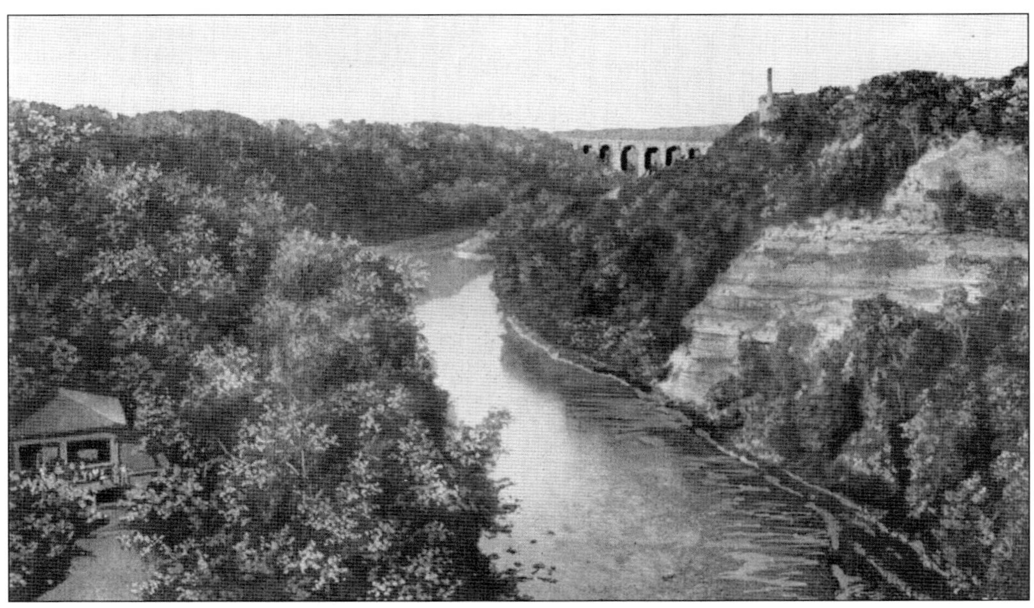

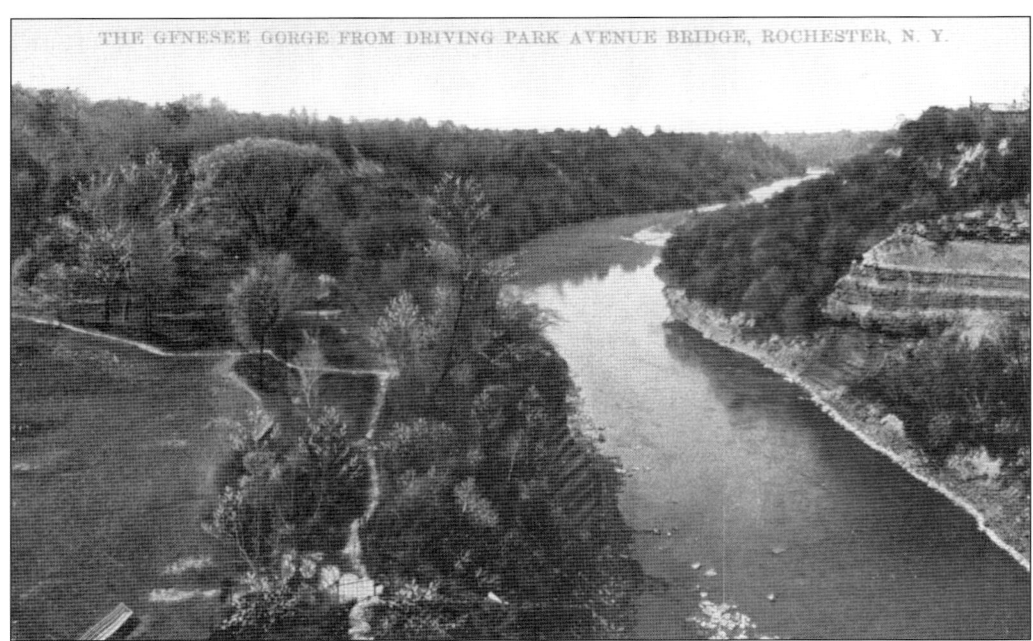

Before the historic 1890 Driving Park Bridge, there were multiple attempts to bridge the Genesee at the Lower Falls. The village of Carthage was in direct competition with Rochesterville, and until 1819, there was only one bridge crossing the Genesee River—at Main Street in Rochesterville. The Main Street Bridge was built in 1812 at a cost of $12,000 paid by New York State. Opponents of this bridge said there was no one to cross it. They had a point that Rochester's population that year was only 15. The community of King's Landing (also known as Hanford's Landing on the west side of the river) was the main port of Great Lakes commerce on the mouth of the Genesee River. Also growing at a rate faster than Rochesterville was Carthage, about a mile farther south on the river, on the bluffs above the last navigable portion of the Genesee downstream of the Lower Falls. (Above, JP; below, RPL.)

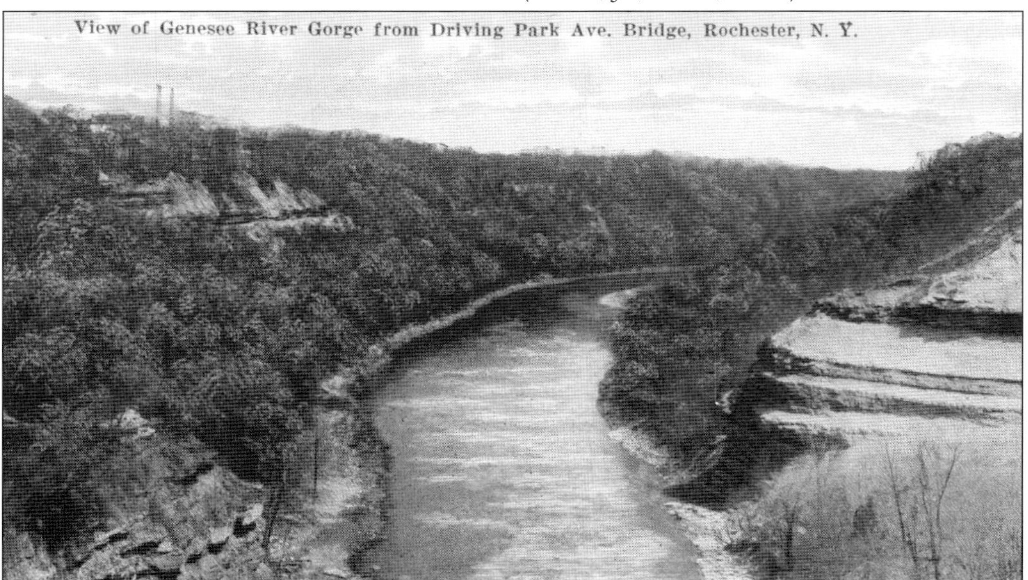

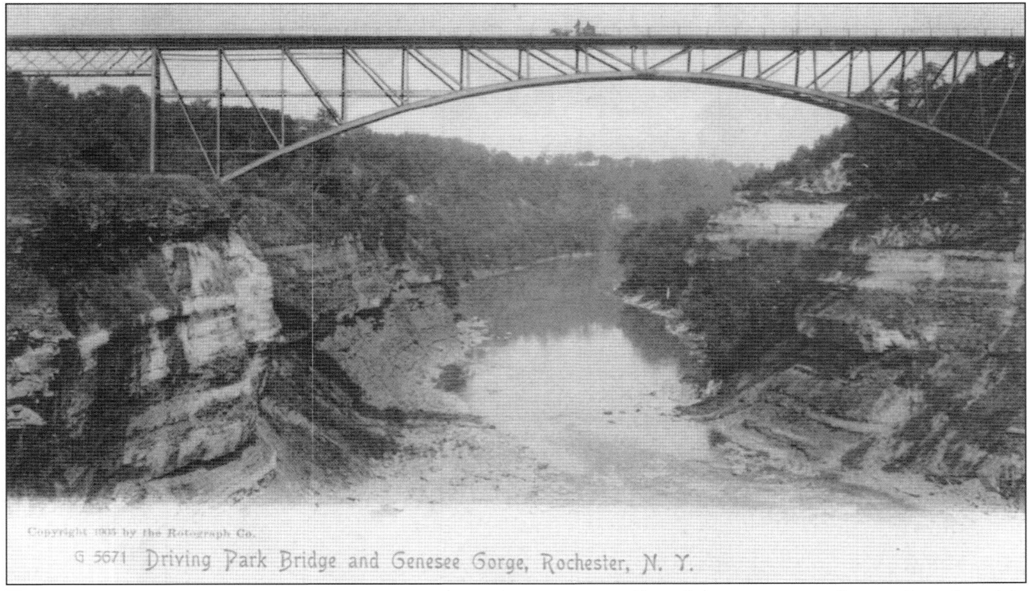

The view of Driving Park Bridge as well as the gorge walls of the Genesee from river level is impressive. River-level bridges were attempted over Middle Falls in 1828 and again in 1835, but in each case floods washed them out. All the while, the Erie Canal was progressing from the east, opening in 1823. That marked the point when Rochesterville dominated the region's development. By 1834, Carthage was incorporated into the City of Rochester. Another attempt to bridge the Genesee Gorge at Driving Park was made, opening in July 1856. This time it was a suspension bridge, but users felt it was unstable, and it was closed. Cables anchored in the gorge were added to stabilize it, and it reopened in September. The city still felt it was inadequate and refused to accept it. In April 1857, the weight of the ice from a storm caused one of the cast iron anchors to snap, and the bridge fell into the gorge. (JS.)

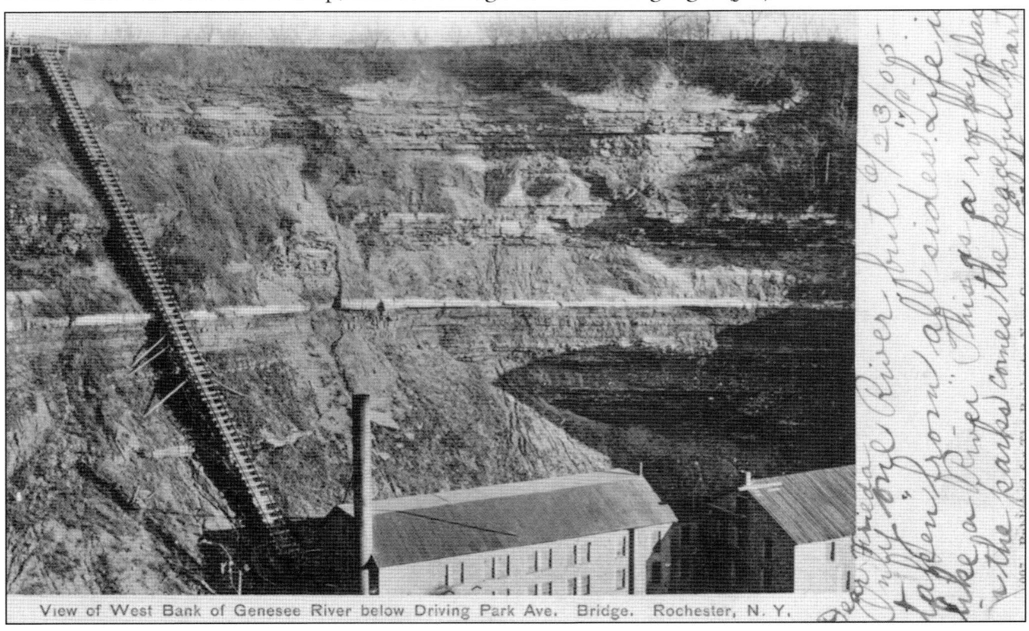

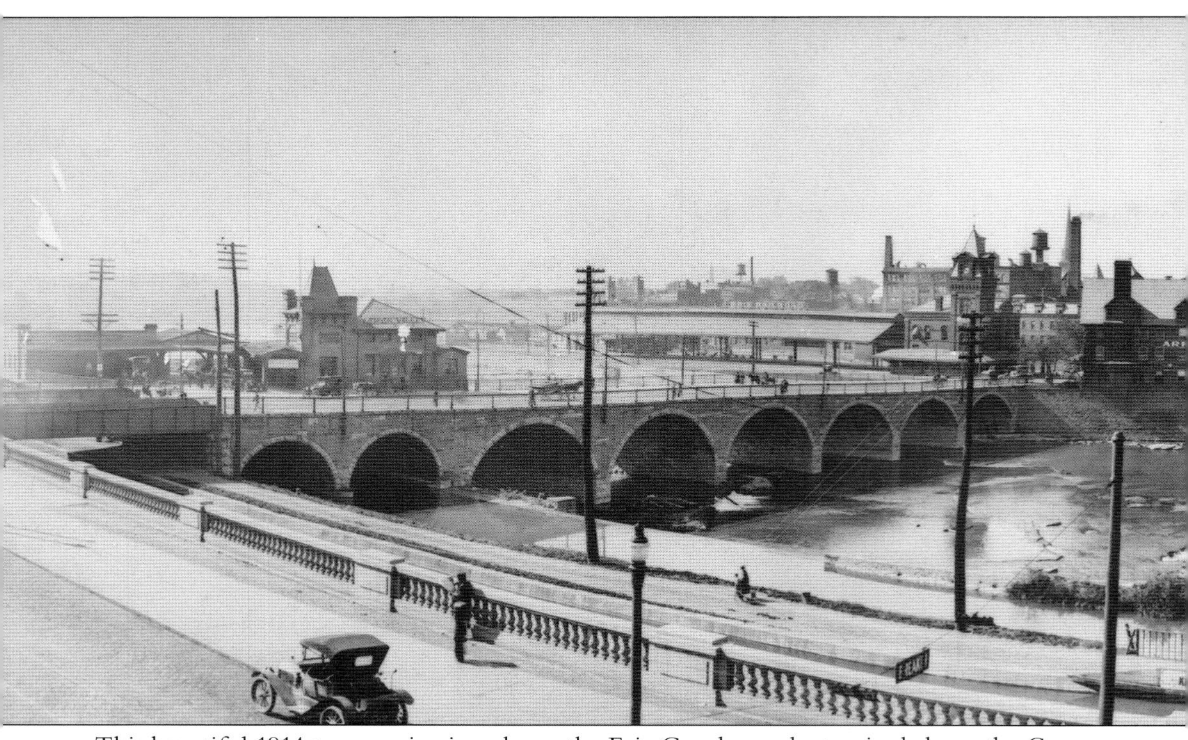

This beautiful 1914 panoramic view shows the Erie Canal aqueduct, raised above the Genesee River, allowing uninterrupted travel. The aqueduct, 802 feet in length, opened in September

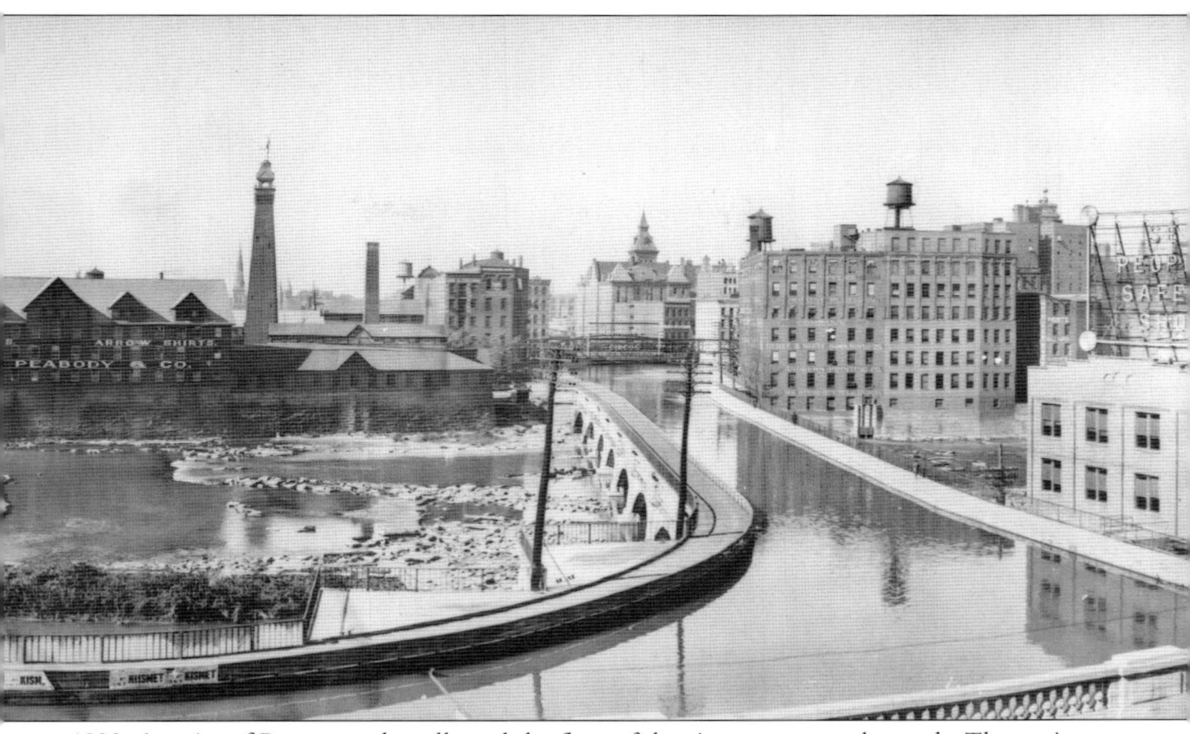

1823. A series of Roman arches allowed the flow of the river to pass underneath. The project took two years to complete at a cost of $83,000. (JSB.)

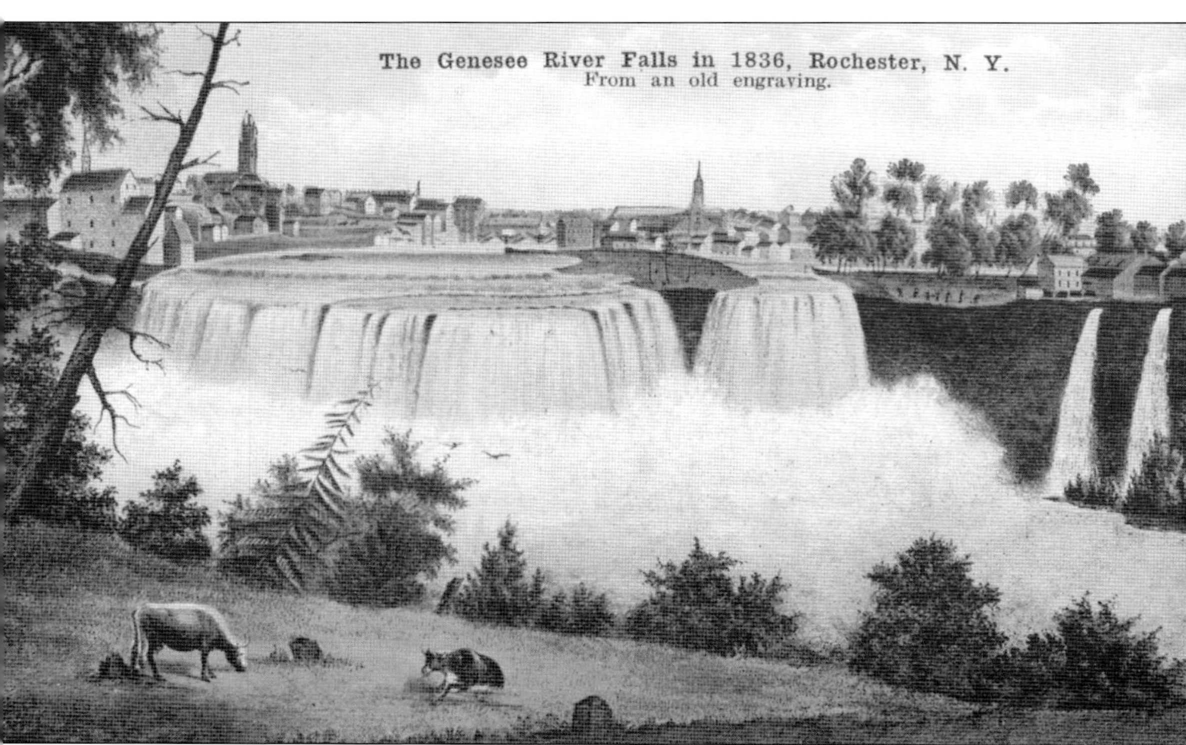

This beautiful postcard shows the Genesee River Middle Falls in 1836 in Rochester, New York. Born in 1752, Nathaniel Rochester, founder of the city of Rochester, New York, spent his early years in North Carolina and then Maryland, where he eventually began to manufacture flour and other products. In his 40s, he became active in local and even presidential politics. In 1800, he visited Genesee country where he had recently bought some 600 acres. In 1810, after purchasing more land in Livingston County, he moved his family first to Dansville and in 1818 to Rochesterville, which had been named for him. Rochester used his political influence to push for the building of the Erie Canal and again in 1821 to have a county centered around Rochester. He named this new county Monroe after the president. While holding several offices in the new city, he helped found St. Luke's Episcopal Church as well as started the Bank of Rochester. After a long life as an influential and successful businessman, helping his namesake city prosper, he died in 1831. His grave is in the well-known Mount Hope Cemetery, not far from the Genesee River.

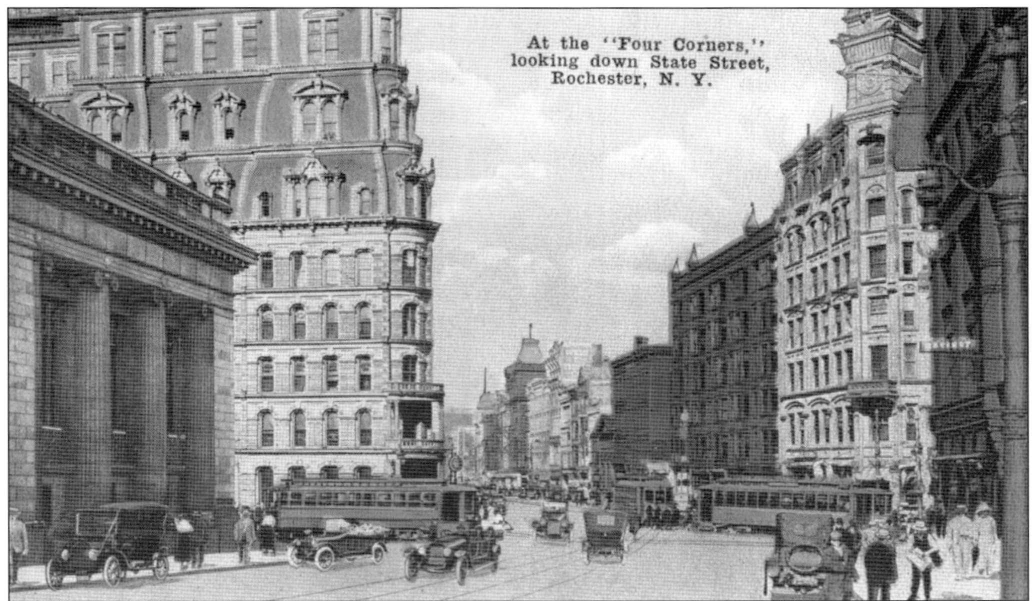

Arch Merrill wrote, "The River not only has given the city being, but it has given it wealth, distinction, and beauty." Rochester is a city in Monroe County, New York, south of Lake Ontario. Known as the "World's Image Center," it was also once known as the "Flour City" and more recently as the "Flower City." It is the county seat for Monroe County. (AHS.)

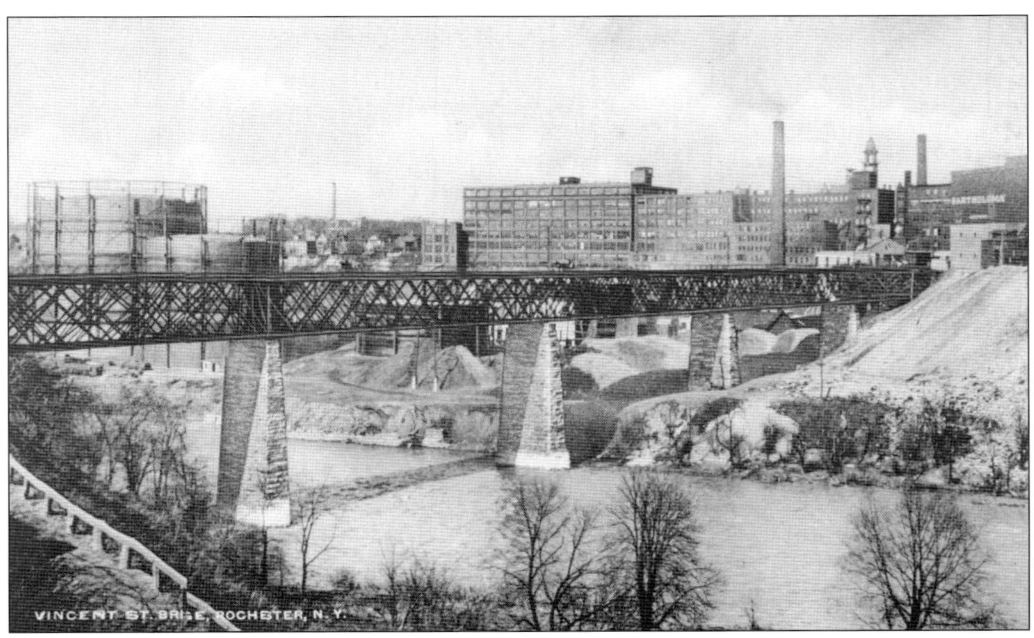

In 1873, the Vincent Street Bridge was erected. In 1882, a boy fell through the decking of the bridge, falling 110 feet to the river below, and lived. The continuous riveted truss was in use until 1892, when it was closed as unsafe by the commissioner of Public Works. It was replaced by the steel Bausch St. Bridge in 1930. (JSB.)

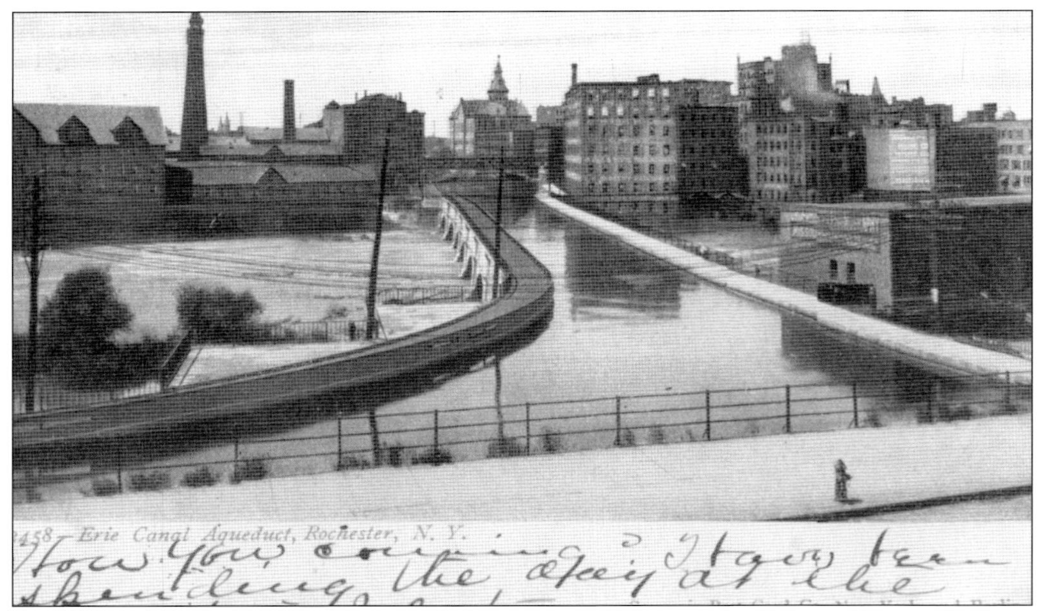

Building of the first aqueduct to carry the Erie Canal over the Genesee River at Rochester was started in the fall of 1821, with completion in September 1823. Built of red Medina sandstone with a coping of Onondaga limestone, it was 802 feet long and 17 feet wide and had 11 arches. This first aqueduct had a problem with leakage, and construction began in 1836 on a new aqueduct a short distance to the south. This second aqueduct, made of Onondaga limestone, was placed in service in 1842. (JSB.)

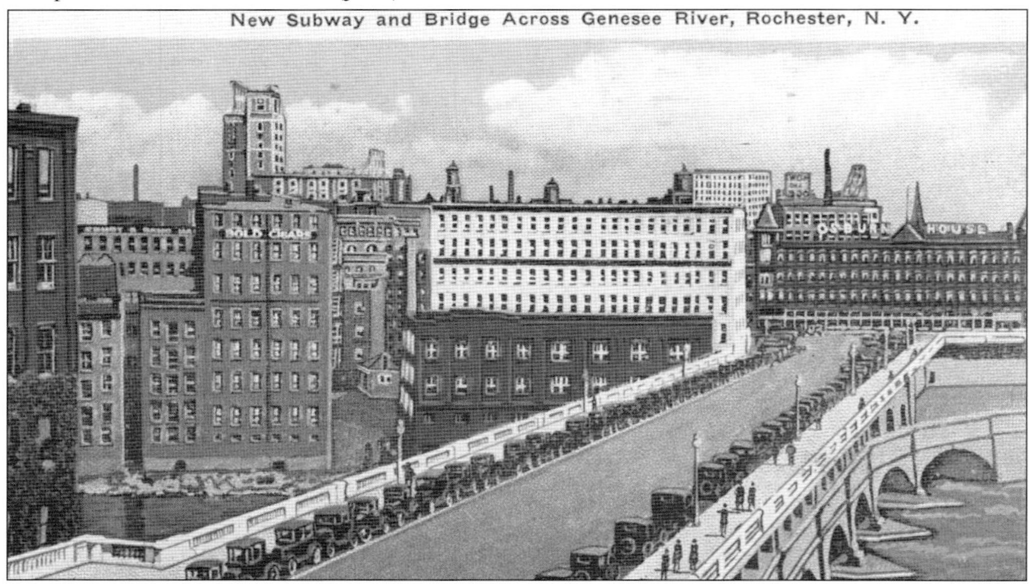

This impressive bridge crosses the Genesee River on seven arches, with a 52-foot span each, resting on six piers and two abutments, each 10 feet thick. The arched portion extends 444 feet, and the whole length, including wing walls, is 800 feet. The original trunk was 65 feet, with an overall width of 70 feet. This is the structure that exists today as the base of the Broad Street Bridge. (JS.)

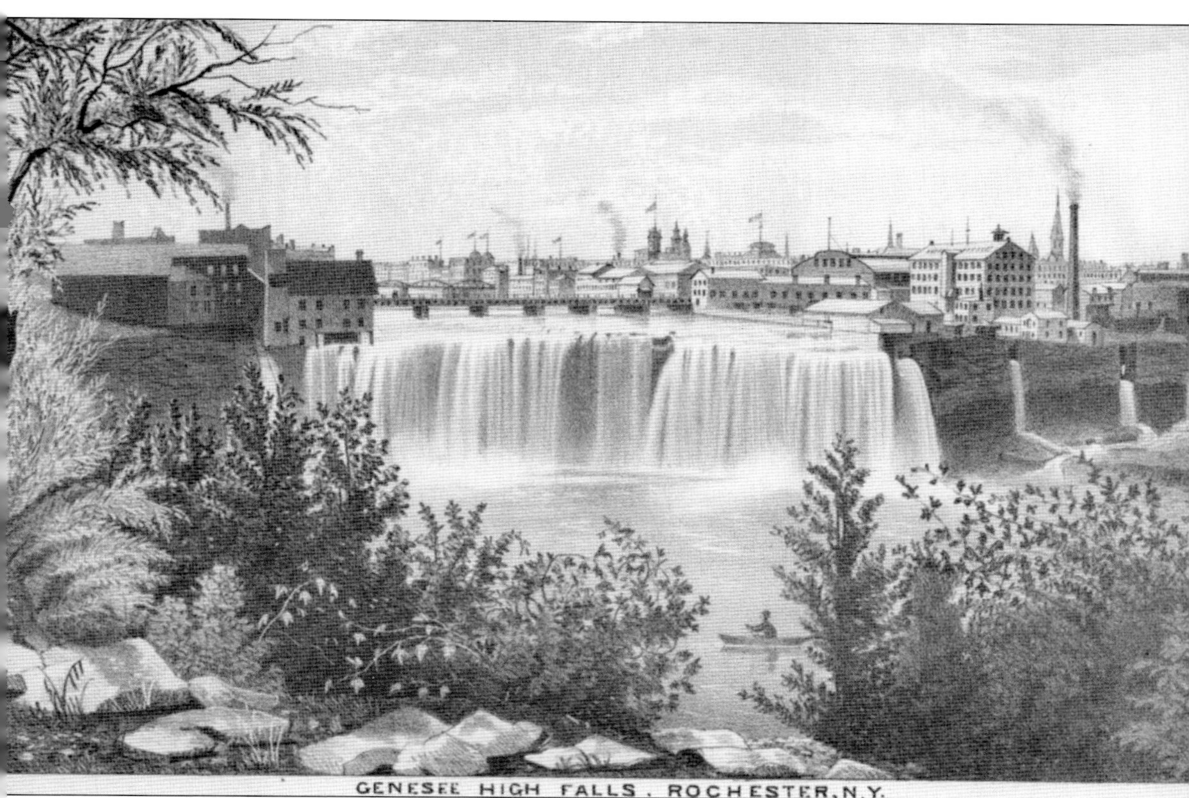

A beautiful illustration from an 1877 engraving shows the Genesee River's High Falls as it was in 1836. Looking at the panorama of the Genesee River lined with mills and factories during the height of the industrial era, one might wonder what the city of Rochester was like even 50 years before this lithograph was produced. Was it always a peaceful, pastoral scene of beauty and splendor, where a person could paddle his canoe in the river below the falls? *The Genesee* by Henry W. Clune tells of a proposal in 1811 to build the second bridge across the river at Genesee Falls, as Rochester was called then. One member of the legislature who knew the proposed site spoke strongly against the project. "Who would use such a bridge at a God-forsaken place, inhabited by muskrats and visited only by straggling trappers, and through which neither man nor beast could gallop without fear of starvation or fever or ague?" However, some of the early settlers, pioneers, businessmen, and women did have a vision that a village, and later a city, could grow out of "this swamp at the edge of the lower Genesee, and which was destined to become the greatest community on the river." (JSB.)

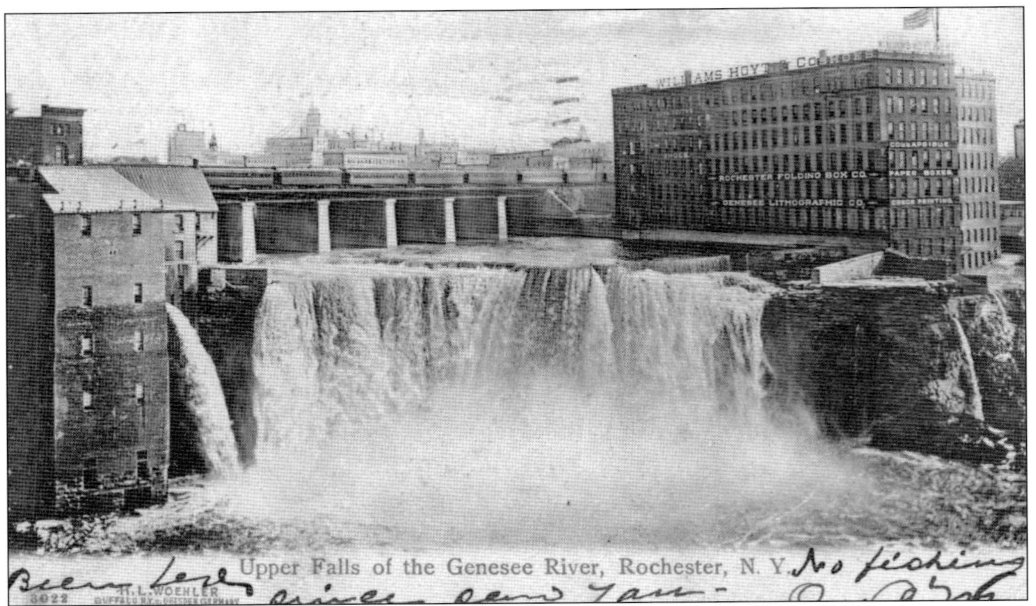

The High Falls, also known as the Upper Falls, Genesee Falls, and the Great Falls of the Genesee, has a height of 96 feet and a crest width of 200 feet. The falls face to the northwest, and the entire crest of the falls is overhung, resulting in a fantastic curtain of falling water. (RPL.)

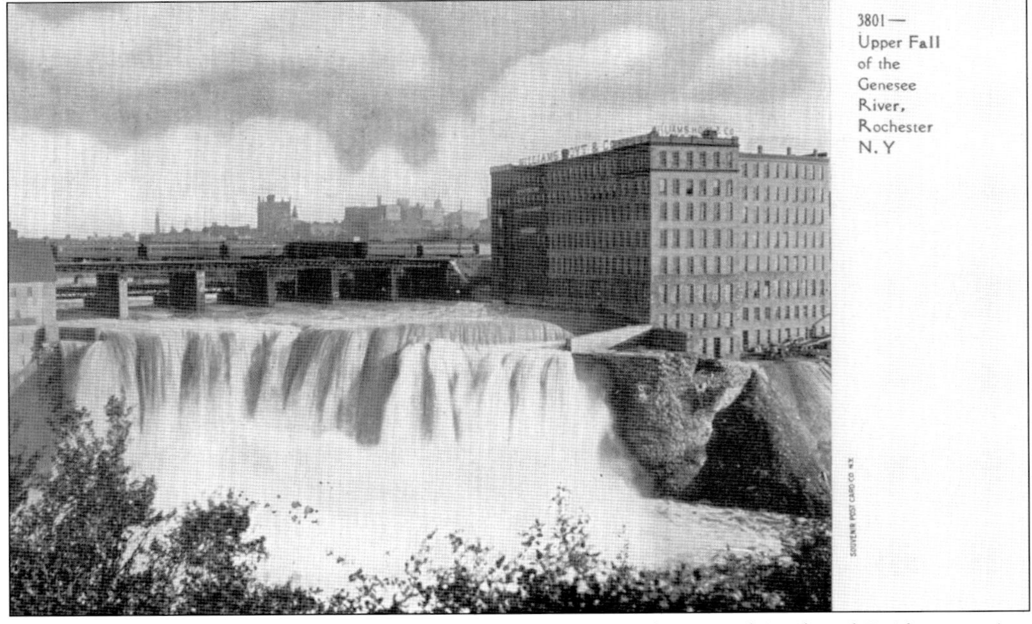

This postcard view, dated July 17, 1905, shows the New York Central Railroad Bridge crossing the Genesee. By the early 1800s, numerous mills were built, and by the 1900s, many industries had developed along the banks. (RPL.)

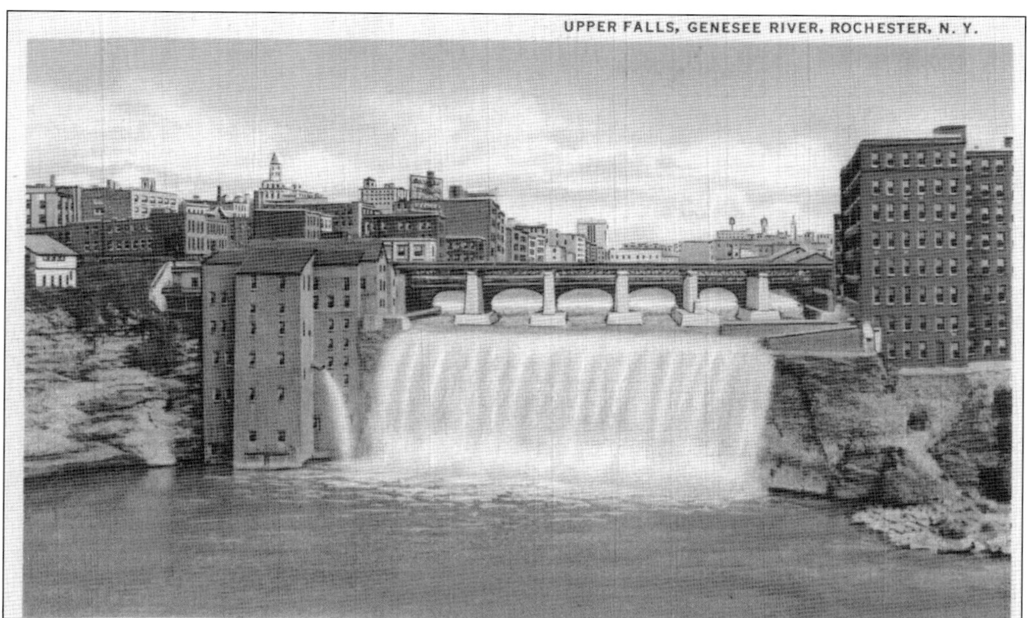

The High (Upper) Falls is a waterfall in the Genesee River that is located just north of downtown Rochester. Because of the falls, that section of town has come to be known as the High Falls District. This area was once the center of Rochester's economic engine, due to scores of factories and businesses on both sides of the gorge using waterwheels to drive their workshops. (RPL.)

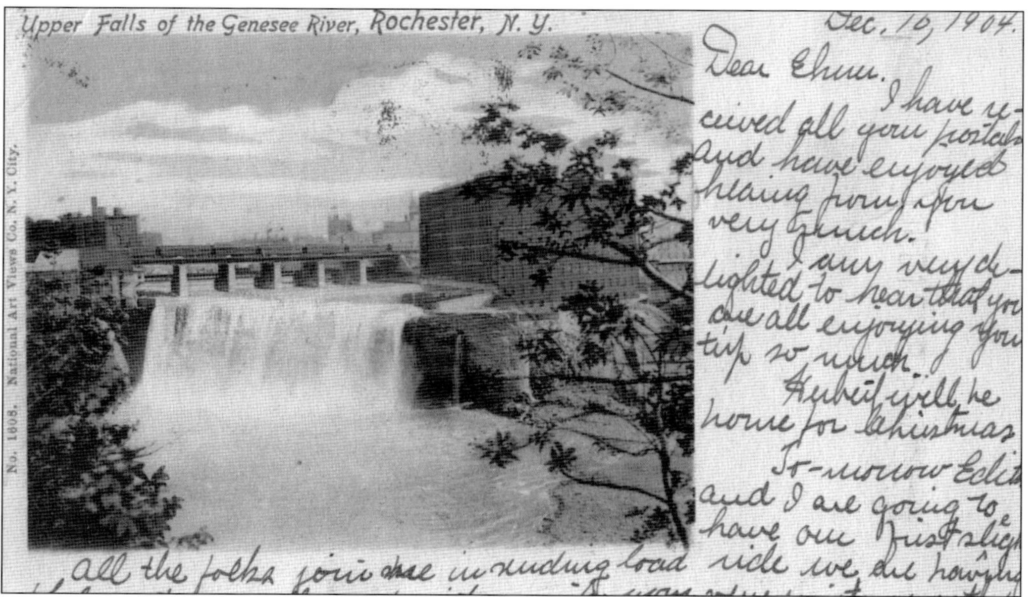

In the early 2000s, the City of Rochester spent a good chunk of money trying to turn this section of the city into an entertainment district, but it never caught on. In recent years, the area has evolved into a residential and business area with loft apartments and office space in tastefully renovated historic buildings. There are still several restaurants serving the area as well as the nearby Frontier Field and Kodak Headquarters. (RPL.)

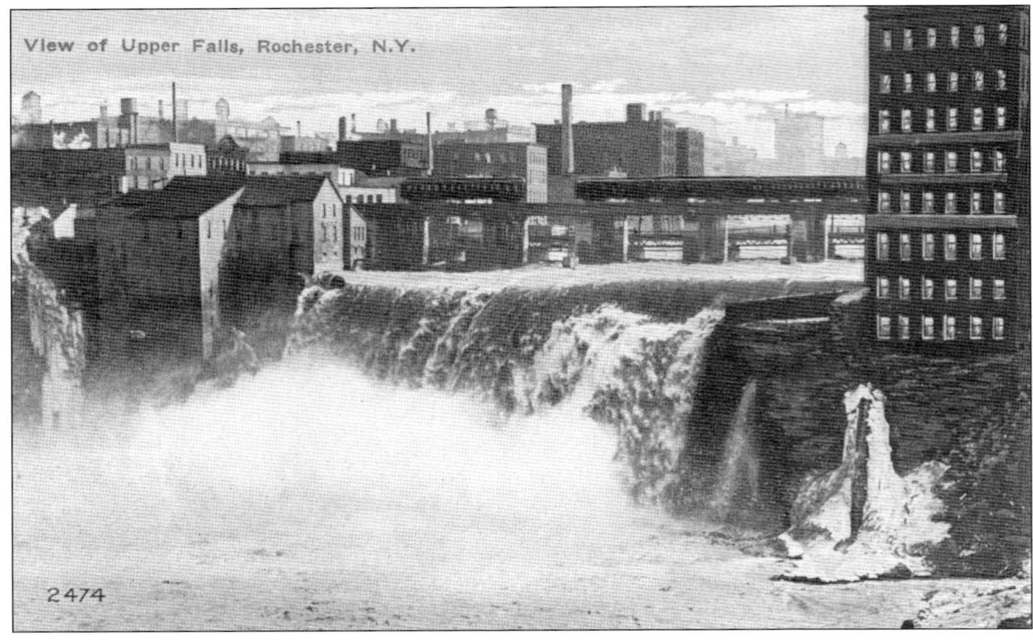

These postcard views of the Upper Falls of the Genesee show how important the river was to the growth of industries along its banks. The High Falls area was the site of much of Rochester's early industrial development, where industry was powered by falling water. Browns race diverts water from above the falls and was once used to feed various flour mills and other industries. Today, the water is used to produce hydroelectric power. (RPL.)

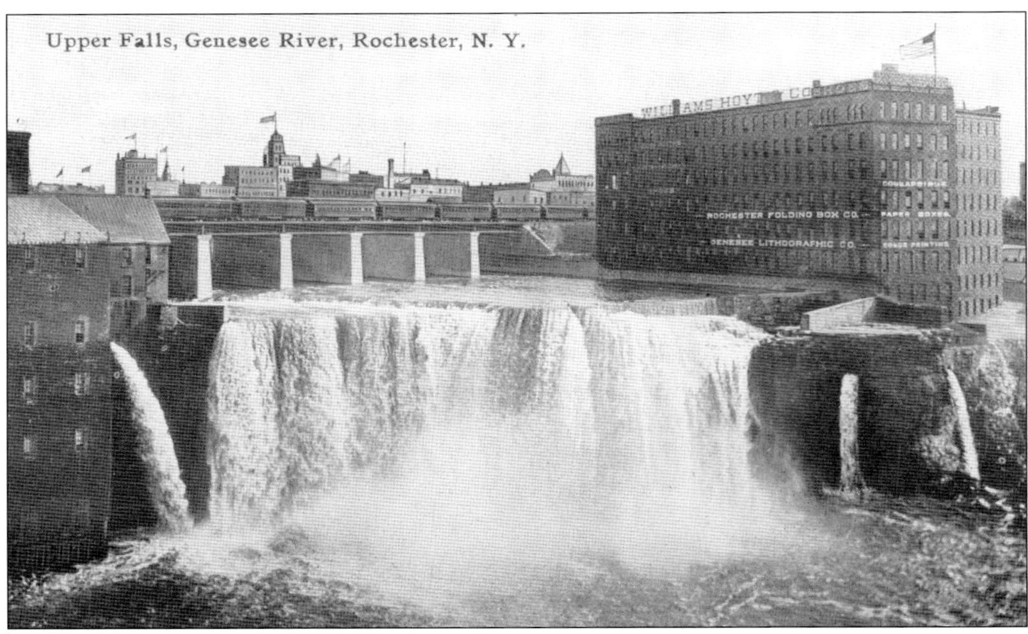

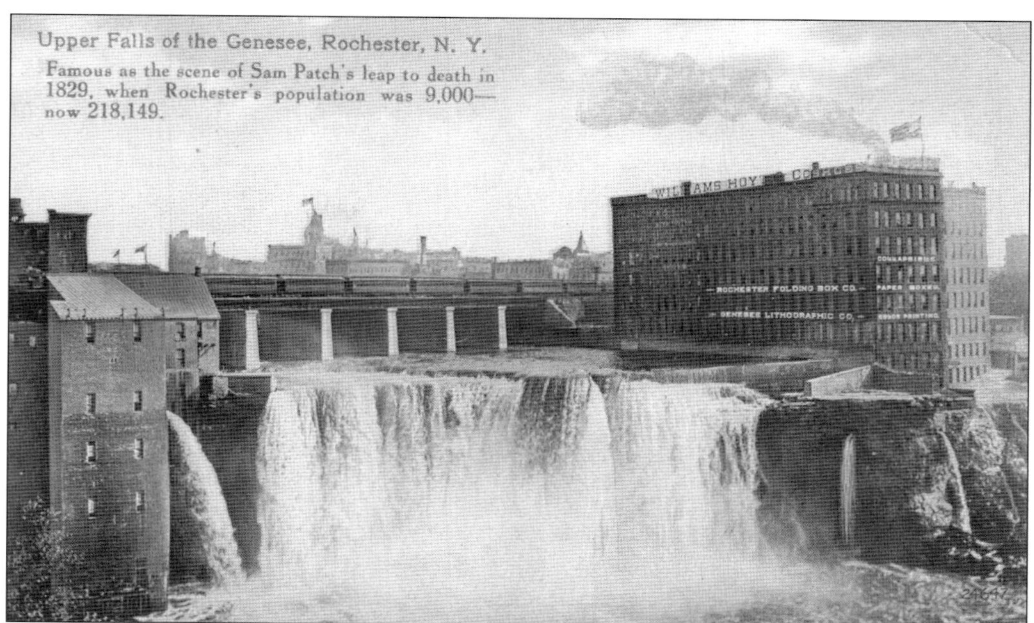

Sam Patch went to Rochester, New York, to challenge the 99-foot High Falls of the Genesee River. On Friday, November 6, 1829, in front of an estimated 7,000 to 8,000 spectators, Patch went out onto a rock ledge in the middle of the falls where he successfully jumped into the Genesee. (CRB.)

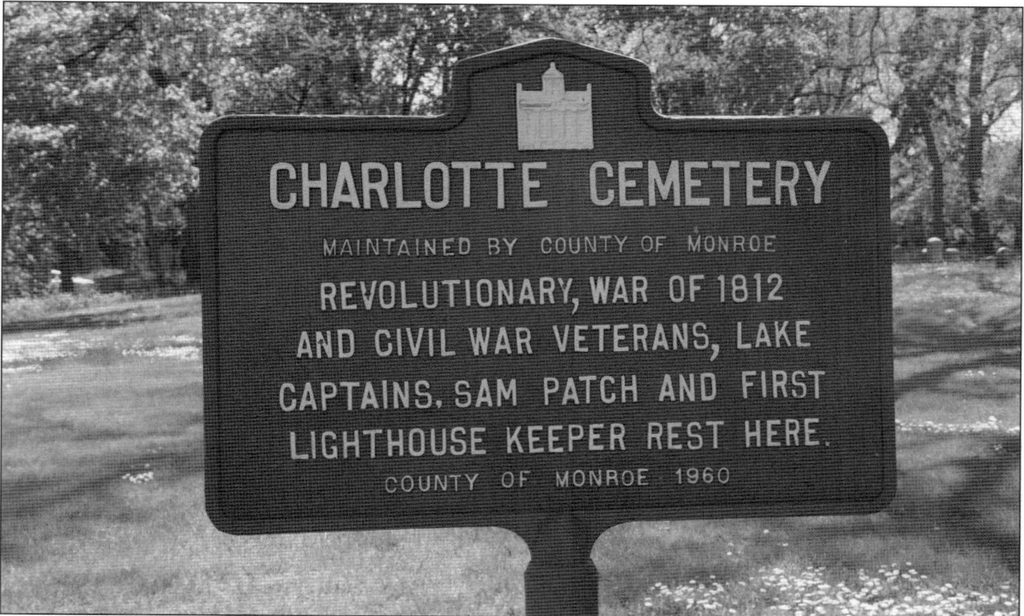

Sam decided to repeat the stunt one week later on Friday, November 13, 1829. This time, he increased the height of the jump to 125 feet by constructing a 25-foot stand. Accounts from the 8,000 present differ on whether he actually jumped or fell. A loud impact was heard, and he never surfaced; his frozen body was found in the ice in Charlotte Harbor (Rochester) early the next spring. He was buried in Charlotte Cemetery, near where his body was found. (JSB.)

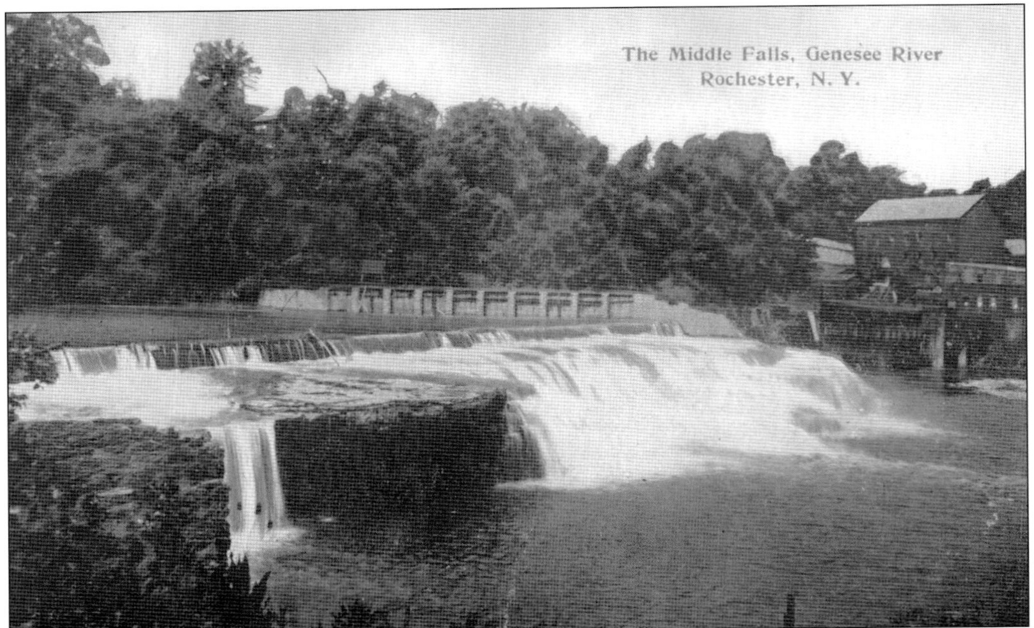

The Middle Falls in Rochester is probably the least spectacular of the three downtown waterfalls. The vertical drop is only around 20 feet, and the falls themselves are funneled through a dam by the Rochester Gas and Electric Corporation. (RPL.)

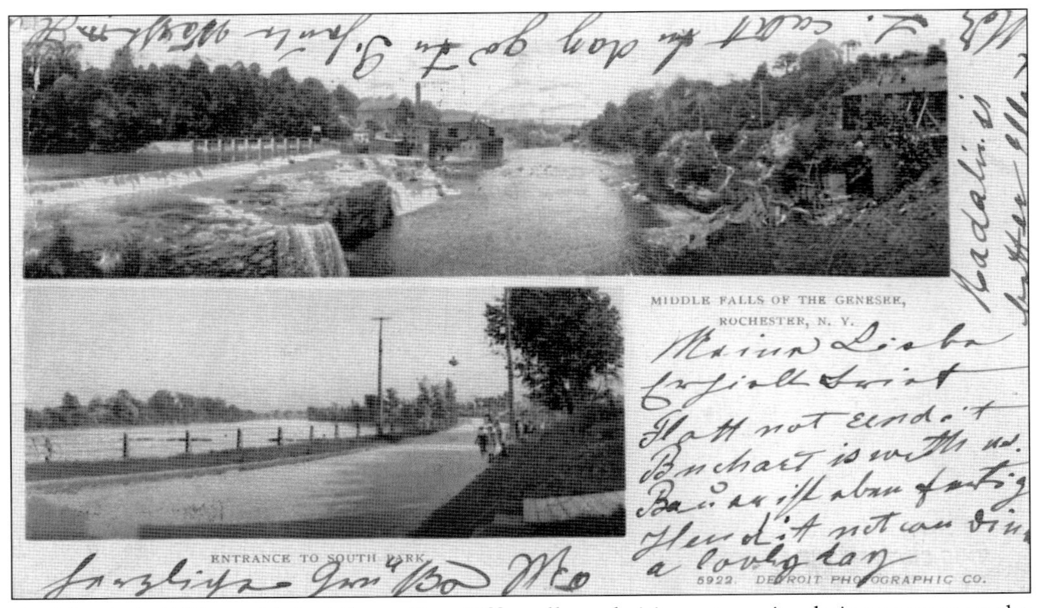

On March 1, 1907, the United States Post Office allowed citizens to write their messages on the address side of the card. Before this date the sender had to be creative, writing greetings where space permitted, often on the printed side of the card. (RPL.)

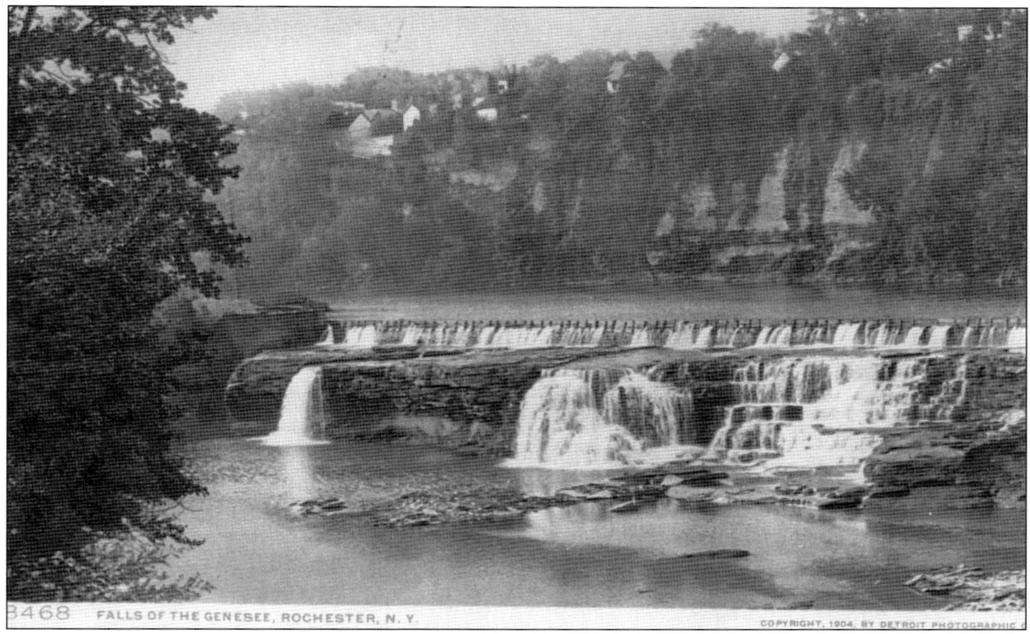

A mile and a quarter downstream from the Upper Falls is the Middle Falls. It has a drop of 20 feet. In the early days it was considered part of the Lower Falls and was called the Upper Step. It is much less impressive than the Upper or Lower Falls. (AHS.)

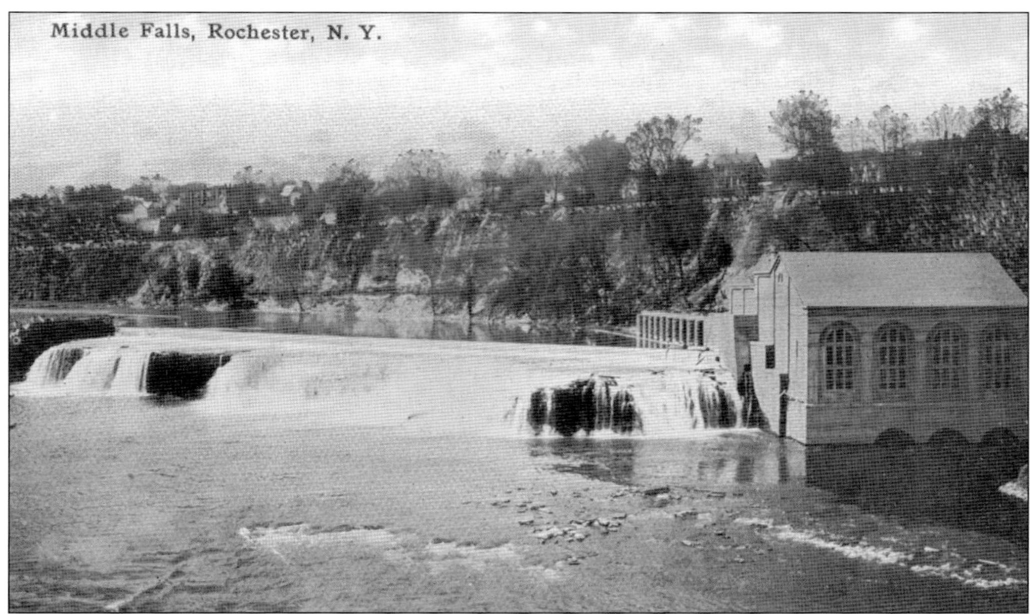

In this view of the Middle Falls, the water has been diverted through a tunnel to the RG&E Substation No. 5 generators at the base of the Lower Falls. It was inaccessible until 2001, when a path was put in leading to a viewing area below the dam, offering the best view of the Lower Falls as well.

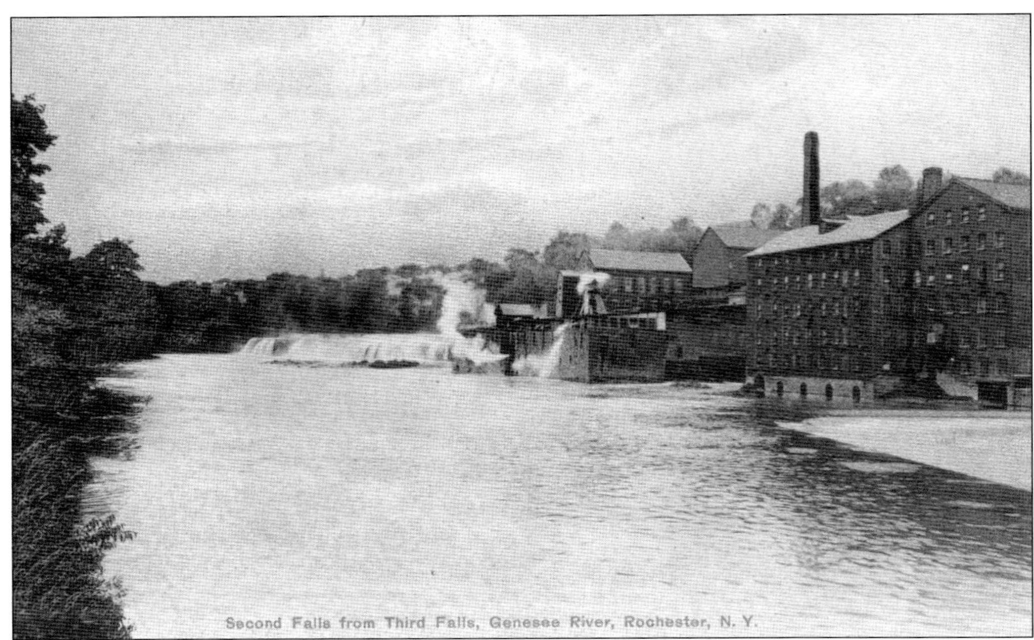

The coordinates given are for a viewing point about 200 yards south of the Middle Falls. The falls are on land owned by RG&E, so the public is prohibited from getting close to the falls. There are descriptive signs and charts in the area telling how the water flows through the RG&E dam. (RPL.)

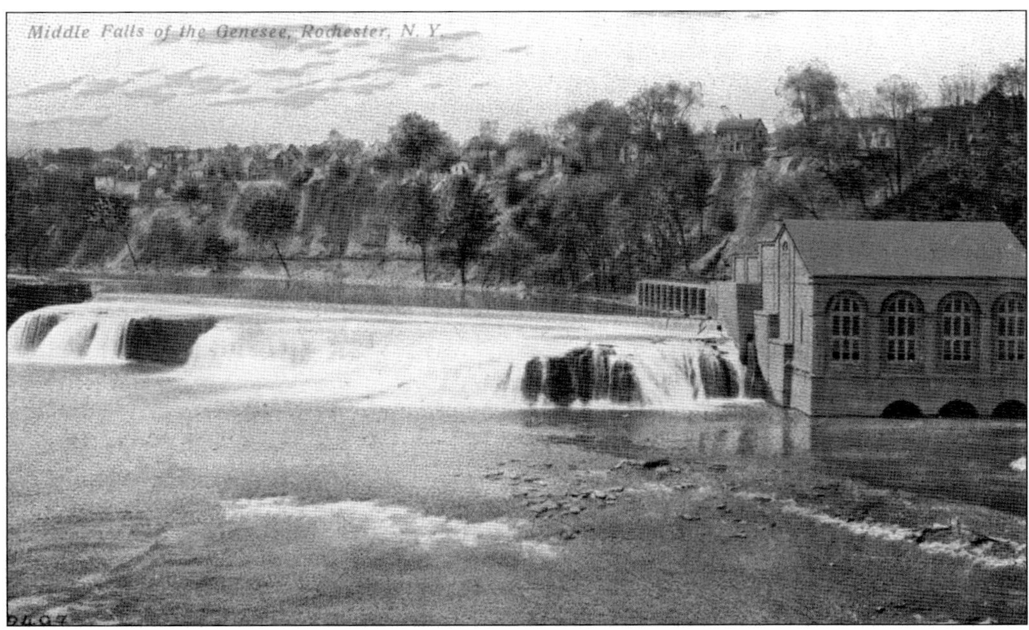

The Lower Falls can be viewed from the Driving Park Bridge. For a closer look, there is a short, improved trail from Maplewood Park to an overlook, and the Lower Falls Park can be seen on the south side of Driving Park. (RPL.)

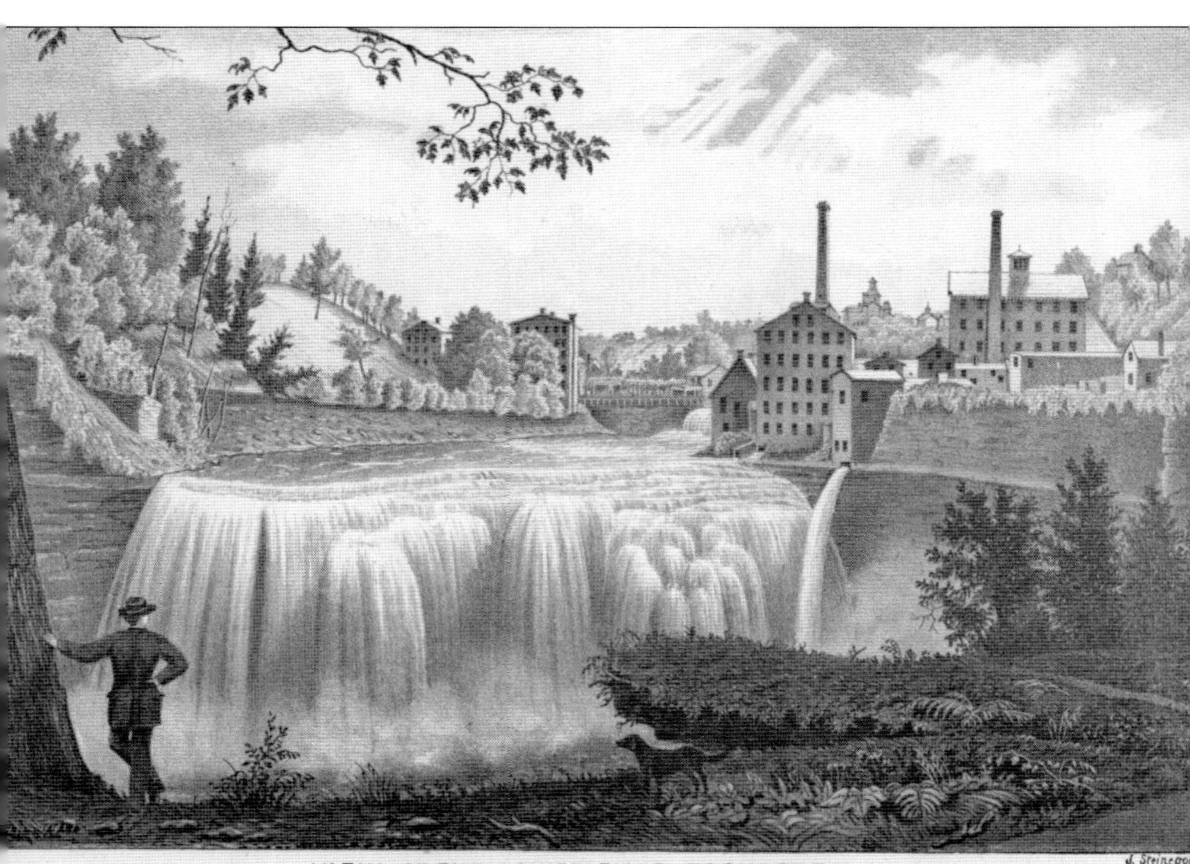

A beautiful illustration from an 1877 engraving showing the Genesee River's Lower Falls in 1836. As Arch Merrill, reaching Rochester, said on his walk along the river, "This area owes its existence to the river and its tossing, power-laden falls." (JSB.)

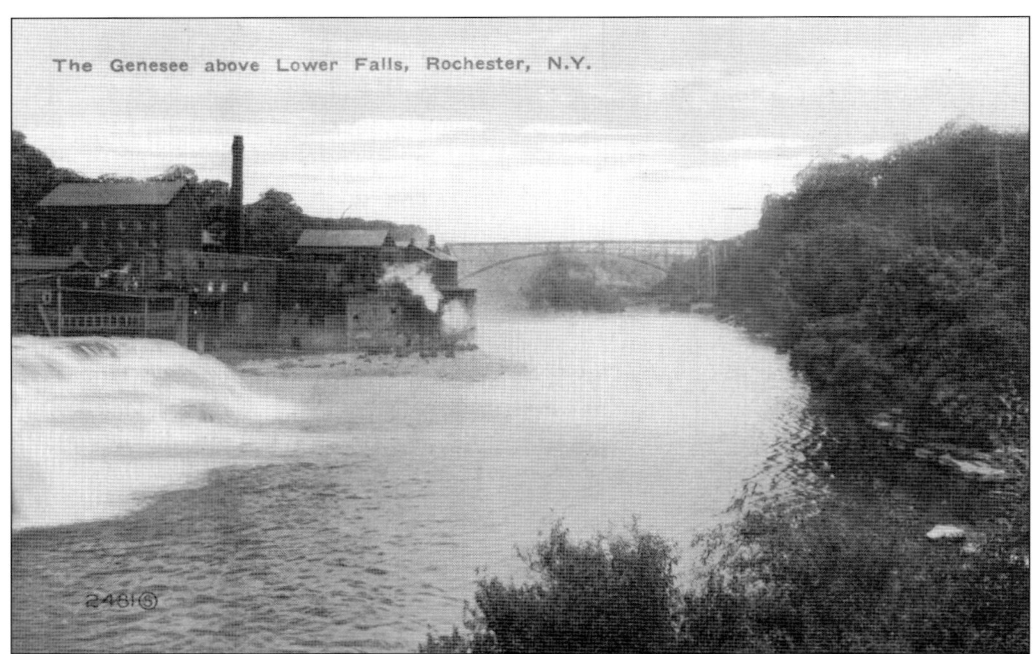

The Lower Falls is located near downtown Rochester. Accessible from Maplewood Park, the falls is 110 feet in height. The Genesee River flows over the falls on its way north to Lake Ontario. The falls faces northwest and has a 276-foot-wide crest. The building nearby is a power plant. The falls is a complex curtain falls, with the eastern half of the falls being overhung, while the western half is a steeply terraced cascade. (RPL.)

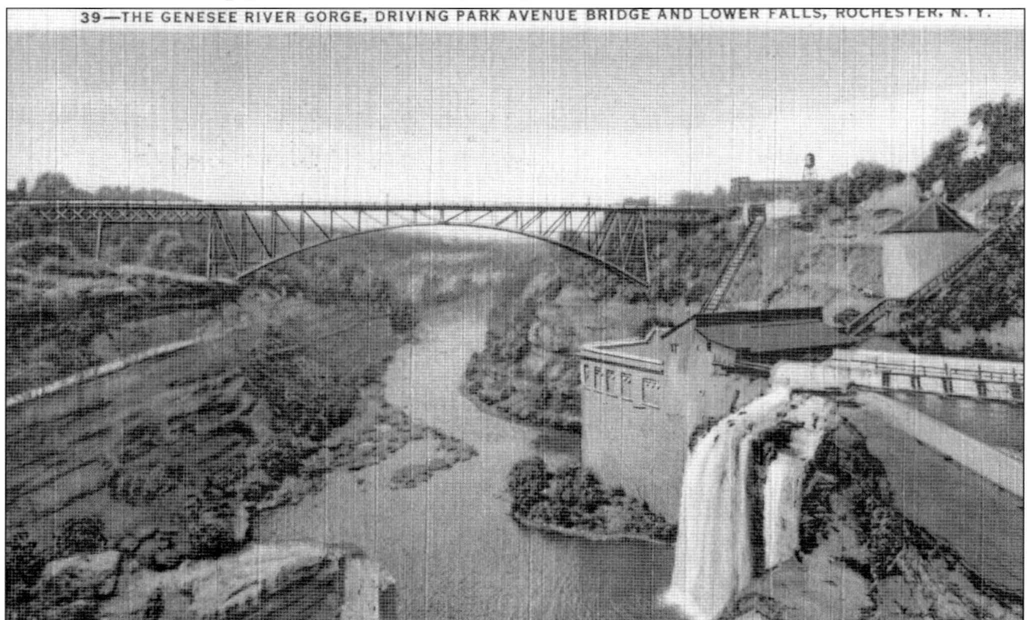

The Lower Falls of the Genesee River is an impressive 110-foot waterfall, crashing over a steep embankment along the river. A nice view of the falls is visible from the Driving Park Bridge. (RPL.)

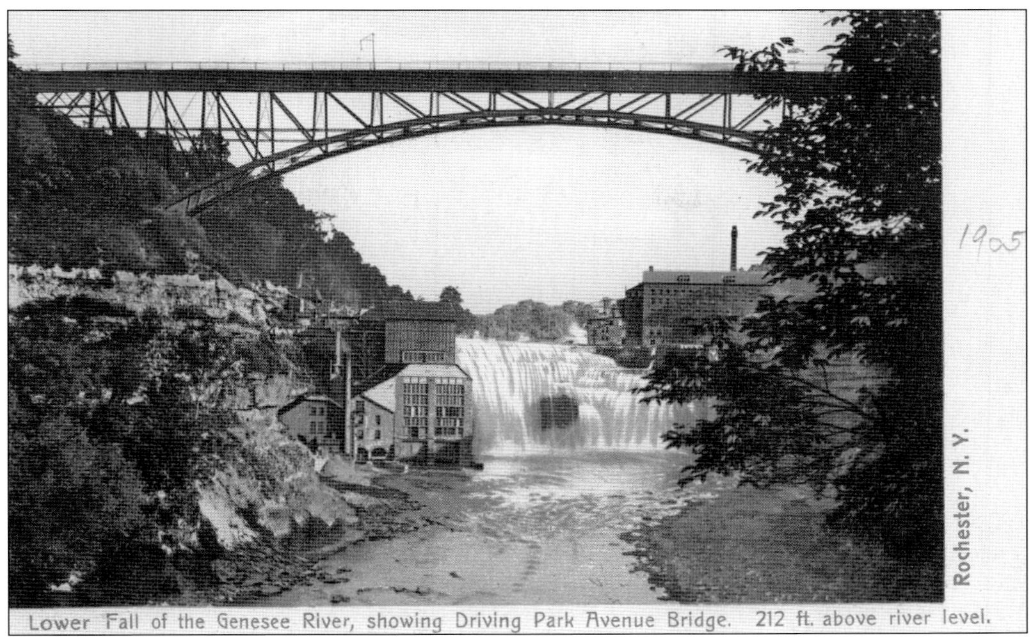

Lower Fall of the Genesee River, showing Driving Park Avenue Bridge. 212 ft. above river level.

The Lower Falls of the Genesee River in Rochester has the potential to be a very scenic waterfall, but its urban setting rather takes away from all it could be. Even with that said, it is hard to stop industrial development, and, to the city's credit, they have surrounded the falls with a parklike atmosphere so at least there is somewhat of an escape from urban chaos, even though the park is surrounded by factories, power plants, and bridges. (RPL.)

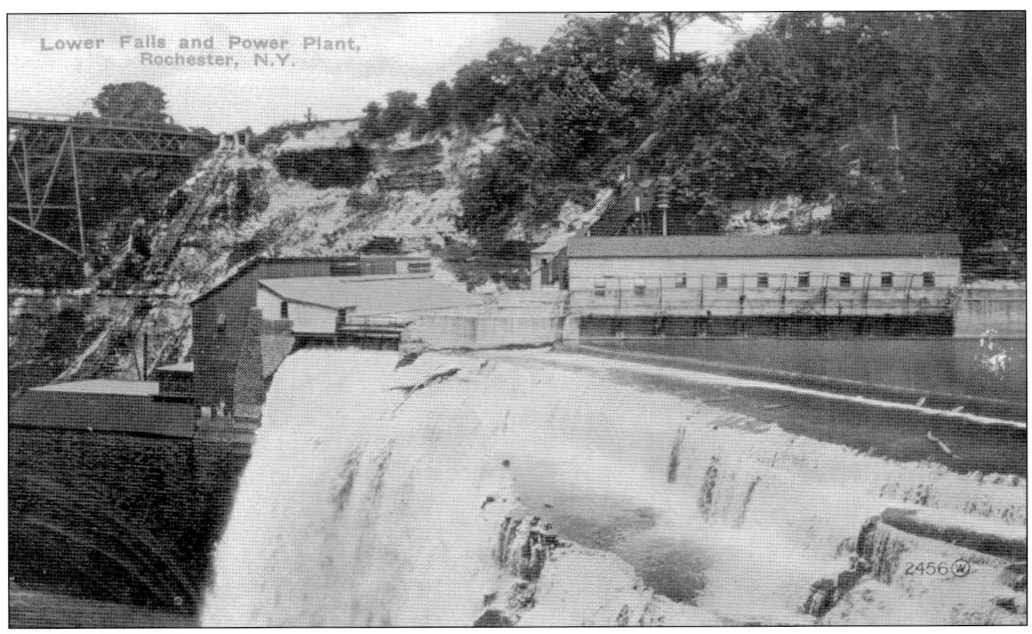

Lower Falls and Power Plant, Rochester, N.Y.

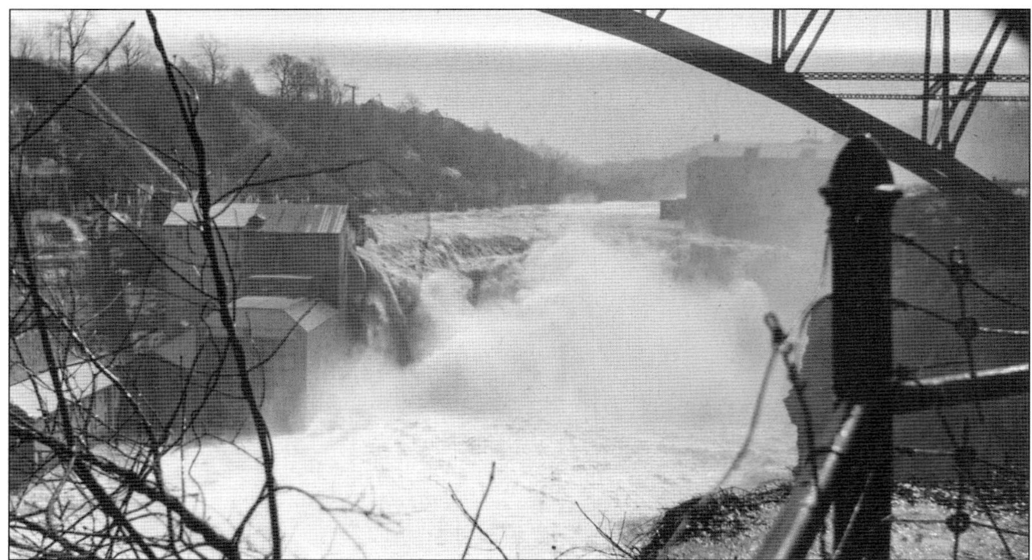

This real-photo postcard shows the Lower Falls at a time of high floodwaters as viewed from Driving Park Bridge. The Lower Gorge of the Genesee River is a wonder of natural and human history, and it is accessible via an array of paths and parks. (RPL.)

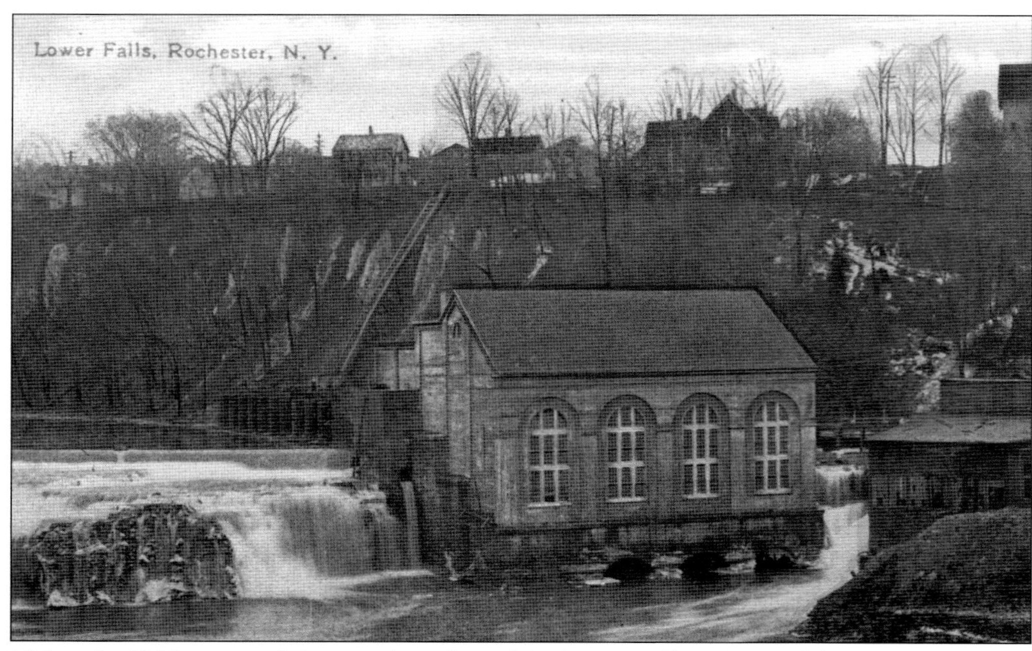

This early-1900s postcard shows a river view of the Lower Falls and one of the generating plants located on the Genesee River in Rochester, New York. This hydro plant supplies power for 30,500 homes and is currently being upgraded. (JS.)

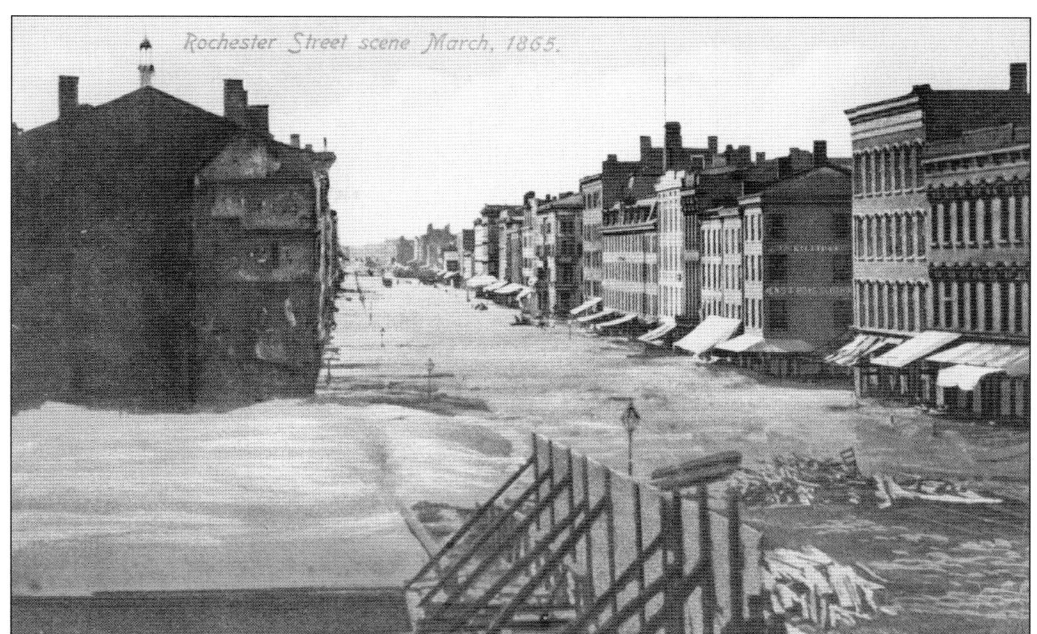

Accumulation of ice in Avon and a sudden March thaw caused the worst flood in the city's history. The flood of 1865, which developed flows exceeding 24 million gallons per minute, resulted in massive destruction. The total damage in western New York exceeded $1 million. (JSB.)

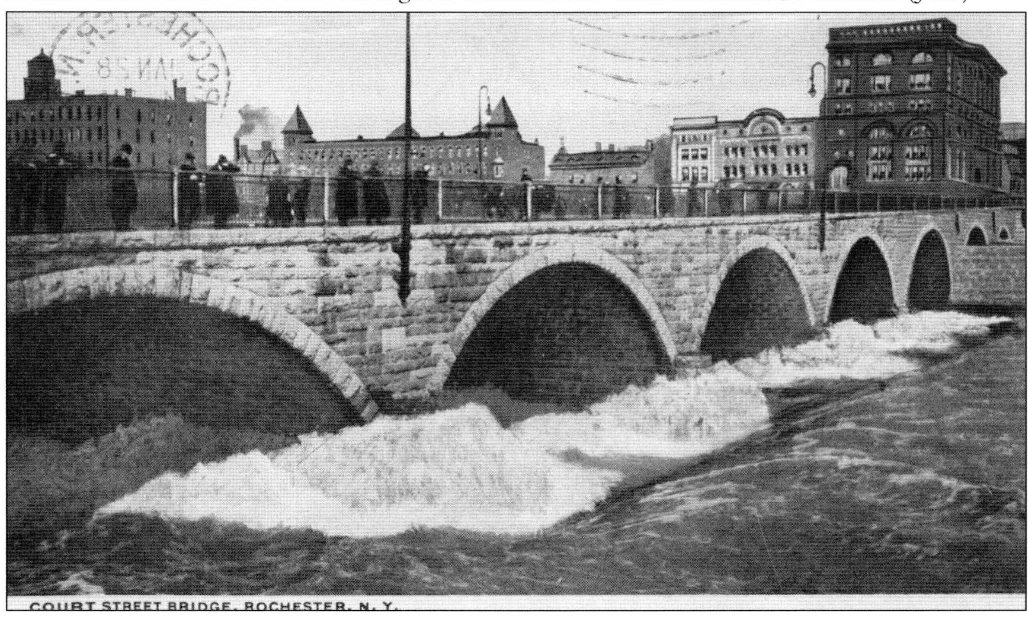

Rochester's Great Flood lasted from March 17 to March 20, 1865. It was caused by a long period of cold weather and heavy snowfall followed by a sudden thaw accompanied by rain. The maximum rate of flow of the river in Rochester was estimated at 54,000 cubic feet per second. The banks of both the river and the canal overflowed into the city. Small boats were used on some flooded streets. The flood began on a Friday, and the river returned to its boundaries within the city on Monday morning. By then, the streets were finally bare. (RPL.)

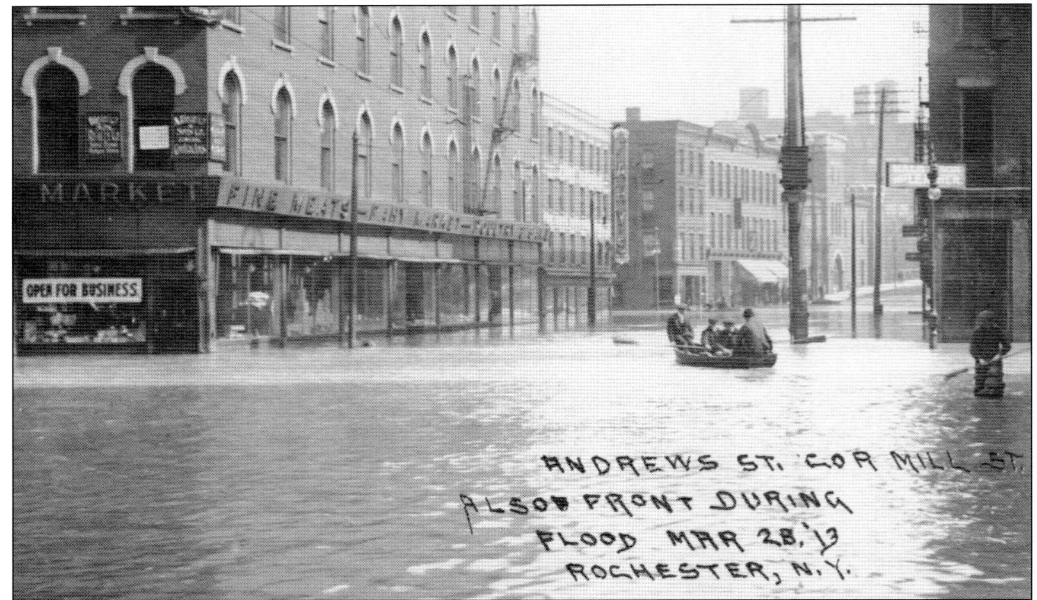

Records show that the Genesee River Valley and the city of Rochester had experienced flooding since 1800. Water was six feet deep on Main Street in downtown Rochester on many occasions. Following the flood of 1865, many businesses feared future floods and moved to higher ground east of the river. Floods also caused extensive damage in Rochester in 1785, 1817, 1818, 1835, 1841, and 1865. (RPL.)

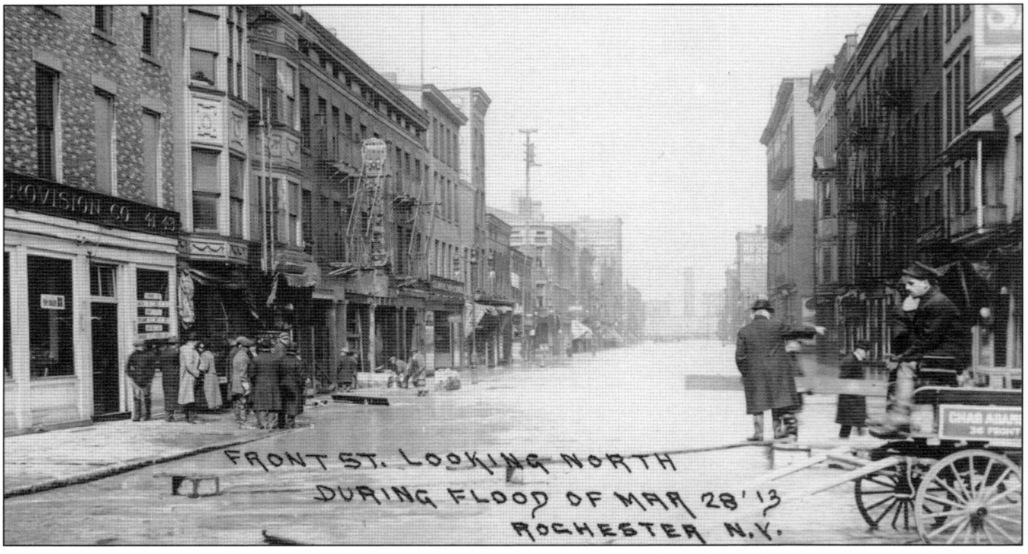

The week following Easter 1913 brought the most geographically widespread natural disaster the United States had suffered up to then in the form of an unusually powerful, long-lived, and widespread winter storm. The first punch came on Good Friday, March 21, 1913, when an arctic high-pressure system swooped down from Canada and a violent windstorm swept the eastern half of the United States from Ontario to the Gulf of Mexico. Hurricane-force winds across the Great Lakes reached record-breaking maximum sustained wind velocities, including 90 miles per hour in Buffalo. (RPL.)

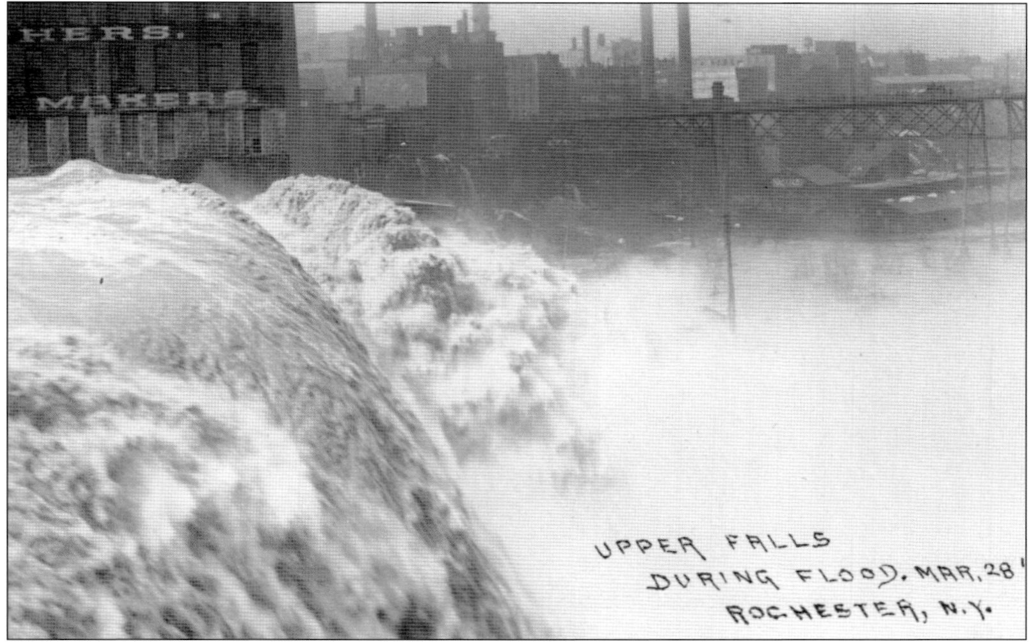

The second colossal punch came on Easter Sunday, March 23, as torrential rains began to fall. The 1913 flood set new record high-water marks and record discharge rates (cubic feet of water per second), many of which still stand, in various New York rivers. The winter of 1912–1913 was unusually warm and wet across all the North Atlantic states. Temperatures ranged from three degrees to 10 degrees above normal. (RPL.)

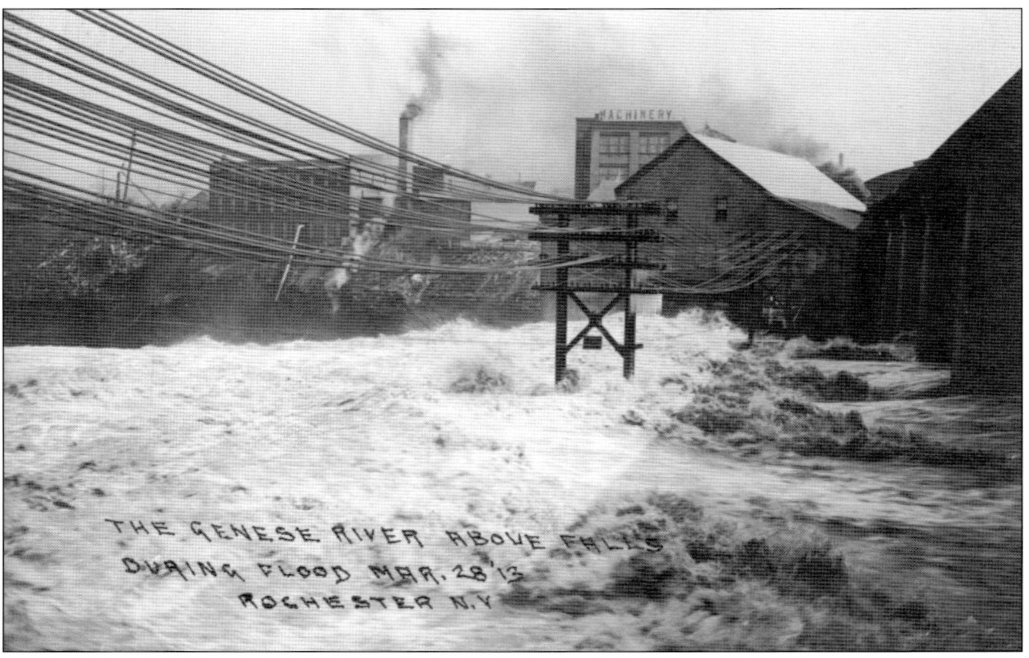

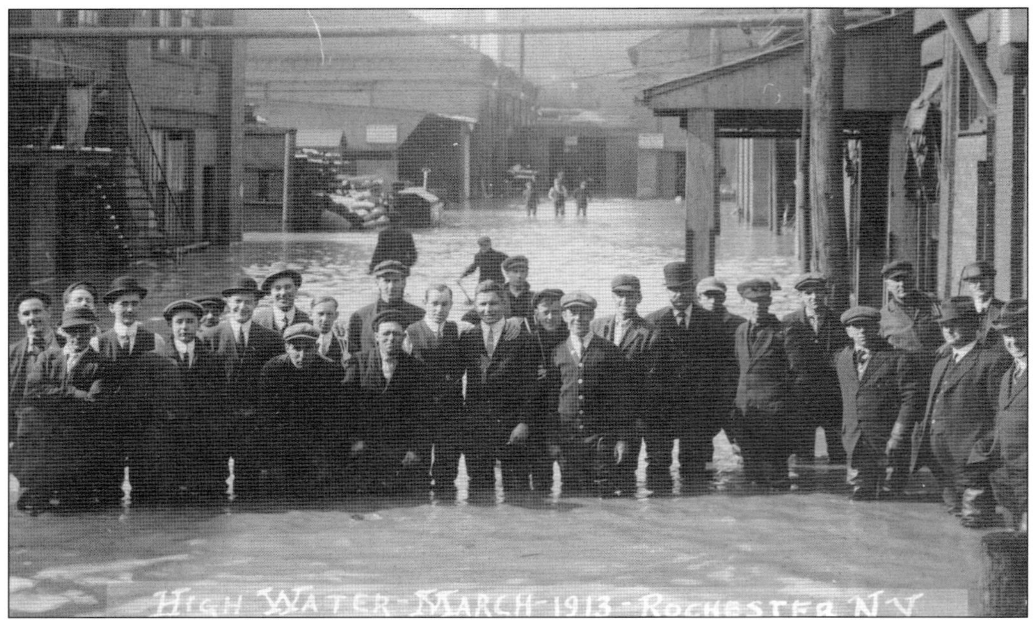

In western New York, the Genesee broke the 1865 record for volume of water and reached a record height of eight feet deep over the Court Street Dam as well as a record discharge rate, flooding a large section of downtown Rochester from one to six feet deep for three days; downtown office basements were flooded 10 to 12 feet deep, putting elevators, lighting, and heating out of commission. Moreover, floodwaters submerged the pumping station of the Rochester water filtration plant and a main pipeline from the distributing reservoir broke, leaving the city without water for two days. (RPL.)

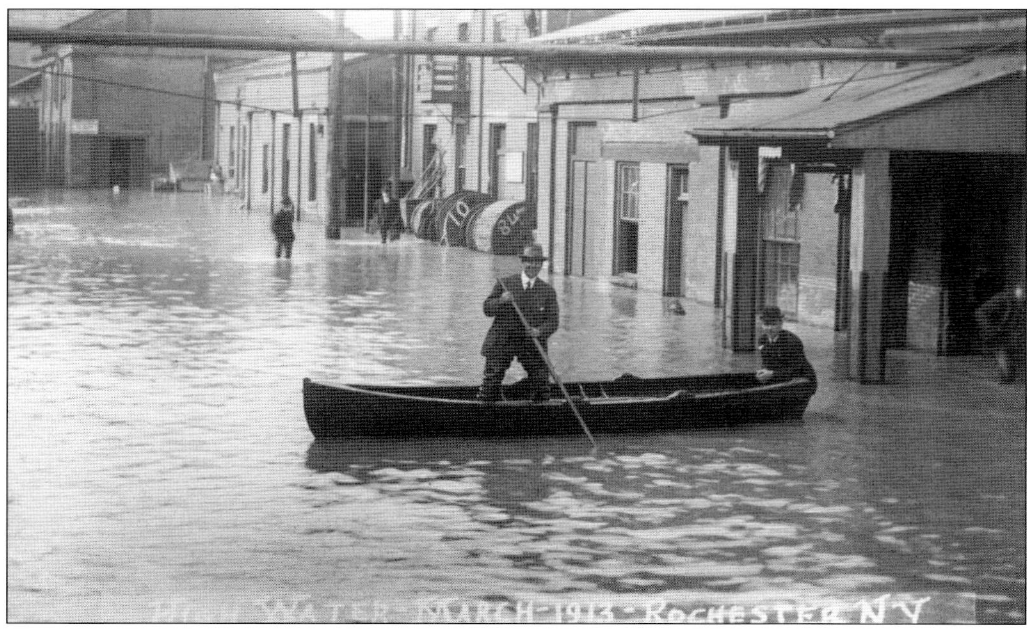

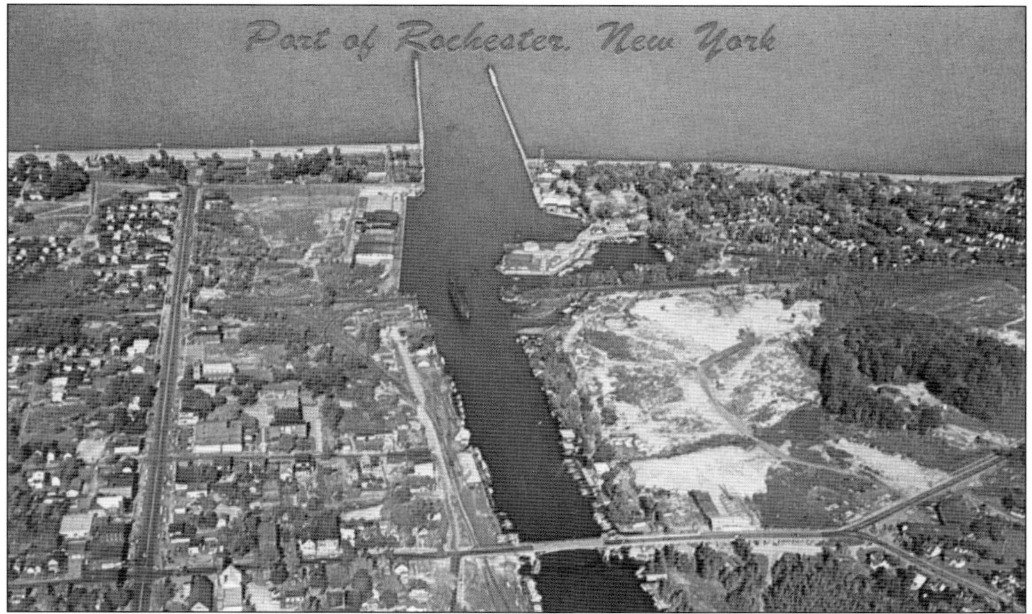

Charlotte is a neighborhood north of Rochester, New York, located at the mouth of the Genesee River along Lake Ontario. It is the home of the Port of Rochester. The Port of Charlotte has been a mute witness to some very interesting history over the years, including Indian encampments, the War of 1812, and more. (JSB.)

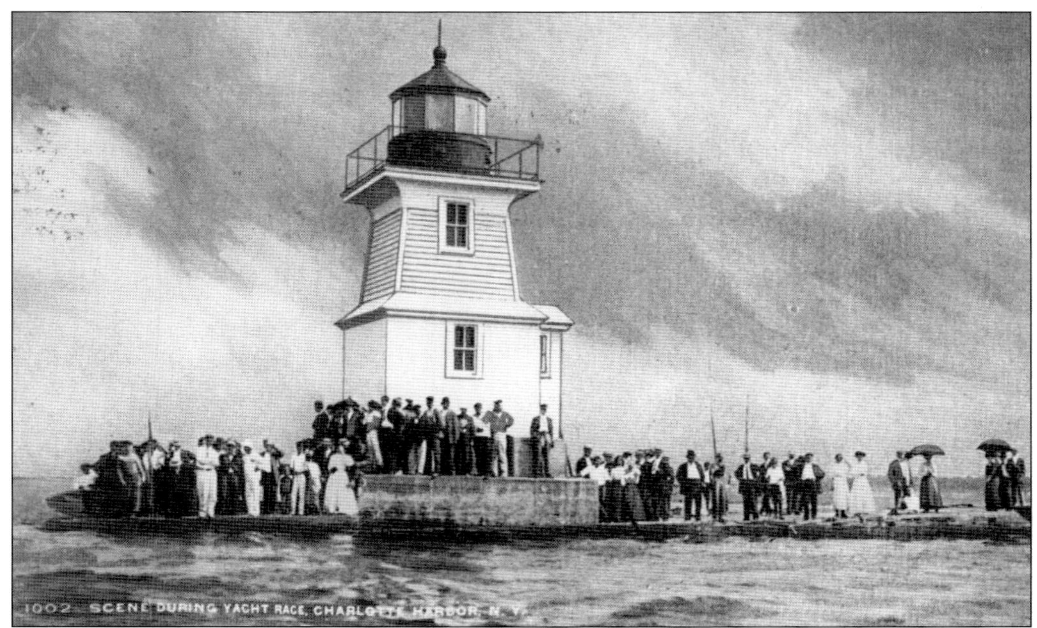

What a way to spend a Sunday afternoon—all dressed up and watching a yacht race from the lighthouse pier in Charlotte Harbor! On January 1, 1916, the Village of Charlotte became a part of the City of Rochester through annexation. It became the city's 23rd Ward. (JSB.)

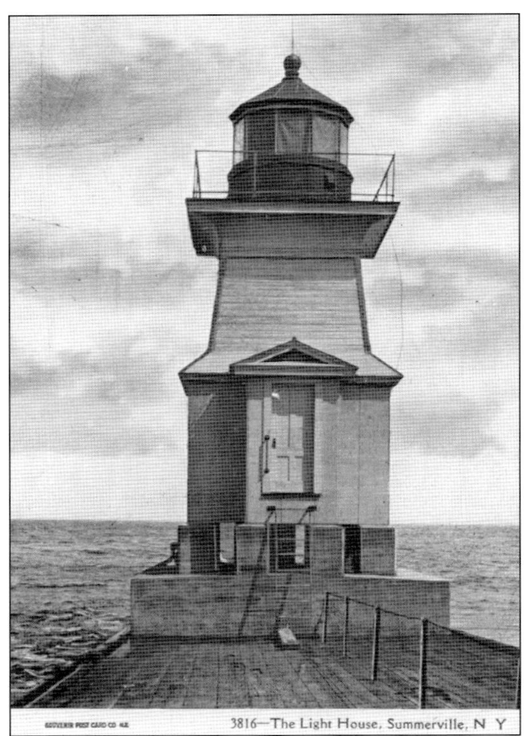

There were two piers at the mouth of the Genesee. Summerville Pier was on the east side, and Charlotte Pier was on the west side. The Charlotte-Genesee Lighthouse, built in 1822, is located on Lake Ontario at the mouth of the Genesee River. It is the second oldest lighthouse on the Great Lakes. The original keeper's quarters was a two-room limestone cottage, which sat beside the 40-foot-high octagonal limestone tower. In 1965, students at the nearby Charlotte High School were instrumental in saving the lighthouse from demolition, and it now houses a museum. (CRB.)

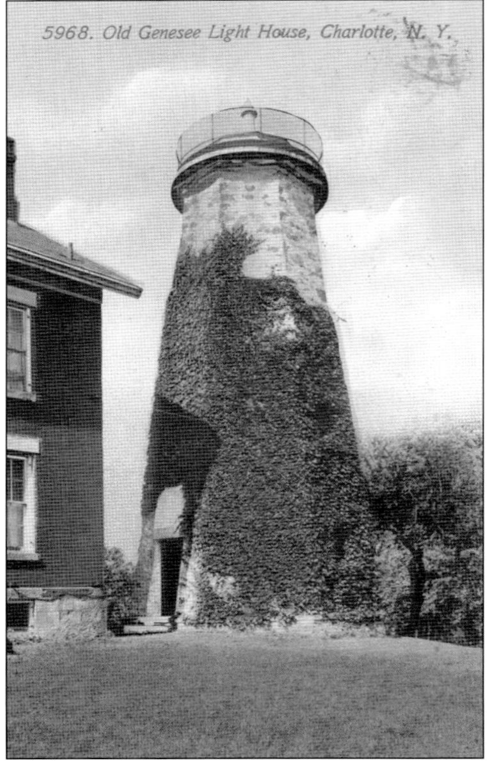

Five

Lake Ontario
Playground of the Genesee

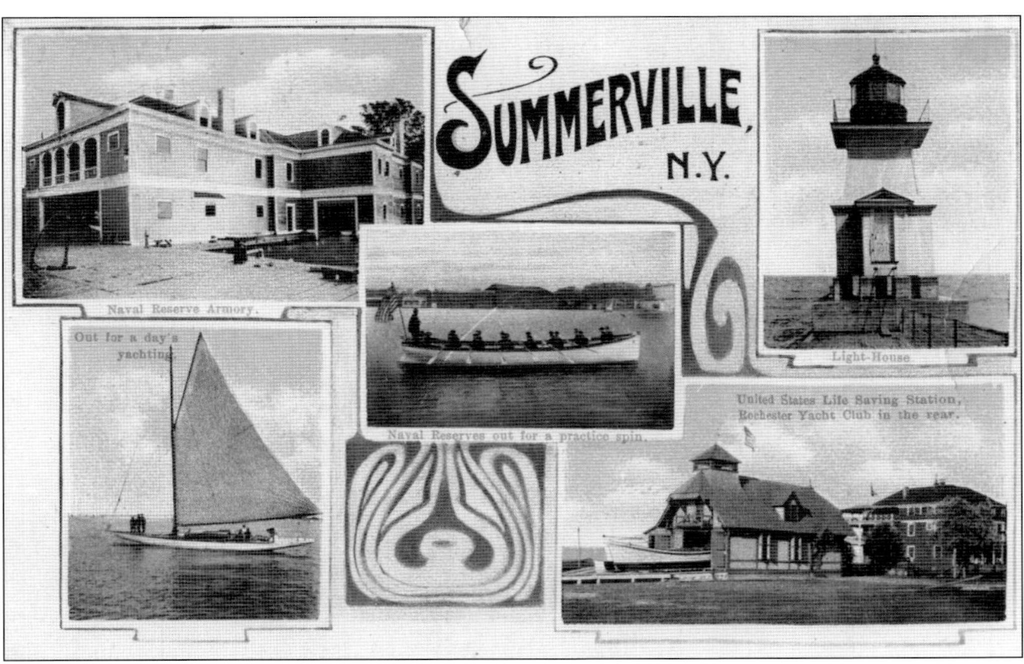

Summerville, at the mouth of the Genesee River, was known for many years as "The Coney Island of the West." It was a favorite spot for weekend and summer outings. It helped Rochester usher out the Victorian Age and introduced it to the Industrial Age. "Whether taking a romantic stroll along its picturesque pier, riding the 1905 Dentzel Menagerie Carousel, swimming, or boating, Ontario Beach Park provided all that is necessary for a perfect summer day at the beach. Ontario Beach Park attracted thousands of visitors over the years. On Labor Day 1919, thirty-five years after its opening, the park closed its doors. (JSB.)

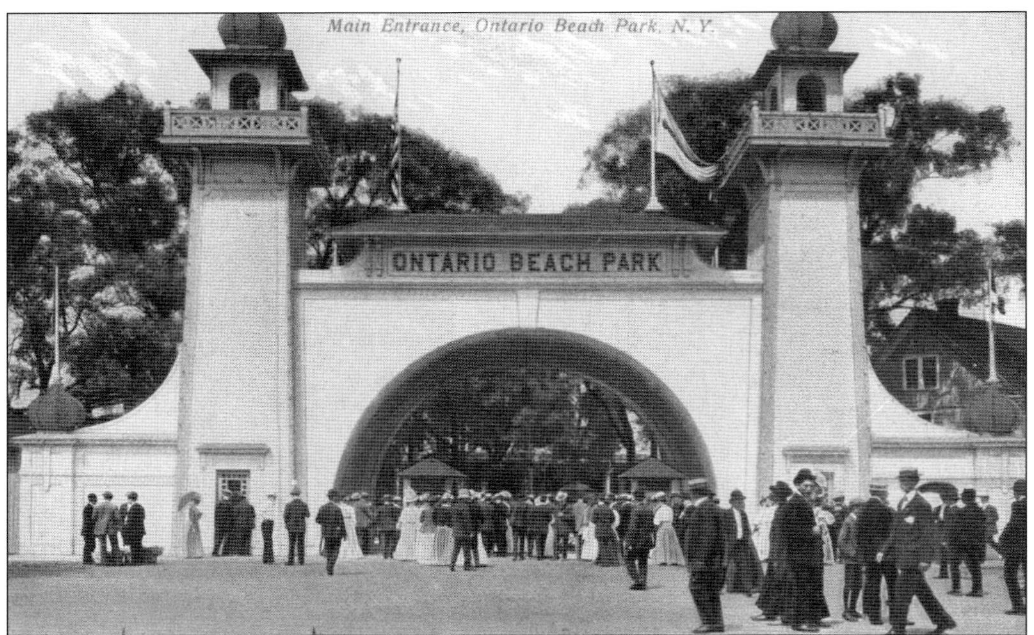

Ontario Beach Park's grand opening was on Saturday August 2, 1884, and it attracted 12,000 visitors. Eight rail coaches were running, each one accommodating 100 passengers. Admission to the park was free if one rode the train from downtown Rochester, otherwise the cost was 10¢. (AHS.)

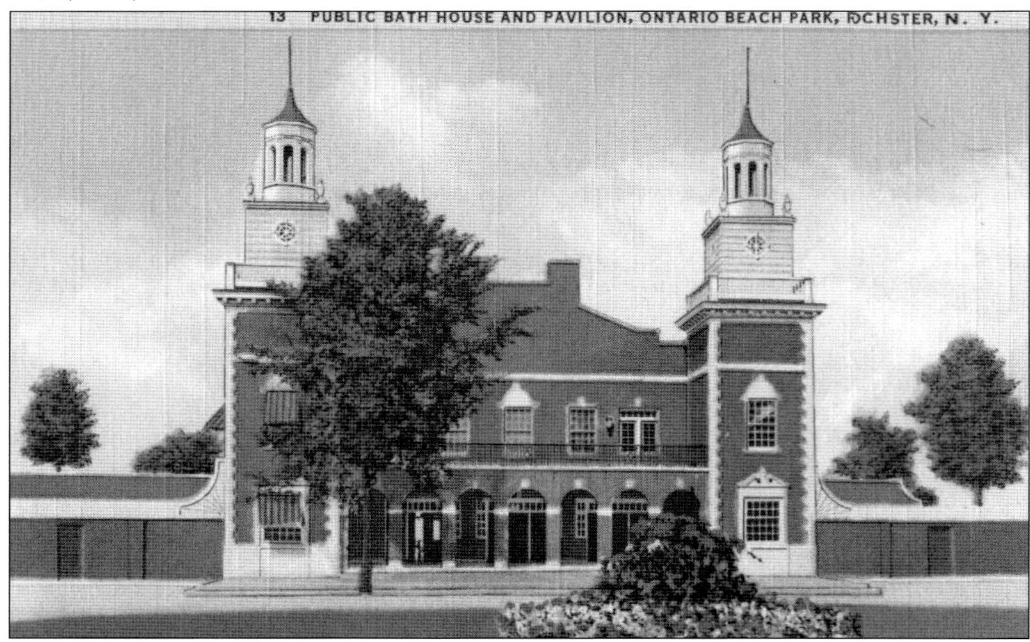

This impressive bathhouse and pavilion was the centerpiece of the park and still stands today, completely restored. On any given day at Ontario Beach Park, one would find numerous folks enjoying its breathtaking panoramic view of Lake Ontario. Rochesterians flocked to its sandy shores on weekends. (JSB.)

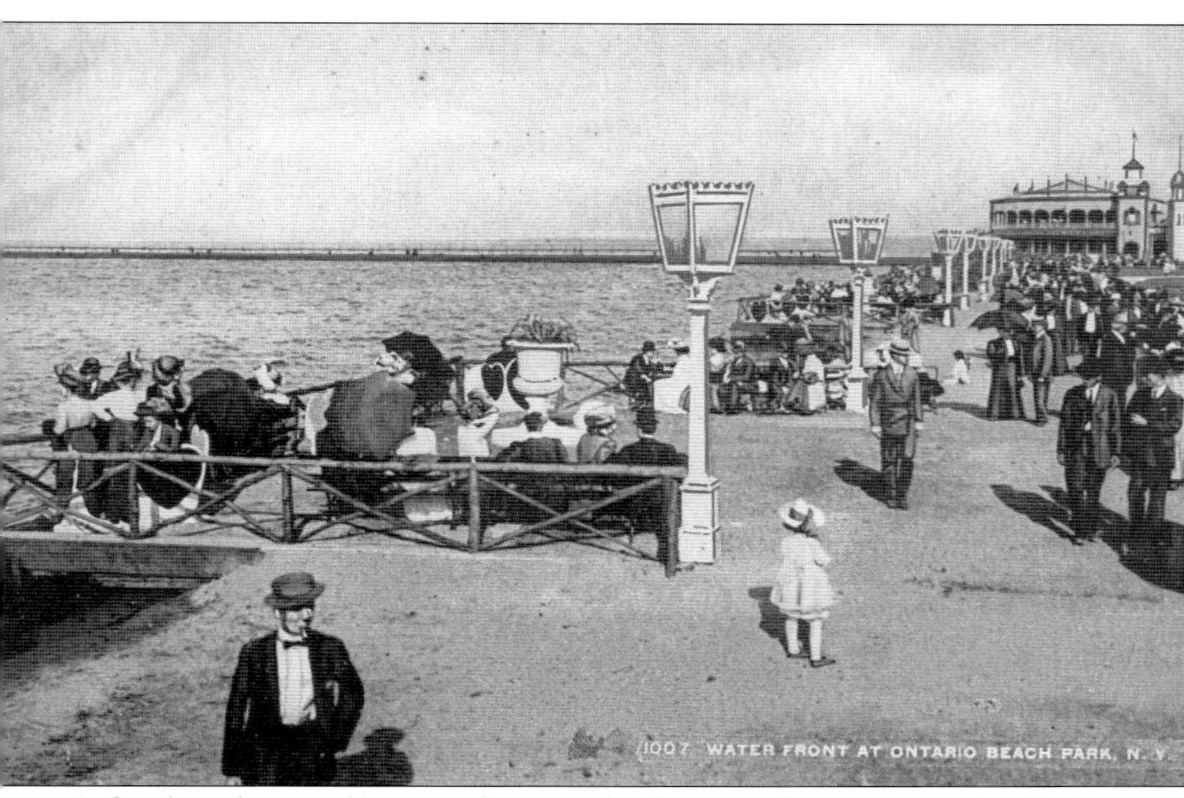

At first the park was nothing more than a popular place to go for a summer outing. Picnic groves, the beautiful lakefront vistas, and pleasant summer breezes were the main attractions. Look at the interesting dress on both men and women that were seen at the park. In 1884, New York Central & Hudson River Railroad built a boardwalk at Ontario Beach Park. In the same year, the Hotel Ontario was built on Charlotte Beach with large pavilions and band shells. Mechanical rides soon followed. On July 4, 1885, the park had a record crowd of 20,000. Every Sunday night had concerts followed by fireworks. (RPL.)

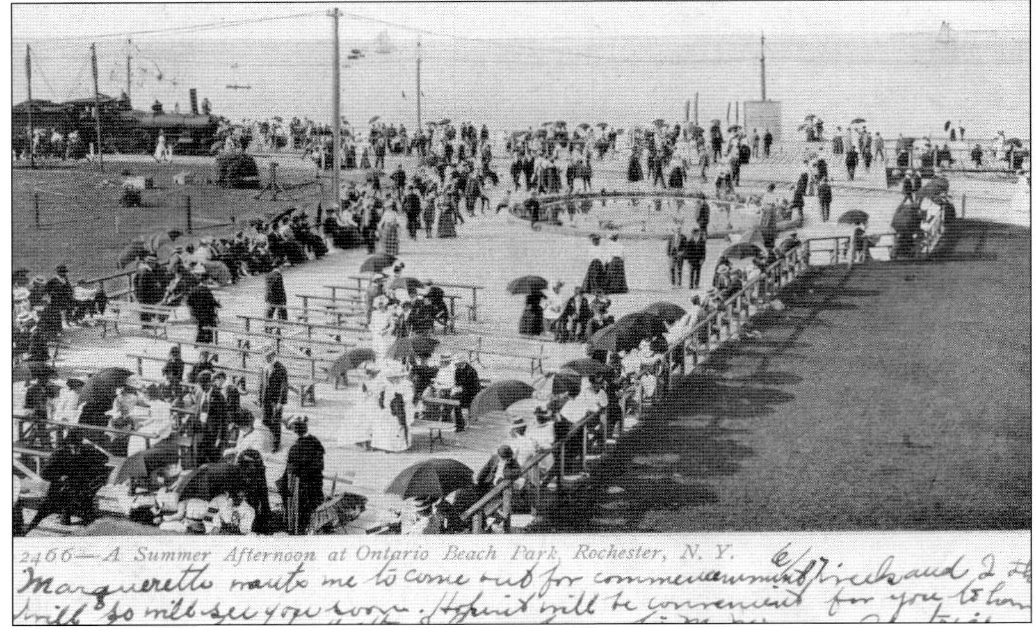

The park was especially popular during the decade of the flapper dresses and the Charleston. These postcards show a typical day at Ontario Beach Park. By far the most popular attractions were the boardwalk and the clean, sparkling beaches that were open to bathers on a daily basis. The boardwalk was constructed of impressive timbers. (RPL.)

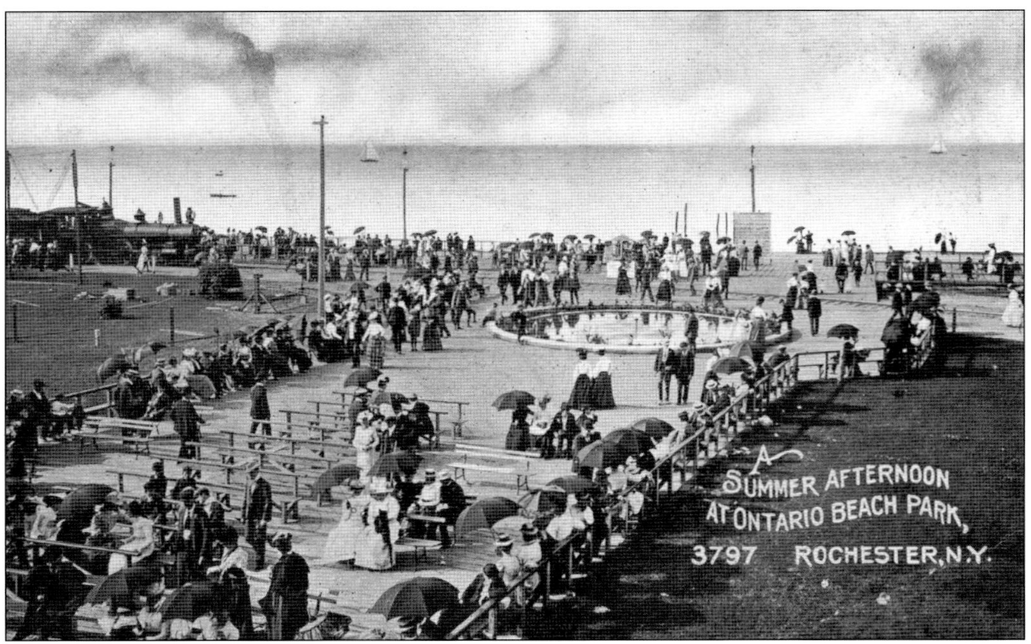

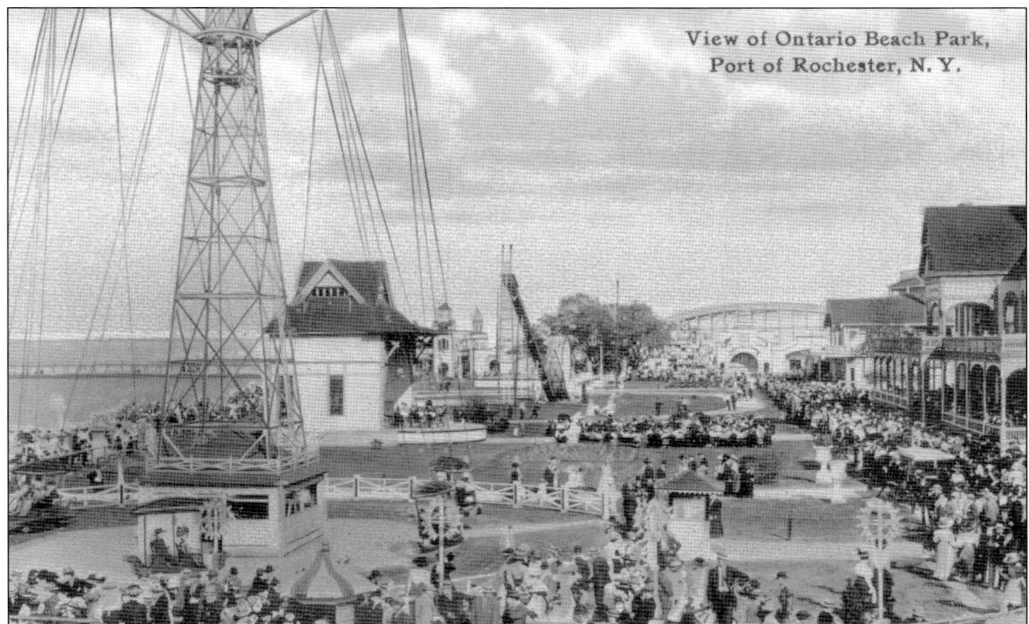

The Chubbuck Wheel Swing was a very popular ride among teens. Its tall structure dominated the skyline and spun riders on a revolving ride. Its popularity soon grew, and this amusement ride was found at country fairs and parks throughout New York State. Today, the ride at local fairs and amusement parks is known as the chair swing. (RPL.)

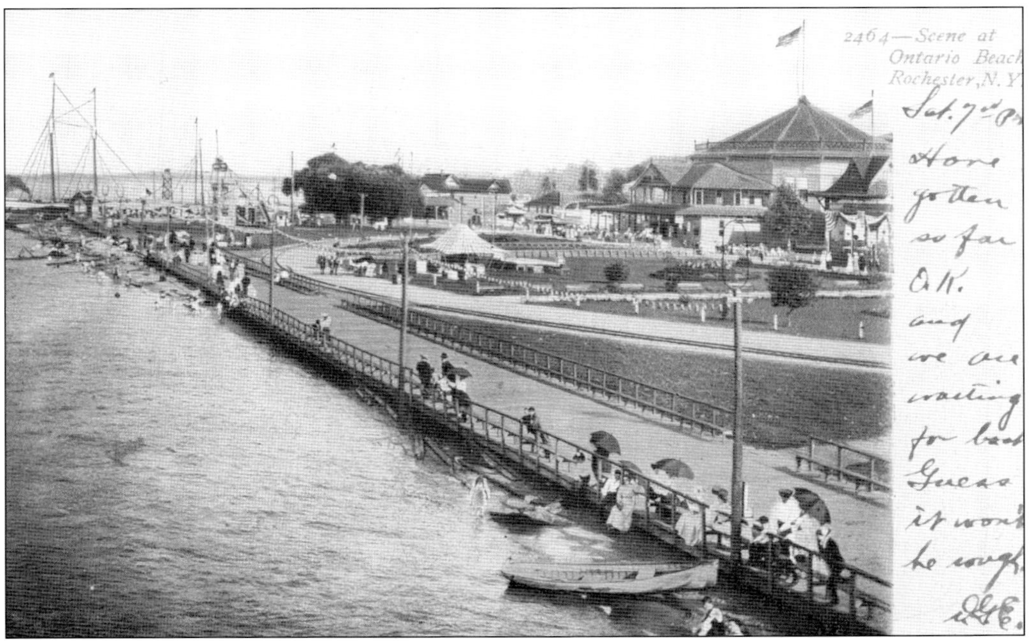

On March 1, 1907, the United States Post Office allowed private citizens to write their messages on the address side of the card. Before this date they had to be creative, writing their greetings where space permitted, often defacing the printed side of the card.

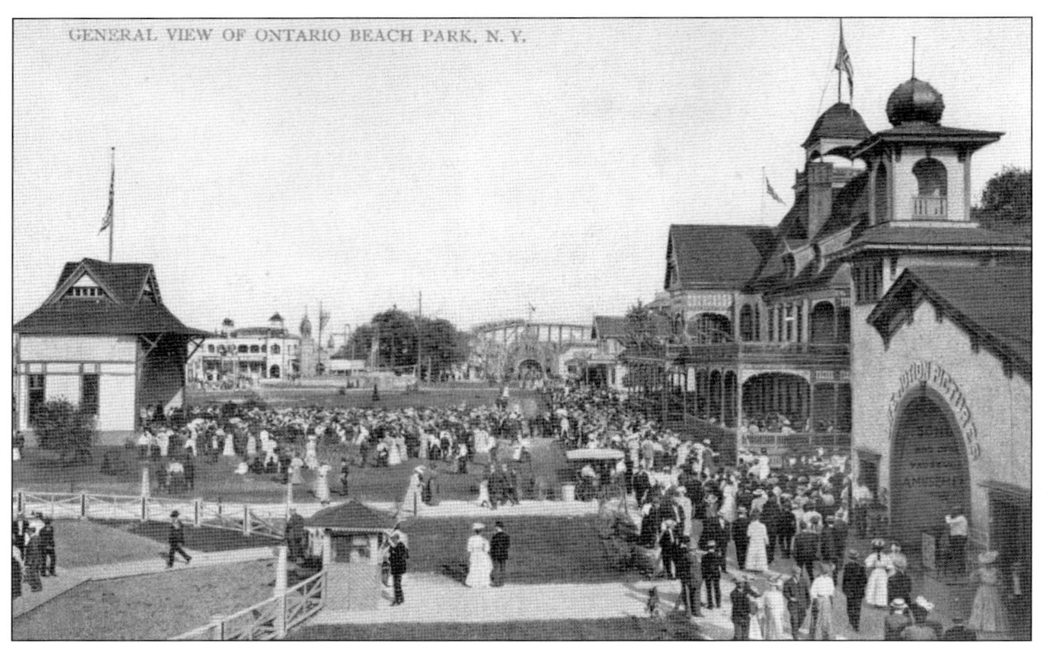

Cottages soon began popping up along the shore and adjacent riverbank. Soon everyone was eager to spend more time near the lake. In 1874, the Cottage Hotel was built on the lakefront, allowing hundreds to stay on-site and enjoy the beach for extended periods. (AHS.)

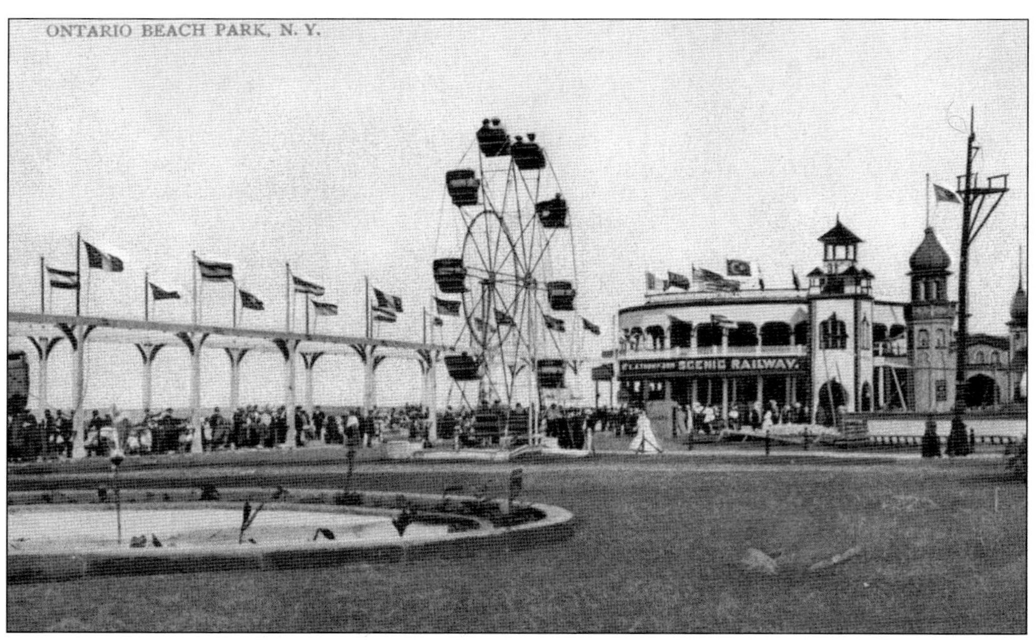

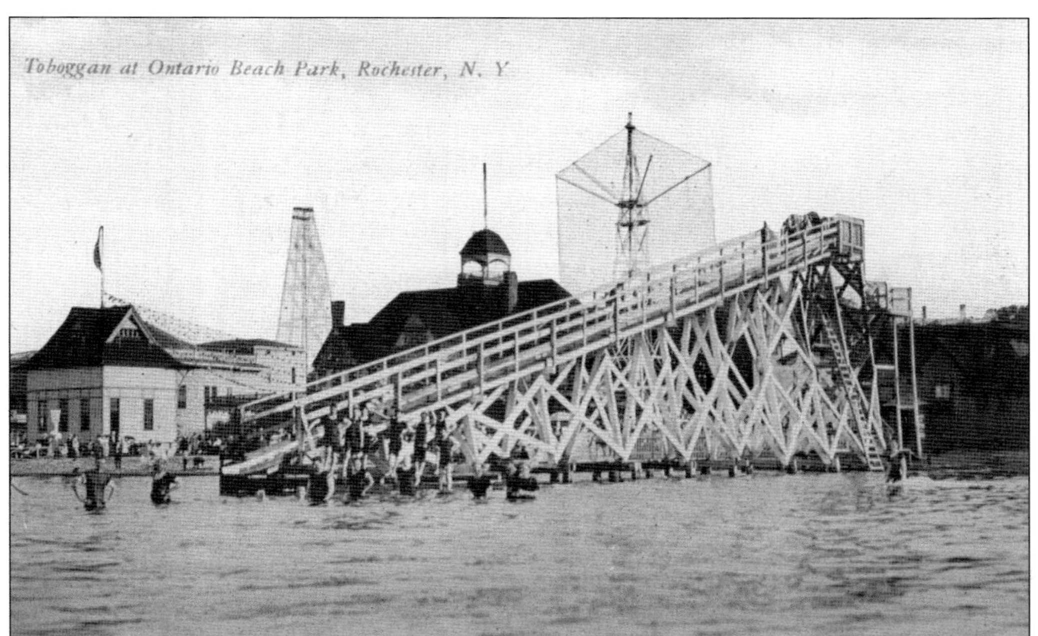

A popular attraction on a hot summer day was the water toboggan ride that took riders right into the lake. It was a source of endless amusement to visitors, young and old alike, who watched the sleds descend a ramp out over the lake, hitting the water at 60 miles per hour. (RPL.)

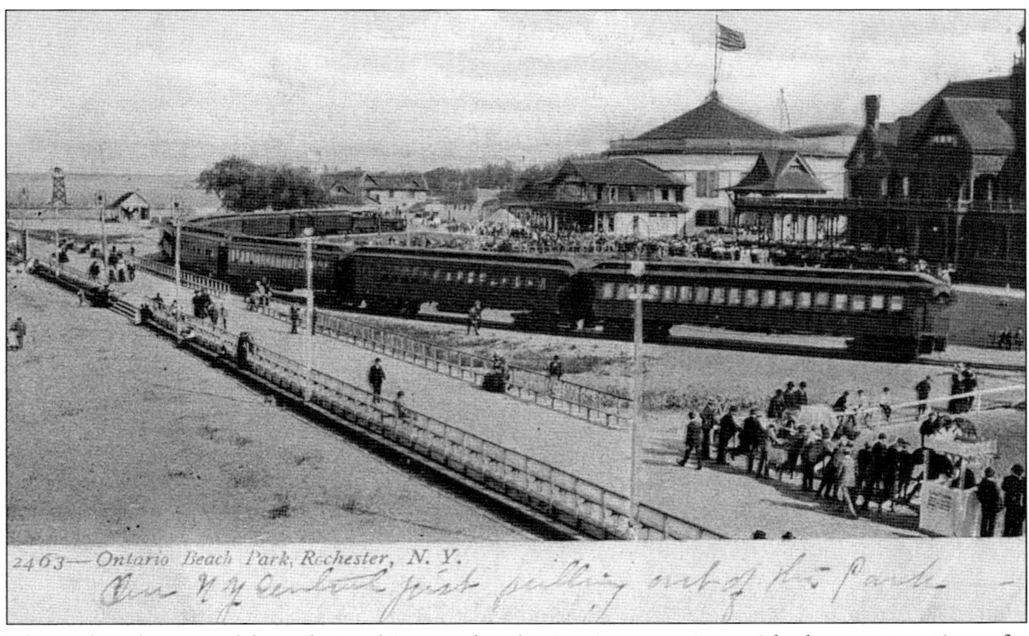

The railroad invested heavily in this popular destination, starting with the construction of a whitewash boardwalk in 1884. The Lake Ontario Beach Improvement Co. leased the surrounding land, constructed attractions, and operated the area around the beach as an amusement park. Ever since the New York Central Railroad built the first line leading to the beach in 1852, it was a popular day trip for area residents, bringing as many as 5,000 people a day. (RPL.)

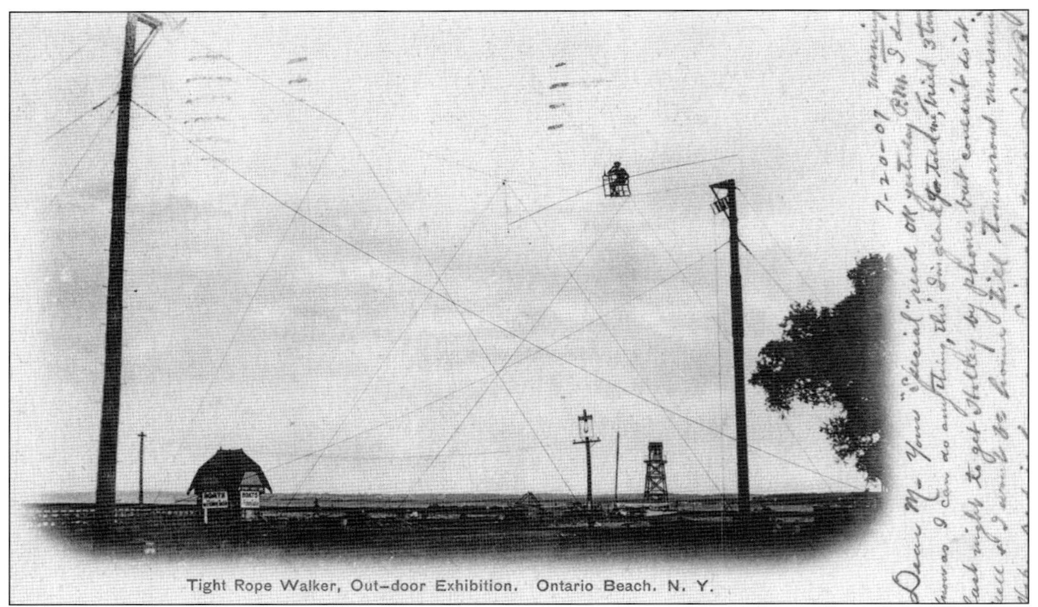

Stunt shows were a frequent occurrence, with tightrope walkers, high-water dives, and car jumps giving the crowds something to talk about. In 1894, the Great Blondin, the famous high-wire performer who repeatedly crossed Niagara Falls, walked atop a 90-foot high wire to the delight of the crowd. (RPL.)

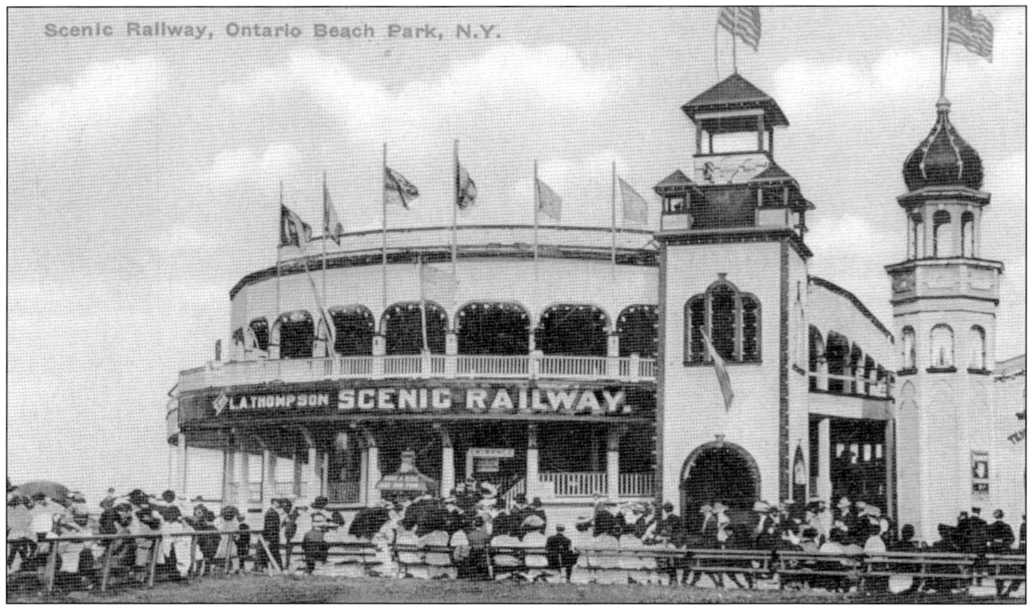

The early 1900s saw the arrival of free, live vaudeville acts that attracted large crowds. Rochester's own electric trolley system was soon extended to the park at a cost of 10¢. Crowds continued to flood in, reaching tens of thousands, while entrepreneurs surrounded the park with businesses. Bars, cheap hotels, makeshift casinos, and other risqué services sprang up in the village. Charlotte was beginning to gain a reputation in the 1890s for being a wild and rowdy place, something the residents blamed on the visitors from the "big city." (RPL.)

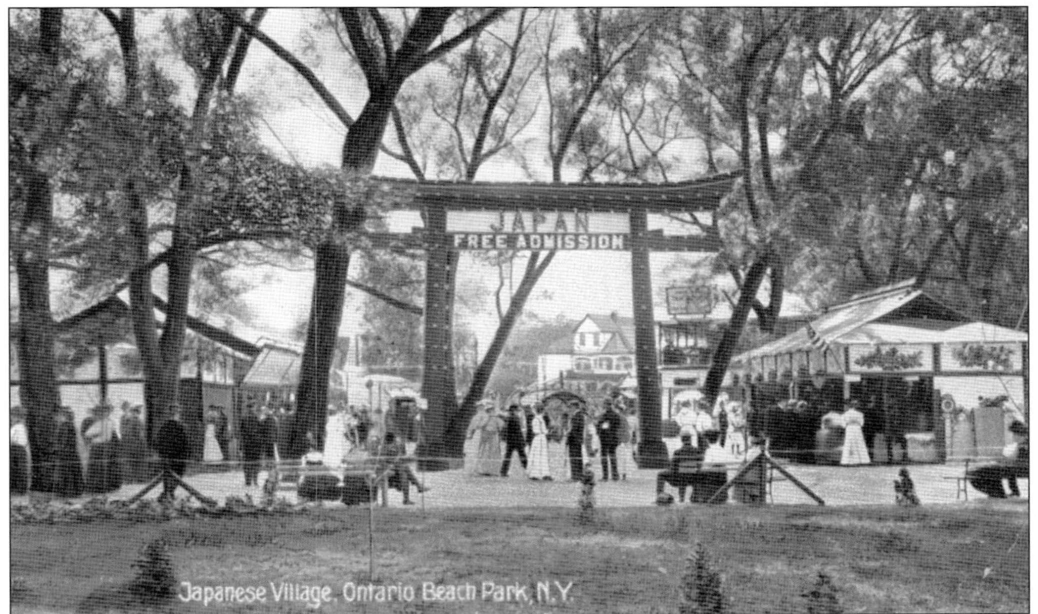

Sideshows lined the midway. For a mere penny, patrons could take a peek at a "wonder of the world" or try a new technology. One unique display was a Japanese Village, filled with interesting items from the other side of the world. The village also boasted a beautiful Japanese-style garden. (RPL.)

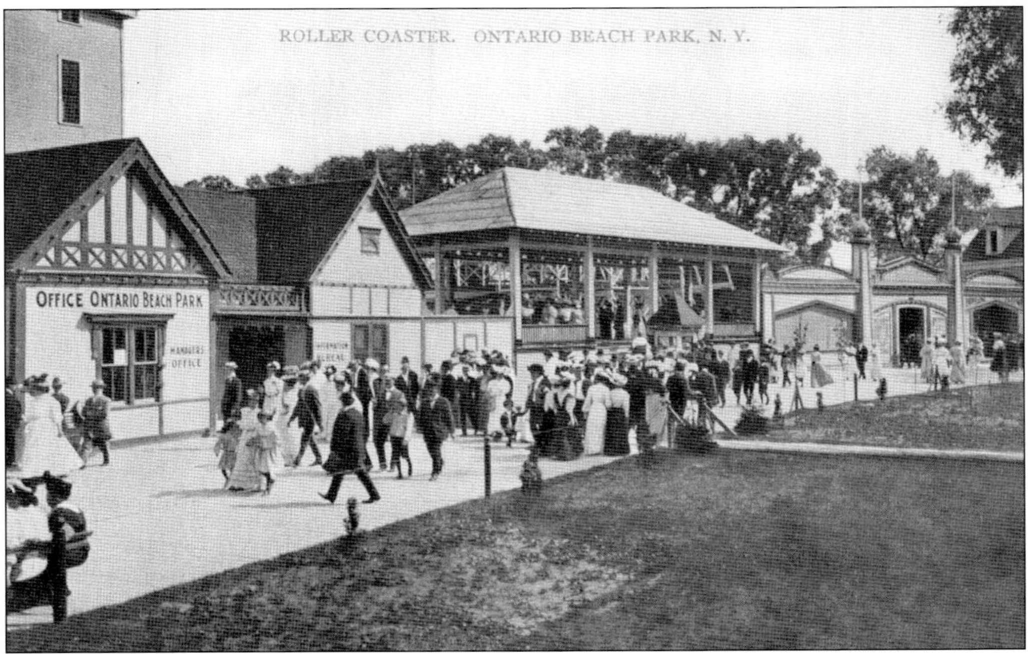

Additional attractions featured favorites like sidewalk concessions, a bandstand, daily stage shows, shooting gallery, arcades, fun houses, and beer gardens, along with a variety of other offerings that attracted people from every class level to the park. (RPL.)

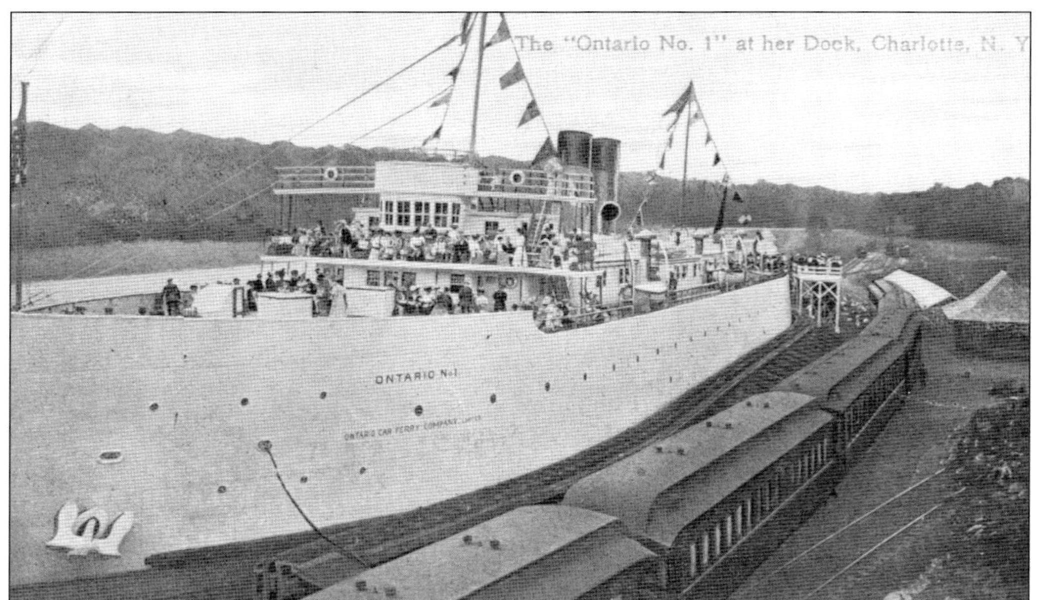

During the Civil War, the entertainment industry faltered, but afterwards, Charlotte rebounded as a summer resort with the arrival of several excursion steamers and with the organization of the Genesee Yacht Club in 1874. The Ontario Car Ferry Company began operating a ferry service for passengers and cargo from the port in November 1907 with the launch of the *Ontario I*, later joined by the *Ontario II* as well as the *Toronto* and the *Kingston*. These large ferries prompted a need to deepen the channel and make harbor improvements. (JSB.)

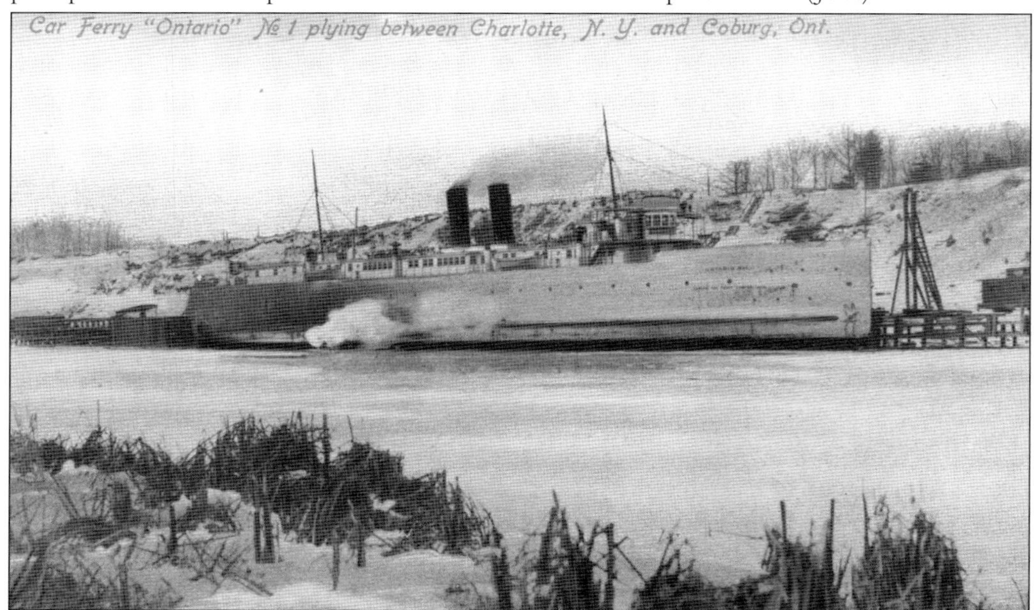

During its heyday, trains and ferries would take multiple trips to the small village of Charlotte, bringing up to 5,000 visitors a day to Ontario Beach Park. Cottages soon began popping up along the shore and adjacent riverbank. Soon, everyone was eager to spend more time near the lake. (JSB.)

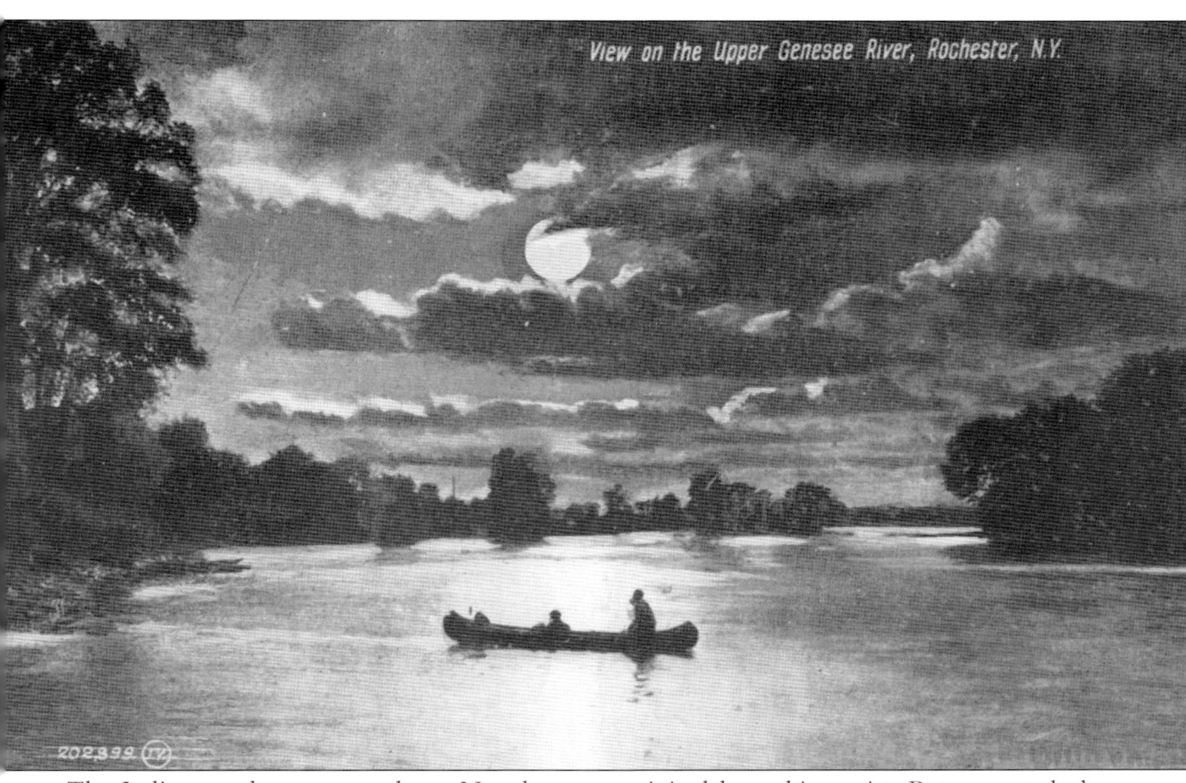

The Indians no longer roam here. Nor do many original log cabins exist. But a great deal of gratitude is owed to the early tribes and rugged pioneers who conquered the wilderness, established communities, and built industries, all the while appreciating the bountiful and beautiful land of the Genesee. To the generous heart of William Letchworth we owe the unspoiled beauty of the "Grand Canyon of the East." This is certainly a remarkable river, and if it could talk, what stories it would have to tell! Roll on, Genesee, roll on. As we say "farewell" to the Genesee River, what could be more romantic than a canoe ride on a moonlit night? (JSB.)

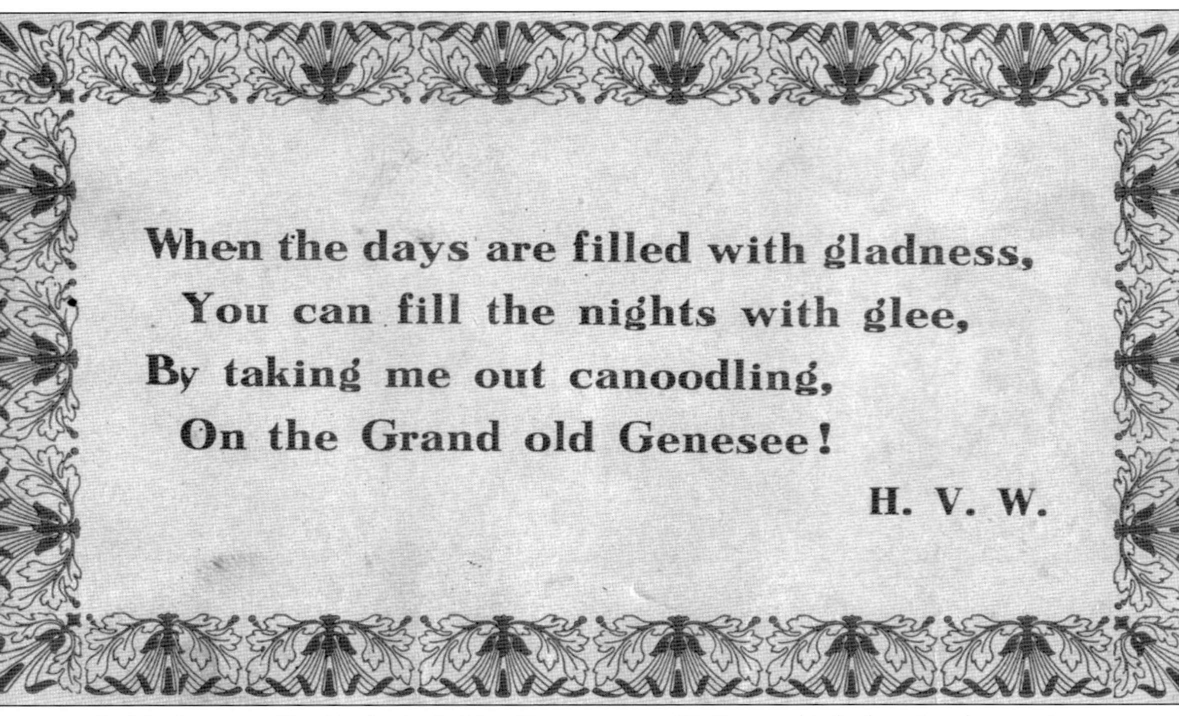

In his *Rochester Sketchbook*, Arch Merrill comments, "I like to think that the changes in our city are only on the surface; that it's fundamental character has not changed." The same could be said of the "Mighty Genesee." Through the centuries of humans living beside the river, as it was harnessed, dammed, diverted, and bridged countless times, the river's fundamental character has not changed. It continues rambling its way north to the Great Lake Ontario.

Consistent with our mission to preserve history on a local level, this book was printed in South Carolina on American-made paper and manufactured entirely in the United States. Products carrying the accredited Forest Stewardship Council (FSC) label are printed on 100 percent FSC-certified paper.

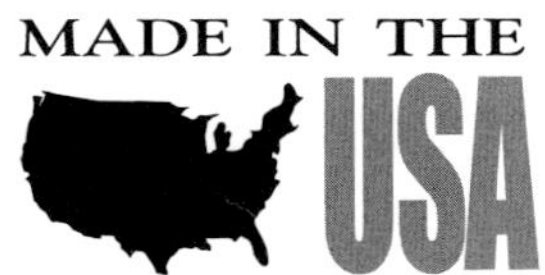

Bibliography

Allegany County Tourism Promotion Council. *Allegany County in the 20th Century: Stories of Change*. Virginia Beach, VA: Donning Company Publishers, 2005.

Anderson, Mildred L.H. *The Genesee Valley Canal: 1836–1878*. Interlaken, NY: Heart of the Lakes Publishing, 1978.

Barnes, Katherine. *Rainbow's End: The Story of Letchworth Park*. Moxon Print, 1967.

Carmer, Carl. *Genesee Fever.* New York, NY: Farrar and Rinehart Inc., 1941.

Clune, Henry W. *Rivers of America: The Genesee.* Holt, Rinehart, and Winston, 1963.

Fairchild, Herman LeRoy. *Geologic Story of the Genesee Valley and Western New York.* Irvine, CA: Reprint Services Corp., 1928

F.W. Beers and Co. 1806 Illustrated History of Allegany County. 1879.

Gillette, Frieda, and Katherine W. Lindley. *And You Shall Remember . . . a Pictorial History of Houghton College.* Houghton, NY: Houghton College, 1982.

Isachsen, Yngvar W. *Geology of New York: A Simplified Account.* New York, NY: New York State Museum, 2000.

McIntosh, W.H. *1788 History of Monroe County with Illustrations.* Everts, Ensign & Everts, 1877.

Merrill, Arch. A *River Ramble: Saga of the Genesee Valley.* Rochester, NY: Democrat and Chronicle, 1943.

———. *Rochester Sketchbook.* Rochester, NY: Democrat and Chronicle, 1946.

Namowitz, Samuel, and Donald Stone. *Earth Science: The World We Live In.* Princeton, NJ: Van Nostrand Co., 1960.

Rosenberg-Naparsteck, Ruth. *Runnin' Crazy: A Portrait of the Genesee River.* Virginia Beach, VA: Donning Company Publishers, 1960.